The Archie/Sabrina Universe

The Archie/Sabrina Universe

Essays on the Comics and Their Adaptations

Edited by HEATHER MCALPINE,
W. RON SWEENEY *and* JESS WIND

McFarland & Company, Inc., Publishers
Jefferson, North Carolina

This book has undergone peer review.

ISBN (print) 978-1-4766-8084-2
ISBN (ebook) 978-1-4766-4933-7

LIBRARY OF CONGRESS AND BRITISH LIBRARY
CATALOGUING DATA ARE AVAILABLE

Library of Congress Control Number 2023006590

© 2023 Heather McAlpine, W. Ron Sweeney and Jess Wind. All rights reserved

No part of this book may be reproduced or transmitted in any form or by any means, electronic or mechanical, including photocopying or recording, or by any information storage and retrieval system, without permission in writing from the publisher.

Front cover: KJ Apa (as Archie Andrews) and Lili Reinhart (as Betty Cooper) in a 2017 episode of *Riverdale* (The CW Television Network/Photofest)

Printed in the United States of America

McFarland & Company, Inc., Publishers
Box 611, Jefferson, North Carolina 28640
www.mcfarlandpub.com

Acknowledgments

This book is the result of nearly five years of discussion, collaboration, and research among the editors and with many people and institutions whose help and support made it possible.

We offer our sincere thanks to the Department of English and the College of Arts at the University of the Fraser Valley for their moral and financial support of the rag-tag and ill-advised *Riverdale* conferences (in 2018, 2019, 2020, organized by Dessa Bayrock, Heather McAlpine, Ron Sweeney, Jess Wind and Alex Wetmore), which formed the basis for this collection.

We also owe a debt of gratitude to the South Asian Studies Institute at UFV, especially to the director, Dr. Satwinder Kaur Bains, and to the coordinator, Dr. Sharanjit Kaur Sandhra, for kindly allowing us to host all three of our conferences inside their welcoming space at UFV. We appreciate your hospitality.

Our editor at McFarland, Layla Milholen, guided us with great patience as we attempted to organize this collection through a global pandemic. We are grateful for your expertise and encouragement.

We offer thanks to the editorial team of *Raspberry Magazine* for their 2019 profile of our contributions to Archie studies.

Finally, our thanks to all of the contributors to this collection and all of our conference presenters over the years, each of whom brought unique insights to our understanding of the extended Archie universe. Conference presenters not represented as contributors to this collection were Rebekah Bielefeld, Ross Chiasson, Riley Dueck, Benjamin Friesen, Tim Haner, Alexandra Johnson, Gabriel Murray, Dani Prince, Alexandra Shuurman, Sarah Sovereign, Rylee Steidle, and Kylie Wall. This book has benefited enormously from your creativity and enthusiasm.

Table of Contents

Acknowledgments   v

Introduction
    Heather McAlpine, W. Ron Sweeney *and* Jess Wind   1

Archie Must Die: On the Many Lives and Deaths
    of Archie Andrews
        W. Ron Sweeney   11

On Becoming a Citizen of Riverdale: Narrative Expansion
    Through Fanfiction, Interactive Fiction, and Other
    Apocryphal (Hyper)Texts
        Dessa Bayrock   28

Endless Authorship: Fanfiction, Copyright, and the Extended
    Archie Universe
        Kirsten Bussière   45

Chilling Adventures in Feminism: Sabrina Is Not the Feminist
    Heroine We Need
        Katie Stobbart   62

"When will the world learn? Women should be in charge
    of everything": Lilith as Villain, Victim, and Feminist
    in *Chilling Adventures of Sabrina*
        Sarah Stang   84

"Put your cape away": *Riverdale*'s #MeToo Moment
        Melissa Wehler   105

Watching Them, Watch Them: The Coded Movement of Betty's Pole
    Dance and Our Passive Audience Gaze
        Hannah Meghan Celinski   124

Punk Rock Prom Queen to Covergirl: Teens and Consumption
in *Riverdale* and *Josie and the Pussycats*
    Kaarina Mikalson   139

Archie Got Hot: How Embracing the Queer Art of Failure
Allows the *Chilling Adventures of Sabrina* to Shift
Queer Readings Away from Identity
    Mat Wenzel   155

Disability in *Chilling Adventures of Sabrina*
    Whitney Tiffany Renville   173

"First as tragedy, then as farce": The *Chilling Adventures
of Sabrina* and Satanic Moral Panic
    Brett Pardy   190

About the Contributors   205

Index   207

Introduction

HEATHER MCALPINE,
W. RON SWEENEY *and* JESS WIND

Chapter 100 of CW's *Riverdale* opens with the now-familiar Jughead Jones voiceover, telling us that we are, in fact, not watching an imaginary story. Well, then, Jughead, what exactly are we watching?

At one point it seemed natural to begin this collection at the beginning—where it started for us as editors—and the journey it took to get here. But when it comes to an academic text stretched through a global pandemic about the social-political discourse at work in a shared television universe, built from 80 years of multimedia content with comic book origins, about all–American teenage hijinks, where precisely it all begins is open for interpretation. Instead, we start at "Chapter 100: The Jughead Paradox," when the shared overlapping mediated universes of *Archie* comics become a central figure in the narrative. Jughead awakens to find himself suddenly aware of a connection between universes which parallel his own. In trying to find answers, he discovers his own dead doppelgänger, long-dead characters returned, and comic books that explain everything.

The fifth episode of season six explains how the season's opening storyline set in alternate-universe "Rivervale" came to be—a reality-splitting explosion originating from a bomb placed under Archie's bed. Jughead learns that the two universes are bleeding into one another and growing increasingly unstable. Importantly, it is in Rivervale that fans were treated to the long-anticipated crossover with *Chilling Adventures of Sabrina* (*CAOS*) after its mid-pandemic cancellation from Netflix, with Kiernan Shipka reprising her witchy role. Read as meta-commentary, "The Jughead Paradox" suggests the television universe of *Riverdale*, itself a layered representation of melodramatic teen media set in small-town America, cannot exist alongside other ever-expanding media-verses in the *Archie* comics landscape. In the show, Jughead strives to separate the universes leaving only the original to continue. Instead, Jughead-as-narrator

1

explains to Jughead-as-writer that Rivervale can continue so long as Jughead-as-writer powers it by continuously writing stories about the town and its inhabitants.[1] Or, read another way, so long as there are writers to produce stories for "the town with pep," the fictional, genre-bending expanded universe of *Archie* comics will forever adapt and endure.

It is within this liminality we situate this collection of essays which examines *Riverdale*, *CAOS*, and the broader *Archie* comics universe for their relationship to the contemporary socio-political media landscape. In his ground-breaking study, *Twelve-Cent Archie*, Bart Beaty (2015) notes that *Archie* comics, across the decades, have always occupied space as low-brow art and become synonymous with inoffensive comics. Because of this, they were devalued in the cultural landscape and likewise largely ignored in academic scholarship. In a Jameson-esque framing of postmodern pastiche, the latest televisual renditions of Archie, Sabrina, and the gang are read by some critics as checking the same low-brow boxes as the comics of a different generation: "They are almost no one's idea of prestige TV. Genre pieces—noir for 'Riverdale,' horror for 'Sabrina'—they are ardently derivative, a homage a minute" (Soloski, 2018). From banal self-referentiality and inconsequential storylines, to limited character growth and camera-winking, shows in the Archie universe proudly flaunt their smorgasbord of popular culture. *Riverdale*, *CAOS*, and other rumored or gone-too-soon spinoffs are simply the latest in *Archie* comics' long line of capturing, shaping, and critiquing American teen culture.

Riverdale showed up all over-dramatic and over-saturated for a twenty-first-century audience. *The Globe and Mail* reported, shortly after the first episode aired, "these aren't your saccharine, sweet teens wiling away the hours at the malt shop" (Janceslewicz, 2017). Having sprung from CW teen television influences like *One Tree Hill*, *Gossip Girl* and the 2008–2013 revival of *90210*, the *Riverdale* we have today makes a lot of sense. And there is no doubt that the series has had success both in terms of popularity and critical appraisal: in its first season *Riverdale* averaged about 1.7 million U.S. viewers, though this doesn't include its audience on Netflix, which acquired streaming rights for outside the United States and releases episodes less than 24 hours after they originally air but doesn't report viewership numbers. The series was also met with generally positive reviews on popular viewer review sites: five episodes in the first season earned 100 percent ratings on Rotten Tomatoes and an overall user review rating of 7.3/10 on Metacritic. Notably, the critic review score for *Riverdale* season 1 on Metacritic is a moderately favorable 68/100. That said, *Riverdale*, now in its seventh season, is discussed online with fan-forum posts like "But WHY did Riverdale become so bad?" (U/Direct-Pineapple-193,

2021) and "Who else thinks Riverdale had huge potential but everything went bad maybe after S4…" (u/Separate_Secretary_5, 2022). At the same time, some fan critics are reveling in the twists and turns: "for fans of the series and the comics that inspired it [Chapter 100] is a perfect hour of television" (Cummins, 2021). These examples highlight divided opinions in audience discourse, though they are largely still concerned with whether *Riverdale* is any good (and therefore valuable). As we editors of this collection argue, and as the scholarship within highlights, whether popular culture is good isn't relevant to the tensions at work in *Riverdale* or *CAOS*. Instead, our focus is on which cultural conversations are foregrounded or erased, how social, political, and historical reality bleeds into contemporary fiction, and how representation, nostalgia, and affect work (or don't) in popular media.

One thing it seems fans, critics, and scholars can agree on is that this isn't our grocery-store digest Archie and the gang from decades past. That said, *Riverdale* does draw on the long history of *Archie* comics, and in many cases, it is much more connected than many critics noticed. Popular and ubiquitous, the collected Archie Comics digests were in many ways the history of comics themselves. Beaty (2015) notes that "despite ongoing attempts to make Archie relevant for new generations of readers, the titles are widely regarded as old-fashioned, outdated, a relic of the way that the American comic-book industry used to work." Even as other comics moved to specialty shops and bookstores, *Archie* was primarily associated with supermarket checkouts and dentists' offices. You could pick up any *Archie* of any era and read nearly the same story. As Beaty states, "If the *Archie* comics are a story-generating machine, one important element to note is that it is a machine that can be endlessly reset" (2015). The characters (and Riverdale as a city) would always return to their default state. The stories themselves may have been less memorable than the core repeated elements of the characters. The comics thus played a key part in reinforcing popular ideas of the American teenager. But even as the *Archie* comics were adapted into television shows and merchandise, in the main *Archie* comics the characters were largely stagnant.

Riverdale represents a turning point for the now 80-plus-year-old Archie Comics, working to capture a new generation of fans (readers, viewers, consumers). *Riverdale* started with a murder mystery so *CAOS* could fly in on a broomstick with its homogenized version of witchcraft, one part wiccan, one part satanism, and whole parts parody of institutional religion. *Riverdale* grounded itself in reality only long enough for Veronica to fast-travel back to New York to introduce viewers to Katy Keene in advance of her short-lived 2019 spinoff. Prior to Archie and the gang making it big on television, they got a makeover on the pages of their original home—comics. Archie's cool is finally updated: he still plays guitar, but his famous crosshatch hair style is gone, in favor of a new choppy "bedhead" look (Waid & Staples, 2016).[2] Additionally, crossover titles like *Archie and Sabrina* (2019), *Archie vs. Predator* (2015), and the horror titles *Jughead: The Hunger* (2018), *Afterlife with Archie* (2015), and *Vampironica* (2019), highlight what "The Jughead Paradox" is trying to tell viewers: the Archie universe keeps expanding into newer and weirder realms. While *Riverdale* and the newcomers to the Archie universe may not resemble the nostalgic Double Digests of our past, what with their weird, genre-bending, transmedia properties and left turns into the realm of the murder-mystery-supernatural-psychological thriller, there is something distinctly familiar about them, suggesting we may have more in common with Jughead the werewolf or the players in a deadly game of Gryphons and Gargoyles than we think.

It Started on Twitter

Turning now to this project's origin story, in 2017 Heather tweeted she was starting to watch *Riverdale*, and Ron with sarcastic foreboding told her to "stop before it's too late." Perhaps it was because the CW's latest iteration of Archie was only on the cusp of its second-season premiere and already a brooding, disturbing, sexy shadow version of its former self. Or perhaps it's because the show's many (many) storylines were already dangling precariously from our short-term memories and anything less than binge-watching would risk forgetting them entirely. Maybe it was because watching *Riverdale*—a show that goes to great lengths to remind us that it is one step removed from the real world, but is juxtaposed with clear markers of place that tie it forever to the Lower Mainland of British Columbia, Canada—is a weird experience. Nevertheless, Ron was already hooked and soon Heather would be too—we all were.

As scholars located in British Columbia's Fraser Valley, we editors were at times thrilled to see so many familiar locales featured on the show—not Pop's but Rocko's Diner in Mission; not the drive-in theater Jughead was living in but the Twilight Drive-in theater in Aldergrove; not Riverdale town hall but Langley Community Centre in Fort Langley—and we were also curious about the connection between a show about a place and the places now about a show. Rocko's Diner now displays a signed photo from the cast and offers *Riverdale*-themed burgers; Tourism Vancouver lists filming locations for Archie sightseers visiting the Lower Mainland. The show's gothic themes teased at a grim reflection of our society. We had as many questions about what *Riverdale* is as we did about what it was doing and where it might be going. Again we ask Jughead-as-narrator—if we're not watching fiction, what are we watching? Is *Riverdale* trying to make meaningful commentary about the falsehoods of small-town America? Is it hinting at the perverseness of today's youth as part of a cycle perpetuated by their also deeply damaged parents? In what ways does this commentary bleed out from the show's writing into its casting, staging, costuming, and choreography?

In March 2018, to a room full of *Riverdale* fans and scholars, Jess pulled at the question we were all asking ourselves: What is *Riverdale*? Is it pastiche? Is it parody? Does it even matter? One needn't look much further than Madeline Petsch's always snappy performance as Cheryl Blossom to know that *Riverdale* is as aware of its status as melodrama as it is of its role as a piece of highly mediated pop culture. That said, is the average viewer in on this parody—are they along for the self-referential ride? After all, Archie did get a reboot during the era of reboots, and nearly everything about the show is steeped in teenage pop culture nostalgia.

No matter when you were a teenager, *Riverdale* has you covered by broadly nodding to some of the most iconic and familiar eras of teenage media. Luke Perry is transported from *Beverly Hills 90210* (1990) to play Archie's father before his death in 2019. We're reminded of John Hughes' films that defined teen culture in the 1980s with Molly Ringwald who plays Archie's mom. The casting of Skeet Ulrich, star of *Scream* as Jughead's dad and *Twin Peaks*' Mädchen Amick as Betty's mom incorporate references to some of the darker and more self-aware moments in teen-centered media. When *Scream* was released in 1996 it was one of the first popular horror films to be entirely aware of the genre in which it existed. It broke convention and parodied the tired formula of teen-slasher films. *Twin Peaks*' surreal and uncanny portrayal of high-school kids, a source of its enduring appeal, is often cited as an influence on later television and film that centers on teenage drama. Looking at the *Riverdale* family tree, it becomes clear that the show is the natural extension of decades of teen and genre cultural production. But let's not forget that *Archie* comics came first, trapping Archie and the gang in a nostalgic time loop: these characters are both the grandparents of teen-centric narrative in their original comic form, and now, in this version, the offspring of teen pop culture itself.

But does all this make it worthy of deeper study? Would it hold up to serious critique? These were the questions we were faced with as Heather and Ron's live-tweeting about *Riverdale* quickly turned to jokes about an academic conference, followed by serious discussion of an academic conference, followed by three actual academic conferences and, as you see now, a book.

Essays on the Chilling Adventures of Archie, Sabrina and the Gang

Why an edited collection? While there is some academic work that focuses on the *Archie* comics universe, its enduring adaptability and place in the history of teen media is deserving of wider examination. We aim to contribute to these conversations by bringing together diverse scholarship which traffics in tensions of cultural representation, feminism, queerness, cultural production and popular media. With critical intersections through fan studies, TV and comics studies, queer and feminist studies, and popular culture and media scholarship, this collection of essays generates rich discussions which can lead to further exploration, including a necessary critical unpacking of racial representation in the Archie expanded universe. While some authors in this collection engage critically with anti-racist scholarship, given Archie's inadequacy in navigating non-white representation historically (Beaty, 2015), we recognize there is more work to be done to attend to the historical strategic erasures of racialized experience in the Archie expanded universe and media more broadly. This project began with the question "Why are we still watching?" But it has been transformed through this collection of essays to ask, more specifically, "What are we watching?" In this edited collection, which follows three semi-academic conferences, authors interrogate *Riverdale*, *CAOS*, and the broader, ever-expanding Archie universe in an effort to make sense not only of the chaos of these shows but of our own ongoing fascination with them.

In the opening essay, W. Ron Sweeney explores the many teased (and actual) deaths of Archie. Building out of comics scholarship, Sweeney suggests that the serial nature of *Archie* comics storytelling pushes the characters toward death and inevitable reboot. In their respective essays, Dessa Bayrock and Kirsten Bussière look at the role of fanfiction in creating space for the show's many fans to see themselves in the story. Bayrock's work examines the role of the fan in active participation with the text while also providing interactive ways to engage with the *Riverdale* gang. Bussière explores the further reaches of Archie fandom by examining fanfiction spaces and their bottom-up approach to diverse representation in the Archie universe.

Described in the media as a feminist pop culture triumph, *CAOS* leaves much to be desired, according to Katie Stobbart. While acknowledging the potential for feminist and intersectional storytelling inherent in the show's focus on witch-figures, its strong non-male leads and its diverse cast, Stobbart's essay traces the many ways in which the series nonetheless fails to deliver "the angry young feminist we're looking for." Along similar lines, Sarah Stang's interrogation of the character of Lilith positions that figure as a potentially liberating example of the monstrous-feminine while considering her problematic role in the third season.

Melissa Wehler's essay also adopts a feminist lens, examining *Riverdale*'s engagement with conversations around sexual assault and survivorship in the context of fourth-wave feminism. Situating the show within the history of the #MeToo movement, Wehler argues that *Riverdale*'s handling of Nick St. Clair's sexual misconduct and its aftermath in season 2, episode 5 ("When a Stranger Calls") intervenes in a nuanced way on these complex issues.

Approaching *Riverdale* from the perspective of dance and movement, Hannah Meghan Celinski's essay closely reads some of the show's key dance sequences in order to decode the problematic messages they convey—many of which, as she demonstrates, stand at odds with the show's professed feminism. Celinski also scrutinizes the layers of "watching" at work both within the show and between the show and its viewers, parsing its mediation of particularly troublesome scenes through a manipulation of the gaze.

Kaarina Mikalson reaches back into the Archie universe archive to 2001, when the feature film *Josie and the Pussycats* offered a post-riot-grrrl feminist vision of the trio that openly mocked the media manipulation of young consumers. Setting this against *Riverdale*'s take on the Pussycats, as much a brand as a band, particularly given the show's extensive use of product placement, Mikalson's essay examines the precarity and racial dynamics at work in both texts and their relationship to consumer culture and adolescence.

The essays by Mat Wenzel and Whitney Tiffany Renville each approach the character of Sabrina as a figure for marginalized identity: working through Jack Halberstam's theory of queer failure, Wenzel argues that Sabrina's failure to move toward either of the "poles" of her identity as a half-witch, half-mortal (a circumstance further complicated by the discovery of her third, satanic essence) makes her a queer character with whom queer viewers might identify. Renville posits that a reading of *CAOS* informed by the social model of disability suggests that the show treats Sabrina's hybrid identity and failures at magic as a kind of disability—and asks to what extent the show might be read reparatively from this perspective.

Finally, Brett Pardy's essay adopts a historical perspective on American popular culture representations of Satanism, which, as he demonstrates, were particularly productive of moral panic in the service of the New Right political agenda in the 1980s. In contrast, Pardy argues, *CAOS*'s engagement with Satanism mounts a critique of the same politics and institutions behind the earlier moral panic.

Ride or Die: Riverdale *and a Global Pandemic*

The last time we were all gathered together was the third edition of our *Riverdale* conference on Friday the 13th, March 2020. As we read our papers (some of which appear in essay form in this book) the pandemic did not yet seem real. We whispered jokes as we hugged and shook hands and wondered if the universities were going to continue to meet in-person. By the end of the day, the school was closed.

Both *Chilling Adventures of Sabrina* and *Riverdale* were impacted by the pandemic. Despite reports from cast and Aguirre-Sacasa that more episodes were planned, Netflix cancelled *CAOS*, presumably due to filming challenges brought on by lockdowns and social distancing measures (Olin, 2021). Additionally, *Riverdale* was one of the earlier shows to be halted in March 2020, after a crew member was in contact with someone who tested positive (Ip, 2020). When they finally returned to filming in September 2020, there were again interruptions with a lack of available testing and the whole experience was traumatic for some of the cast members, who felt trapped by travel restrictions and filming rules (Todisco, 2020). While these shutdowns affected the entire industry, there's something particularly fitting about *Riverdale* being impacted: *Riverdale* is a show that constantly responds to cultural events but doesn't really know what to do with them. And, in fact, *Riverdale* had once already briefly teased a mysterious quarantine, only to immediately abandon that storyline ("Chapter 43: Outbreak"). Will the Archie universe, which has seen zombie plagues and werewolves and vampires and superheroes and time travel and so much more, bring a pandemic into future episodes? We are looking forward to it.

In 2023, as Canada returns to a "new normal" and *Riverdale* continues forward into its final season, we return to our earlier questions about this show and its expanding universe and why we remain so fascinated by it. This collection comes at a time when critical questions about whose stories get told and how in our media abound—a time when the unexpected and, at times ridiculous, (mis)adventures of the Archie expanded universe are only barely different from the world we experience. It provides these characters some much needed critical attention given their enduring place in the cultural milieu of teenage-turned-mid-twenties-adult media.

Amid a global pandemic, an international race revolution, climate crises, and war, we return as we have always done, to Riverdale and Greendale. As we watch Veronica sing at her nightclub in front of a university recruiter and then get raided by her father who was mayor for a stretch, we again ask "Why are we watching this show?" And the answer is that we just watched Veronica sing at her nightclub in front of a university recruiter and then get raided by her father who was mayor for a stretch and so she's going into the rum business to make some extra money. As prestige television spawns fan theories, extensive YouTube explainers, and long essays in magazines, sometimes it is nice to just bask in the chaos of the Archie expanded universe, a universe where sets look like the inside of a highly curated antique store; where characters fight, kiss, scheme and sing their troubles away; where magic and ghosts make perfect sense beside supervillains and superpowers; and where critical social-political issues are addressed and resolved faster than you can drink your milkshake.

Notes

1. Similarly, in 2018 producer Greg Berlanti said of *Riverdale* and *Chilling Adventures of Sabrina* showrunner Roberto Aguirre-Sacasa that "he just genuinely is bursting with stories to tell" (Soloski, 2018).

2. Don't worry, you can still get "classic Archie" titles in their familiar digest format in print or digital through the Archie Comics website.

References

Cummins, C. (2021, December 15). "Riverdale's 100th Episode Is a Multiversal Celebration of All Things Archie." *Den of Geek*. https://www.denofgeek.com/tv/riverdale-100-episode-celebration-of-all-things-archie/.
Ip, S. (2020, March 2). "Hollywood North: Riverdale Filming Shut Down After Crew Comes in Contact with COVID-19." *Vancouver Sun*.
Jancelewicz, C. (2017, January 3). "Netflix Canada: What's Good in January?" *Global News*.
Ketchmer, J. (Director), & DeWille, J. (Writer) (2018, December 12). Chapter 43: Outbreak [television series episode]. In J.B. Moranville, *Riverdale*. Warner Bros. Television.
Metacritic (2017). "Riverdale: Season 1." https://www.metacritic.com/tv/riverdale/season-1/user-reviews.
The Metro Vancouver Conventions and Visitors Bureau (2021). "Riverdale Filming Sites in Vancouver." https://www.destinationvancouver.com/vancouver/filmed-in-vancouver/suggested-vancouver-itineraries-and-maps/riverdale-filming-sites-in-vancouver/.
Olin, B. (2021). "Chilling Adventures of Sabrina Canceled Because of COVID-19." *Fansided*. https://netflixlife.com/2020/10/08/chilling-adventures-of-sabrina-canceled-covid-19/.
Rotten Tomatoes (2017). "Riverdale Season 1." https://www.rottentomatoes.com/tv/riverdale/s01.
Soloski, A. (2018, November 18). "He Makes Archie Deep and Sabrina Dark. Meet Roberto Aguirre-Sacasa." *New York Times*. https://www.nytimes.com/2018/11/08/arts/sabrina-riverdale-roberto-aguirre-sacasa.html.
Todisco, E. (2020, September 3). "Lili Reinhart Feels 'Like a Prisoner' Filming *Riverdale* in Canada During COVID-19." *People.com*. https://people.com/tv/lili-reinhart-feels-prisoners-filming-riverdale-canada/.
u/Direct-Pineapple-193 (2021). "But WHY did Riverdale become so bad?" [forum post]. *Reddit*. https://www.reddit.com/r/television/comments/rq2f6j/but_why_did_riverdale_become_so_bad/.
u/Separate_Secretary_5 (2022). "Who else thinks riverdale had huge potential but everything went bad maybe after s4 …" [forum post]. *Reddit*. https://www.reddit.com/r/riverdale/comments/u8d1a9/who_else_thinks_riverdale_had_huge_potential_but/.
Waid, M., & Staples, F. (2016). *Archie*, vol. 1. Archie Comic Publications.

Archie Must Die

On the Many Lives and Deaths of Archie Andrews

W. RON SWEENEY

> All plots tend toward death.
> —Don Delillo, *White Noise*

> In the same comic book, or in the edition of the following week, a new story begins. If it took Superman up again at the point where he left off, he would have taken a step toward death.
> —Umberto Eco, "The Myth of Superman"

Introduction

To mark its departure from the traditional *Archie* comics, *Riverdale* opens with a death. Throughout the first season, iconic characters from the history of the comics are threatened and the show teases Archie's own death. For many fans of the classic *Archie* supermarket digest comics or the classic animated television shows, *Riverdale* felt like a breach in the canon with Archie far removed from the innocence of old. However, this essay will show how *Riverdale* specifically builds on previous incarnations of Archie, particularly the *Archie: The Married Life* series and the *Afterlife with Archie* horror series. And I argue that *Riverdale* is particularly inspired by Archie's death at the end of the *Archie: The Married Life* series. By the third season of *Riverdale*, Archie's death has been foreshadowed multiple times. As Archie is mauled by a bear in the ominously titled ninth episode of the third season, "Chapter 44: No Exit," fans could be forgiven for thinking the death of Archie is inevitable. And I would suggest it is unavoidable. In examining the many lives and deaths of Archie,

I wish to show how the move from mythic time to historical time dooms Archie.

Archie Got Hot

In the very first episode of *Riverdale*, Kevin Keller proclaims, "Archie got hot!" It is an attempt to create a new reality for the comics property. In fact, *Archie* comics was not hot at all. While *Archie* comics had dominated the comics charts of the '50s and '60s, in recent decades it was all but dead (Comichron, 2014). The CEO of Archie Comics, Jon Goldwater, accurately proclaimed that "Archie was a dormant property when I arrived. It was frozen" (Weinman, 2015). *Archie* was perceived as out-of-date and old-fashioned, and while it still existed on those supermarket shelves, there was very little connection between those books and the larger cultural spaces of comics media. In working with comics creators like Mark Waid (*Daredevil*, *Kingdom Come*) and Fiona Staples (*Saga*), and especially through the efforts of eventual Chief Creative Officer Roberto Aguirre-Sacasa, Archie Comics attempted to create a new status for the inhabitants of Riverdale. Out of these collaborations come a few notable projects: the 2015 relaunch of an *Archie* serial comic, an *Archie* horror imprint, and *Riverdale*.

The difference in tone between Waid and Staples' 2015 relaunch of *Archie* and the television series *Riverdale* could not be more striking. While *Riverdale* attempted to completely upend the Archie mythos, writer Mark Waid and artist Fiona Staples start from a principle of continuity. In her introduction to the first volume, Staples exclaims, "A redesigned Archie? No one wants that!" (Waid & Staples, 2016). She agrees to draw Archie when Waid tells her, "There's nothing wrong with Archie." This idea of Archie as an iconic and unchanging character had already been challenged in previous serial comics, however Staples shows that there is still a dominant idea of Riverdale's redhead. In the introduction, Staples suggests that while many artists have drawn Archie, he has remained the same (Waid & Staples, 2016). She saw her task in reworking Archie as a continuation rather than a transformation. Her version of Archie brings him more in line with contemporary art styles, particularly of other young adult comics, while still clearly building on the classic art.[1] Furthermore, it was the iconic aspect of the Archie character that fascinated Staples:

> And it was incredibly endearing! Archie and the gang would never graduate and go to university or get boring full-time jobs. They'd never even had to go through puberty—they just went from being li'l to being teens. Awesome! [Waid & Staples, 2016].

Archie comics were innocent in part because they never had to follow through to consequences. No matter how many times the gang approached conflict and disaster, the next issue would allow for a reset. Waid and Staples' opening images feature Archie giving the reader a tour of a new Riverdale High in an attempt to modernize the school and diversify the student body, which had been incredibly homogenous throughout its history. It is a delicate balancing act for the comic: Archie needs to be both stationary and also to develop into a contemporary character. Likewise, *Riverdale* needs to be timeless and also brand new. And so there are classic elements of the *Archie* comics still present in the comic, most notably the school's architecture and Archie's jacket.

While the opening of *Riverdale* involves murder and rape, the first story arc of Waid and Staples is concerned with a #LipstickIncident that does not even end with infidelity (Finn, 2015).[2] It does, however, lead to the breakup of Archie and Betty and the arrival of Veronica in Riverdale. But the two types of storytelling are not as divergent as it appears at first glance. While Riverdale is determined to radically reimagine the characters, and Waid's *Archie* series attempts to stay close to tradition, the serial storytelling style links them. Serial storytelling forces the characters into longer and more dramatic arcs, and by *Archie: Volume 4*, Betty is in a coma! So much for the same old Archie and friends. To change the story by introducing ongoing plots into the world is to radically rework the nature of the *Archie* comic. Archie will now be consumed by time, and possibly by his friends.

In moving from the supermarket anthology format to serial narrative forms, Archie as a character moves from icon to individual. As Bart Beatty argued in *Twelve-Cent Archie*, the iconic version of Archie was

> an atypical comic-book protagonist. He is a young man to whom things happen; he is not someone who makes things happen. Only rarely is he the central actor in any of the plots in which he is involved. Only on occasion is he the character who takes the first action. In character terms, he is actually little more than a cipher—a blank space on which stories are written [2015, p. 16].

In fact, in the old supermarket digest comics it is difficult for Archie to act: for him to decide between Betty and Veronica would introduce a different type of plot to the book.[3] In *Understanding Comics: The Invisible Art*, Scott McCloud argues that simplified and less "realistic" character representations in comics provide an "amplification through simplification" (1993, p. 30). As we move from the historic image of Archie, through the animated image of the cartoons, to the modern representations, and finally to the television adaptation, the relationship to the character transforms. What *Riverdale* then presents is a different concept of narrative time from the traditional *Archie* comics. The Archie of *Archie* comics was ageless; he existed in a permanent state of youth.

Bart Beaty notes that characterization is often haphazard in these *Archie* comics (2015, p. 26); he finds that Archie can be "a good student or a bad student, a strong athlete or a poor one, nimble and agile or clumsy and maladroit, all depending on the particular needs of any given story" (2015, p. 17). Whatever happened to Archie didn't matter: by the next issue, whatever plot elements had been advanced would simply be reset (2015, p. 20). Because of the format of the comics, it was less important for *Archie* to have consistency than it was to have the setup to a good joke. Even the location of Riverdale itself was inconsistent in the comics. As Beaty's study finds, in some issues it existed as a three-hour drive to New York City, while other times there was a long plane trip involved; what mattered was "not the idea that it might be an actual place but rather that it could be any place" (2015, p. 30). These narrative inconsistencies are mostly unnoticed when the story resets each issue. The reader can simply assume that the town is as flexible as the characters. It only becomes more of a problem when the story switches to a continuous storytelling. In *Riverdale* and in Waid and Staples' *Archie Vol. 1*, the audience starts to learn more about the town and its place within America. Time no longer stands still for the characters or the city.

The Myth of Archie

To understand the transformations of Archie in *Riverdale*, I turn here to Umberto Eco and translator Natalie Chilton's essay "The Myth of Superman." Of particular importance is the way Eco examines the relationship between time and continuity in the classic superhero comics. While Eco's essay primarily concerns the superhero, Beaty notes, "They should have written about Archie comics" (2015, p. 210). Originally written in 1962 as a review of *The Amazing Adventures of Superman*, the essay was translated and revised with Natalie Chilton and published in *Diacritics* in 1972. Perhaps no article has had as much influence on studies of comics' storytelling structures as Eco's "The Myth of Superman." Eco's essay examined the ways in which time and continuity worked in the superhero tradition, and in particular contrasted Superman with the heroes of traditional mythic stories. In a particularly important passage, Eco comments, "In the same comic book, or in the edition of the following week, a new story begins. If it took Superman up again at the point where he left off, he would have taken a step toward death" (1972, p. 17). Instead, Superman and Archie do not age, and could continue their adventures without any danger.[4]

The challenge for the superhero comic is to keep the story balanced between mythic time and novel time, since it is taking place in the contemporary world. On the level of the individual issue or story, time progresses as in realist fiction. So instead, the comics reset, story to story and issue to issue. Eco writes:

> Superman, then, must remain "inconsumable" and at the same time be "consumed" according to the ways of everyday life. He possesses the characteristics of timeless myth, but is accepted only because his activities take place in our human and everyday world of time. The narrative paradox that Superman's script writers must resolve somehow, even without being aware of it, demands a paradoxical solution with regard to time [Eco, 1972, p. 6].

The solution developed in the classic comics was to pretend that the previous story did not influence the following story. Superman—and his writers—must "forget" what he has done the day before. Writes Eco, "In Superman stories the time that breaks down is the time of the story, that is, the notion of time which ties one episode to another" (1977, p. 17). So Eco notes that the stories use an oneiric or dreamlike state in their storytelling:

> The stories develop in a kind of oneiric climate—of which the reader is not aware at all—where what has happened before and what has happened after appears extremely hazy. The narrator picks up the strand of the event again and again as if he had forgotten to say something and wanted to add details to what had already been said [1977, p. 17].

Time is actually less of a problem for stories like *Archie* that don't have to operate in the adventure mode like Superman. For Superman has to save the day, over and over again, defeating Lex Luthor only to have to face him again the next month. Archie, with the exception of the occasional adventure, mostly lives in the day to day. And in most *Archie* comics of the same era, readers will find that Archie's choices don't make a difference. The things that happen to Archie are erased by the beginning of the next story.[5] But if Archie's actions in one month's comic lead to action in another comic, he has, in Eco's terms, stepped toward death. If Archie is to age, then like Superman, he will have taken a step toward death.

Eco's essay was primarily an analysis of the Superman of the '50s and '60s (Singer, 2017, p. 38). By 1972, as Eco was revising his review, superhero comics had begun to move away from this traditional story structure and Marvel in particular had developed their own shared universe of stories. While some critics used this transformation to claim that superhero comics had moved beyond Eco's ideas, Marc Singer shows in *Breaking the Frames: Populism and Prestige in Comics Studies* that Eco's ideas still have a great relevance to the current comics landscape. Singer argues that some comics scholars, in overly celebrating the populism of current comics, refuse the critique in Eco of the ways in which popular comics (and superhero comics in particular) reinforce the status quo (37). Singer is particularly interested here in the "oneiric climate" of comics. Comics have moved away from the "oneiric climate" of suspended time toward a system of continuity (Singer, 2018 p. 36). This transformation, identified by many scholars, has likewise occurred in *Archie* comics, although not in the main supermarket digests (Singer, 2018). However, this does not mean that Eco's ideas are irrelevant. In fact, the new model of continuity just prolongs the crisis that Eco identified. Singer cautions against discarding Eco's insights too hastily: "Eco's oneiric climate is not a simple state of timelessness so much as it is one strategy for managing a contradiction faced by any character in a popular serial narrative" (Singer, 2018, p. 40). Works such as *Life with Archie: The Married Life* or *Riverdale* feel the challenge of narrative time very quickly. As the characters develop, they move further away from their mythological origin. The danger is always that they will move too far from a recognizable iconicity, and in the process fundamentally alter the status of the character in the public consciousness.

Since the time in which Eco wrote, Superman has in fact died multiple times. But as Singer suggests, the death does not counter Eco's argument: in fact, "the finality of their deaths had been erased in favor of the type of never-ending seriality that is still the norm in superhero comics" (2018, p. 57). The first time Superman dies, many fans were distraught. Fifteen deaths later, and it is no longer quite so shocking (Karbank, 2017). In fact, comics fans are quite used to having whole universes destroyed and recreated. Singer writes:

> worlds are destroyed and reborn, continuities are purged and restored, and the only constant amid the constant change is the certainty that any character eventually will be returned to their most popular and durable form. Supported by nostalgic creators and fans and supporting lucrative licenses in turn, the dream always wins in the end [Singer, 2018, p.57].

Archie Comics has also attempted to appeal to new fans and nostalgic fans simultaneously, by generating headlines in the media and in producing numerous golden age collections. There was certainly never any danger that they would stop producing *Archie* comics following the death of Archie, anymore than DC Comics has stopped producing Superman comics following the various deaths of their icon. For Singer, claims that comics worlds have moved away from Eco's analysis overlook the complexity of the schemata idea and also overestimate the ability of mainstream corporate storytelling to move away from this oneiric climate. The model of storytelling in Marvel Comics, DC Comics and *Archie* comics must maintain the characters as properties: they cannot risk losing their intellectual property by moving the characters too far away from the traditional version of the character. And so even when writers within the company are allowed to create revised versions of the canonical stories, there is an inevitable return to the status quo.

Angela Ndalianis explores the limits of Eco's understanding of time and continuity in "Enter the Aleph: Superhero Worlds and Hypertime Realities." Using *Smallville*, the 2001 television adaptation of the Superman backstory, Ndalianis argues that the show "unsettles Eco's schema but it also calls into question his assertion that the myth value of the superhero collapses when the myth layer succumbs to serial logic" (2009, p. 284). I want to spend time on this example, because much of what Ndalianis suggests regarding *Smallville* can be asked of *Riverdale* as well. Much like *Riverdale*, *Smallville* set out to challenge the status quo of the Superman mythology. Unlike *Riverdale*, it did not radically rewrite the ideas of the characters or the setting. And its relationship to the source material, because it was set *in the past*, was not as contentious. It was dealing with the history or backstory, while *Riverdale*'s plot moves forward into the characters' futures.

Singer's criticism of Ndalianis is that she simplifies Eco's critique in order to praise the television adaptation of Superman: *Smallville*. While Ndalianis claims that *Smallville* "unsettles Eco's schema" (qtd. in Singer, 2018, p. 44), Singer suggests that this *is* Eco's schema. Singer writes, "Far from collapsing the mythological value of Superman, Eco's iterative seriality preserved it for decades" (2018, p. 44). Singer notes that when the television adaptation does reach outside of itself, it is "devoid of any commentary or critique on their source material" but tends to consist of "in-jokes, homages, or derivative imitations" (2018, p. 46). This sounds like a direct description of *Riverdale*, which has taken great joy in its constant allusions and references, but has not ever been clear about what it is using them for. Core to Singer's argument is the idea that the earlier comics (and this applies to *Archie* comics very closely) were far more experimental in form than they are often given credit for. But for Ndalianis what matters here is not so much how *Smallville* fits into Eco's categories, but how differently the viewers of contemporary television adaptations react to the myths. She is correct that the schemata is unsettled: instead of the stable concept of character, there is a constant revision of these characters, and even if they end up returning to familiar forms, they bring some of their transformation with them. Ndalianis writes: "In *Smallville*, the anticipated metanarrative—Eco's mythic layer—is both worshipped as static entity and revealed to always be in a state of process, an interplay that problematizes Eco's distinction between the mythic and the serial" (2009, p. 276). With a story like *Smallville*, the serial becomes part of the larger myth, particularly as that story is then revised into the larger Superman canon. Archie can go back to his iconic version, but for readers and viewers the events of *Riverdale* will have forever shaped their understanding of the character.

Life with Archie

As had happened in superhero comics, Archie Comics turned to promoted event storylines to freshen up their comics. In the runup to *Archie* #600, Archie Comics announced that their protagonist would finally choose between Betty and Veronica in a special wedding themed series (Boesveld, 2009). In the three-part special, "Archie Marries Veronica," writer Michael Uslan has Archie encounter the aptly named Memory Lane, and of course he decides to explore it, saying, "Hey, I've never walked up memory lane, only down! Think I'll explore the opposite direction this time" (Uslan, 2009, p. 3). Archie then walks into his future with Veronica, beginning with a proposal, then marriage, and finally ending with the birth of twins. Not all fans were happy when they found out that Archie would choose Veronica, but the surprises were hardly over. Following the initial three issues, the following three issues explored the possibility of Archie's life with Betty. "Archie Marries Betty" followed a similar structure: proposal, wedding, and finally twins. The doubling cannot ever be stopped. Even when the comics promised a resolution to the classic Archie dilemma, they could not resist an immediate reset and the 6-issue run ended with Archie wandering back into his ordinary life and into his ordinary problems: two dates on a Saturday, leading to milkshakes dumped on his head by both Betty and Veronica.[6]

While the story covers Archie's two possible decisions, in many ways it is just a continuation of the "Imaginary Tales" style of storytelling popularized in earlier eras of comics (c.f. Singer, p. 39). The event would also shape the following decade of *Archie* comics, leading to the 2010–2014 series *Life with Archie: The Married Life* and to spin-offs such as the horror series *Afterlife with Archie* and eventually the television series, *Riverdale*. Inspired by the success of the series (if not in sales, at least in newspaper and magazine articles), Archie Comics published an ongoing serial Archie: *Life with Archie: The Married Life*.[7] Once again published as a monthly magazine title, *Life with Archie* was this time written by Paul Kupperberg, and only loosely based on the earlier series. It was not, however, a direct sequel, and specifically avoided the pregnancy storylines of the earlier *Archie Marries Veronica/Archie Marries Betty* series. *Life with Archie: The Married Life* again worked around the problem of Archie choosing by presenting two alternative timelines. Again, Archie and Veronica's stories come first, because historically, Varchie is endgame.[8]

Throughout *Life with Archie: The Married Life*, Kupperberg explores what would happen to an Archie that had to move through time. His actions have consequences: in the world with Veronica he is forced to navigate a business he is starkly unprepared for and with Betty he has to find a way to pay rent and follow his dreams of musical success. But it is not which decision Archie makes that has mattered here. It is that he has chosen. To those who would say Archie has simply chosen "both," Kupperberg retorts: "And no, the answer is not 'both.' Because in each storyline, Archie makes the only choice he can for that particular reality" (Uslan, 2011). This very idea of a "particular reality" for Archie is the break from the previous idea of the comics.

The series partially transforms *Archie* comics from operating according to a mythic narrative time to a novelistic time, but this does not fully destroy the oneiric time of the comic. The reader is frequently reminded that what they are reading is just one possibility. As readers flip back and forth between the stories with Archie and Veronica or Archie and Betty, they have to realize that neither story is strictly canonical. These are part of the larger dream of the Archie mythology. Within the story, only Dilton Doiley recognizes that something is off and even suggests the possibility of an Archie multiverse.[9] In each story, the changes to storytelling mode also affects the minor characters: Miss Grundy will die, Pop will leave the diner to Jughead. Once-sidelined characters like Moose Mason and Kevin Keller will be placed front and center in the story. These characters, because they are less influenced by Archie's key decision to marry Betty or Veronica, allow the *Married Life* to keep the universes loosely connected. This becomes particularly important in the conclusion of the series.

The Death of Archie

In July 2014, *Life with Archie: The Married Life* comes to a conclusion in issue #36. Once again, the news of the issue superseded the actual release. Published with 5 variant covers, the most notable here features the art of Francesco Francavilla, who was soon to collaborate with Roberto Aguirre-Sacasa on the horror series *Afterlife with Archie*. The Francavilla cover shows Jughead, flanked by Betty and Veronica, standing in the rain with umbrellas in front of the tombstone of Archie Andrews. For anyone buying the issue, what happened inside was not going to be much of a surprise. But within the narrative itself, the death of Archie is only barely set up. While there had been hints across a few issues that danger was approaching, there was no logical reason for the series to end here. Rather, it is fairly clear that the series' time was running out, with low consumer interest.

The most interesting decision of the issue is that rather than alternating between the two storylines—as previous issues had done—Kupperberg merges the two timelines. As a consequence, a number of elements are vague: the couples that have been the feature of the series to this point need to be kept separate. The issue is overtly nostalgic, dropping back and forth between past moments of Archie's life before moving the cast to Pop's Diner. As so much of the series had revolved around the status of the diner, it is the only logical place for the final scene. This space had remained in many ways the heart of the series, centering concerns over changing cities and economic strife. But more importantly it was the place that connected the current series to the timeless climate of the original comics. When Archie arrives, Jughead gives him a milkshake with three straws (Kupperberg, 2014, p.27). Throughout this issue, pencillers Pat and Tim Kennedy and inker Jim Amash return to this particularly evocative image of the Archie mythology. Here it suggests that this issue contains both timelines simultaneously, and indeed it draws in the many worlds that Archie has inhabited.

Life with Archie: The Married Life gives Archie a heroic death, as he is shot trying to save the new Senator Kevin Keller from a homophobic assassination attempt. A splash page shows Archie jumping at the gunman, with the large caption "BLAM" dominating the top third of the page (Kupperberg, 2014, p. 37). It is an unusually active image of a character more prone to pratfalls than heroic action. More memorable is the final image of Archie dead in the diner, surrounded by the main cast of the comic (Kupperberg, 2014, p. 41). The image mirrored the cover, except here it is Jughead who holds Archie as he dies, with Veronica and Betty comforting each other to the side (Kupperberg, 2014, p. 41). There are no clues as to which universe this is: the reader is expected to look for clues, but conclude that this is in fact both universes. Archie's final words are ambiguously addressed to both Betty and Veronica: "I've always loved you" (Kupperberg, 2014, p. 40). As a final issue, *Life with Archie: The Married Life #36* is more about the history of *Archie* comics than it is about the death of Archie. A series of flashbacks reconnects Archie to his past as a comics icon, reinvigorating the classic version as it kills off the serial version. Victor Gorelick, the editor-in-chief of Archie Comics, writes in the Foreword to *The Death of Archie: A Life Celebrated*:

> So, why does Archie have to die? It's not because Riverdale has changed, or that the fundamental basics of what made Archie great have been altered—what's changed is reality [Kupperberg, 2014].

The reality that has changed for Archie is due to the introduction of narrative time. But updating Riverdale and placing it into a modern context, the comics have to grapple with contemporary politics, such as the homophobic violence that targeted Kevin Keller and resulted in Archie's death. As soon as Archie steps forward into a novelistic time structure, his death becomes inevitable. It is important then for Gorelick to assure the reader of *Archie* comics that this is only one ending: "Yes, in *Life with Archie*, Archie Andrews dies. It's a sad ending, but comic books are still here and Archie will live on in our comics, digests, graphic novels" (Kupperberg, 2014). Even his death cannot stop Archie from returning, or stop the writers from returning to the *Married Life* plot.

The Sweet Hereafter

The final episode of the first season of *Riverdale* encapsulates the many issues of continuity and death Archie faces in *Riverdale*. Drawing heavily on the conclusion of *Life with Archie: The Married Life*, "Chapter 13: The Sweet Hereafter" moves toward an inevitable Archie death, while temporarily denying it (Aguirre-Sacasa, 2017). The season's major plotlines had wrapped up, and the Archie gang gathered at the diner. Jughead's voiceover suggests a return to the idyllic Riverdale that preceded the season's events:

> We had many milkshakes that night. And we all felt that as dangerous as the world around us had become, here, at least, in this booth, we were safe [Aguirre-Sacasa, 2017].

The events following Jughead's narration show the different understandings of safety found in *Riverdale*. Cheryl torches her family home, while Jughead puts on a Serpents jacket, joining the protection of the South Side gang. Archie, after spending the night with Veronica, goes back to the diner. There is a moment in which he looks in the mirror and sees the iconic happy-go-lucky Archie that we are familiar with from the comics. The moment is immediately broken by a commotion in Pops. While in Kupperberg's series, Archie throws himself in front of Kevin Keller, protecting the character from homophobic violence, here *Riverdale* keeps the story within the family. Archie tries to prevent his father from being shot, but is too slow, and Fred Andrews is shot by a masked man. The show even mirrors the image from the comic, in which Jughead had held a dying Archie. As the credits roll, Jughead again picks up his narration, suggesting that this is "the last moment of Riverdale's innocence." It is not until the opening of season two that *Riverdale* reveals that Fred Andrews survives.

In both cases, the shooting marks an end point and the diner was the place that best represented the way Riverdale as a city was from a perceived "innocent" past. Both show and comic need to break from that past in order to move the plot forward, while simultaneously recuperating it for future incarnations of the Archie mythos. For Archie as a character, the teased deaths would continue. *Riverdale* operates under an assumption/rule that Archie must always be under threat. The villain here is not "The Black Hood" but the nature of plot in *Archie* comics. As Eco, Singer, and Ndalianis each show in their own way, comics properties—as with many of the franchises built from these comics—are deeply invested in exploring their own status quos. At the same time as there is a movement away from the static starting point, there is also a push back toward reset and stasis. But a show like *Riverdale* cannot circle back in the same way that the comics do: the actors age—far more quickly than the characters they are portraying—and the show must continue forward.[10] It is the nature of the plot that pushes them toward mortality. And given how much of *Riverdale* is concerned with interweaving plots, the threats begin to pile up around Archie.

And it is not just Archie whose death is foreshadowed in *Riverdale*. In season three, Betty is nearly decapitated. Season four teases the murder of Jughead. Readers of the *Archie* comics, and the horror imprint in particular, will recognize many allusions: the Black Hood is a significant plot point in season two; Jughead's possible turn to werewolf; the arrival of zombies, and even *Vampironica*. As with many of the allusions in *Riverdale*, they connect back to the multiple decades of multiple Archie identities and stories, as well as pointing toward an atmosphere of impending doom. What disaster will eventually claim the lives of the four main characters? The plot can only move forward toward some calamity.

Afterlives of Archie

In the comics, the afterlife of Archie has been particularly eventful. Archie Comics had always published multiple titles monthly, and that's before even considering some of the strange crossovers and co-published comics.[11] Roberto Aguirre-Sacasa had even worked on *Glee* cross-overs.[12] The *Archie Crossover Collection* demonstrates that Archie can even crossover with the real world, as the gang meets George Takei and The Ramones. So it isn't surprising that Archie Comics continued experimenting with new models even as the *Life with Archie: The Married Life* series continued. The significant moment occurred when Francesco Francavilla drew a horror variant of *Life with Archie: The Married Life* #23. The popularity of Francavilla's dark imaging of the Archie universe prompted the creation of a horror imprint at the comics company. *Afterlife with Archie* written by Roberto Aguirre-Sacasa featured a full zombie takeover of Riverdale, and *Jughead: The Hunger* turned the favorite side-kick into a werewolf, while *Vampironica* really needs no further explanation. Archie Comics has even begun exploring crossovers between the horror series. In her review of *Jughead: The Hunger* and *Riverdale*, Sylvia Herrera argues that, like *Riverdale*,

> The Hunger therefore successfully transitions the wholesome image of Archie and his friends to the gothic comic-book genre, where our characters find themselves in darker storylines and conceal secretive pasts [2017, p. 222].

As with *Riverdale*, we begin with death and the body counts rise in shocking but predictable ways. Even stories not clearly marked as a part of the horror imprint now explore the impact of Archie's death. In Mark Waid's 6-part miniseries *Archie: 1941*, Archie heads off to fight in World War II, is lost and presumed dead, and readers are again given the image of Archie's tombstone in the comics, as his friends again mourn his death. The repeated imagining of Archie's death in the new comics speaks to the need to simultaneously reinvent the character and then return to the series' origin, as in Waid's *Archie: 1941*, which literally returns to the year *Archie* was first published.

Alongside the *Riverdale* television show, Archie Comics has released a series of interconnected comics, including two series of graphic novels specifically working through the *Riverdale* brand. The first was sold as *Road to Riverdale* and featured stories from across the Archie Comics line of serial comics. But these storylines did not tie into the actual plotlines of *Riverdale* the tv show and may have been confusing for readers. The second series was called *Riverdale: All New Stories* and these books were in fact based on the versions of the characters from the television show. The first book is mostly backstory and exposition, showing major characters as they approach the beginning of *Riverdale*. Volume 2 was published after season two. The stories here are about establishing some of the characters from *Riverdale* whose stories don't always get told, such as Kevin Keller and Reggie Mantle and Pop Tate. Of particular interest is a *Riverdale Vol. 2* story involving Dilton Doiley titled "Apocalypse Now!" Here Dilton predicts an imminent catastrophe and we get to see his survivalist bunker. Jughead briefly thinks he will be trapped here as Doiley locks the door and refuses to let Jughead leave. It's all standard survival storytelling, with a bit of *10 Cloverfield Lane* thrown in. But that only lasts for one night and then the key is stolen back by Jughead and the doors are opened revealing no apocalypse. This is *Riverdale*, after all, not an Archie horror series. But before Jughead can return to the city, we see him reading the signs in the clouds: there are four horsemen there. Perhaps there is something more coming to *Riverdale*.

No Exit

The end of *Riverdale* season one, with its relatively straightforward mysteries and teases, seems very innocent compared to the convoluted plots of seasons two and three. I argue that season three of *Riverdale* makes the show about Archie Comics and the place of Archie in the modern world. The metafictional element is most clear through the "Gryphons and Gargoyles" subplot. As a full-blown satanic-panic parody of *Dungeons & Dragons,* the game functions within the *Riverdale* universe to collapse the distinction between reality and fantasy. The season embraces Eco's "oneiric climate": as Jughead states in "Chapter 40: The Great Escape," "It's all one big narrative that's still being written and played" (Murray, 2018). In the episode, they literally play Gryphons and Gargoyles to influence Archie's escape, thereby suggesting that the game has real world effects. In "Chapter 44: No Exit" Archie plays Gryphons and Gargoyles while unconscious, after a near-fatal bear attack (Anderson, 2019). The episode begins with Jughead invoking the hero's journey and directly comparing Archie to Luke Skywalker. This is a long way from the "atypical comic-book protagonist" from the classic *Archie* comics (Beaty, 2015, p. 16). When Archie is told, by people he has seen die, that he has to play Gryphons and Gargoyles in order to escape, he recognizes the oneiric climate, responding: "This isn't real. You guys are all dead.... I'm dreaming" (Anderson, 2019). But to get out he has to complete a series of quests which will take him back over pivotal moments in the series. Archie returns first to the diner, the point at which he should have died, or should have acted sooner. He tackles the gunman and kills him, holding the black hood as if to become the revenging assassin himself. But the task is not over. He gets another quest from the deceased prison warden who tells him he needs to find "the place and time where it all went wrong." For fans of the show, this suggests the possibility of a reset. Here, it is clear that something has gone wrong.[13] Archie identifies his failure to kill Hiram Lodge as the core problem. The fact that Archie is dominated by Lodge is key to the mythology. Archie again kills, and again finds he is not out of his game; he faces one last round with Jughead, Betty, and Veronica, who tell him "it's the only way back." In this last quest, Archie must confront himself. He is shown holding a baseball bat, standing over his younger self. It is a direct return to the opening night of the *Riverdale* show. In trying to stop Archie from this self-destruction, Fred Andrews suggests "you could forgive him" (Anderson, 2019). But Archie cannot imagine forgiveness. While there is a chance here to return to innocence, Archie cannot find it. And while his father tells him, "there's always another path home," Archie knows that this version of Riverdale cannot let him live. Innocent Archie will have to wait for yet another reboot. This is who he has to become, he thinks, in order to survive in this Riverdale. Archie claims, "If I ever want to go back to Riverdale again, I have to destroy that part of me that's weak, that's bad, that's stupid" (Anderson, 2019). He has to fight himself, the sleeping self, oblivious to the danger that was in Riverdale from the beginning.

Riverdale, after having directly invoked *Star Wars* in the opening, must enact it in the conclusion. Archie strikes the innocent version of himself and that version disappears, leaving only the more experienced Archie facing what is to come. Archie does not yet wake up and the episode ends with Archie seemingly dead, but of course it is another tease. Jughead begins the following episode: "At 8:47, on a Wednesday morning, Archie Andrews died. At least, the Archie we knew. What returned to Riverdale was something far different from the redheaded boy next door" (Paterson, 2019). The death required by *Riverdale* has again been deferred.

Conclusions

Both Superman and Archie have now died multiple times and will continue to die until the audience finally grows tired of them. In the *Married Life* comic, Archie's death serves to close the narrative loop, and fix the rupture that had been introduced by having him marry Veronica (and then Betty). In *Riverdale*, the problem for Archie has been much less how to choose between Veronica and Betty. Archie's problem is one of being out-of-place in the contemporary world. The show demands his death—real or symbolic—as an acknowledgment of the problem of mortality for the icon. Archie's death in *Riverdale* is the logical end point for the series; however, even if Roberto Aguirre-Sacasa and the other writers choose to recuperate Archie, there's no escaping mortality. As he has moved from mythic figure to a character in the serial *Riverdale* universe, he faces the constant problem of choosing what happens next. Eventually, even the teens on *Riverdale* graduate and get jobs, and that, in Umberto Eco's terms, constitutes "a step toward death" (1977, p. 17). For the show to end, Archie will have to die.

Notes

1. C.f. "The Evolution of Archie Comics" from *Riverdale: All-New Stories*.
2. However much the show wishes to ignore it, Archie is abused by a Riverdale teacher in the opening episodes. It is the first of many traumas he will endure over the course of *Riverdale*.
3. Beaty notes that it wasn't ever really up to Archie in the first place. This was a decision for Veronica and Betty (2015, p. 38).

4. For the comics, according to Eco, it's important that Superman is both mortal and immortal. He cannot die, because then the story would be over. But if he is immortal, then "the public's identification with his double identity would fall by the wayside" (1977, p. 16). It is less certain that this applies to Archie.

5. As some viewers of *Riverdale* have found, the show often forgets its own past as well. But these omissions are not part of the deliberate strategy of the world-building.

6. Archie Comics is currently publishing *Archie: The Married Life 10th Anniversary* further exploring the two possible futures.

7. There is some confusion about the title, as it was published differently in its monthly issue and in its eventual graphic novel collection. The individual issues parodied teen magazine covers and were titled *Life with Archie: The Married Life* and ran from issue #1 up to issue #37. The graphic novels were titled *Archie: The Married Life* and were collected into six books.

8. Stated by Veronica during *Riverdale*'s season-three episode, "Chapter 56: The Dark Secret of Harvest House." It is also confirmed historically in Beaty's *Twelve-Cent Archie* (2015).

9. Archie Comics suggested that this would be addressed in an upcoming series (Ferguson).

10. I might make an exception here in *Riverdale*, as the actors are so far removed from the actual ages of the characters, they could reset to the beginning without much difference. *Riverdale* has also explored the past generation using the current cast of characters in "Chapter 39: The Midnight Club."

11. In one of the stranger examples, Archie Comics licensed the characters to Spire Christian Comics (https://comicsworthreading.com/2010/05/14/archies-christian-comics/).

12. Aguirre-Sacasa was chief creative officer at Archie Comics and a writer for *Glee* and naturally wrote the crossover comics. The comics noted numerous similarities between the Archie universe and the *Glee* universe.

13. But since the show still cannot admit that Archie was abused and manipulated by Miss Grundy in the opening arc of the series, it cannot actually return Archie to innocence.

References

Aguirre-Sacasa, R. (2017). *Riverdale All-New Stories Vol. 1*. Archie Comic Publications.

Aguirre-Sacasa, R. (Writer), & Krieger, L.T. (Director) (2017). Chapter One: The River's Edge [television series episode]. *Riverdale*. United States: Berlanti Productions and Archie Comics Publications.

Aguirre-Sacasa, R. (Writer), & Krieger, L.T. (Director) (2017). Chapter Thirteen: The Sweet Hereafter [television series episode]. *Riverdale*. United States: Berlanti Productions and Archie Comics Publications.

Anderson, A. (Writer), & Hunt, J. (Director) (2019). Chapter Forty-Four: No Exit [Television series episode]. *Riverdale*. United States: Berlanti Productions and Archie Comics Publications.

Beaty, B. (2015). *Twelve-Cent Archie*. Rutgers University Press.

Boesveld, S. (2009, May 27). "Archie Commits—Finally." *The Globe and Mail*. Retrieved from https://www.theglobeandmail.com/life/archie-commits---finally/article4315990/.

Comichron (2014, July 14). "The Life of Archie: 54 Years of Circulation History." Retrieved from https://blog.comichron.com/2014/07/the-life-of-archie-54-years-of.html.

Eco, U., & Chilton, N. (1972). "The Myth of Superman." *Diacritics* 2(1), 14. https://doi-org.proxy.ufv.ca:2443/10.2307/464920.

Ferguson, J. (2019). "Can Dilton Doiley Restore Order in Archie: The Married Life—10 Years Later #5 First Look?" Retrieved from http://www.comicon.com/2019/11/30/can-dilton-doiley-restore-order-in-archie-the-married-life-10-years-later-5-first-look/.

Finn, C. (2015). "ICYMI: We Found Out What the #LipstickIncident Was in 'Archie' #4." *Comics Alliance*. Retrieved from http://comicsalliance.com/icymi-archie-lipstick-incident.

Herrera, S.E. (2017). "Riverdale, Season 1 and Jughead: The Hunger." *Irish Journal of Gothic & Horror Studies 16*, 219. Retrieved from https://search.ebscohost.com/login.
Karbank, O. (2017, 15 October). "Superdead: 15 Times Superman Actually Died." Retrieved from https://www.cbr.com/times-superman-died.
Kupperberg, P. (2014). *The Death of Archie: A Life Celebrated*. Archie Comic Publications.
Kupperberg, P. (Writer) (2014). *Archie: The Married Life Book 6*. Archie Comic Publications.
Murray, G. (Writer), & Romanowski, P. (Director) (2018). Chapter Forty: The Great Escape [television series episode]. *Riverdale*. United States: Berlanti Productions and Archie Comics Publications.
Ndalianis, A. (2009). *The Contemporary Comic Book Superhero*. Routledge.
Paterson, B. (Writer), & Kiley, M. (Director) (2012). Chapter Forty-Five: The Stranger [television series episode]. *Riverdale*. United States: Berlanti Productions and Archie Comics Publications.
Rosenberg, M., Segura, A., & Parent, D. (2017). *Archie Crossover Collection*. Archie Comics Publications.
Singer, M. (2018). *Breaking the Frames: Populism and Prestige in Comics Studies*. University of Texas Press.
Uslan, M., & Breyfogle, N. (2011). *Archie: The Married Life Book 1*. Archie Comic Publications.
Waid, M., & Staples, F. (2016). *Archie Vol. 1*. Archie Comic Publications.
Waid, M., & Woods, P. (2017). *Archie Vol. 4*. Archie Comic Publications.
Weinman, J. (2015). "Golly Gee, Is That... Archie?" *Macleans*. Retrieved from https://www.macleans.ca/culture/books/golly-gee-is-that-archie/.

On Becoming a Citizen of Riverdale
Narrative Expansion Through Fanfiction, Interactive Fiction, and Other Apocryphal (Hyper)Texts

Dessa Bayrock

It's Thursday night and I'm yelling at my television. I know the characters on screen can't hear me, and I know they won't take my advice, but all the same: here I am. The television in front of me. Archie Andrews refusing to sleep, instead intent on hunting down a serial killer. The incredulous words leaving my mouth. If I had popcorn, I would throw it. *In what world is this your responsibility?!* I shout. *Who do you think you are, you sexy teen?!*

I yell this despite myself—despite the fact that Archie Andrews isn't real, and can't hear me, and will never, ever stop being a dramatic teenager. And yet I feel compelled by this urge to save him, warn him, protect him—and not just Archie, but all the sexy teenagers of CW's *Riverdale* television show.

This one of many urges which can inspire traditionally passive readers and viewers to write fanfiction: *if the characters won't listen to my advice, fine. I'll create a world in which they have to listen to me, in which their logic matches mine, in which I control the narrative and can ensure it goes the way it should.* Fanfiction writers rewrite the narrative. They translate it. They expand it.

The combination of these two things—yelling at my television, and becoming preoccupied with possibilities of narrative expansion—is how I found myself on a flight across the country, hunched over my laptop and feverishly coding descriptions, tags, and alternate endings into a program called Twine.[1] I was traveling to the first annual *Riverdale: A Land of Contrasts* conference in beautiful British Columbia, where I would present a strange hybrid project called *Citizen of Riverdale*.[2] As I would explain to a room of scholars, academics, and students just a few days later, the project

I was building was a strange combination of worlds. On one hand, this chimera was a digital humanities project concerned with the ways in which readers make meaning in partnership with a text—something I would call narrative expansion, whereby stories expand through and with a reader even after they're edited, published, and theoretically "finished." On the other hand, an argument could be made that this project was, simultaneously, nothing more than a piece of fanfiction—which is, after all, a genre of writing that falls neatly under the umbrella of "narrative expansion."

After weeks of frenzied work, I titled my project *Citizen of Riverdale*; as I explained to the audience at the first *Riverdale* conference we organized and held in Abbotsford, B.C., in 2017, it is an interactive, Choose-Your-Own-Adventure-style text-based game. The opening sally of its narrative situates the player as a newcomer to the community of Riverdale—importantly, the version of the town portrayed by the television series and not the version portrayed in *Archie* comics—and gives the reader opportunities to meet and interact with the main characters of the show. This construction mimics the show's use of its *Archie* comics source material; I likewise preserved key elements from the original texts, both *Archie* comics and *Riverdale* television show, but re-contextualized them in an environment which allowed a new plot to take place.

In other words: fanfiction. In other words: narrative expansion. In other words: the thing that happens when the audience takes hold of the story and begins fitting new pieces together—whether the original author is in favor or not.

Using *Riverdale*, *Archie* comics, and my construction of *Citizen of Riverdale* as a focal point, this essay explores exactly this idea of narrative expansion—or, in other words, what happens to a narrative after its initial publication puts it within reach of readers, viewers, and fans to do with it what they will. Many consume it and forget it; some become invested or obsessed; a good portion might wish things happened a little differently; and, finally, a select few (such as fanfiction authors and video game developers) not only wish things might have happened differently but build a world in which things *did* happen differently. The result: narrative expansion. The world begins to grow, to change, to extend tentacles into other genres, other stories, other mediums.

Riverdale itself is already an example of narrative expansion; the show is particularly suited to rewriting and re-contextualization (such as that found in fanfiction and other fan-created media) because the television show's universe is really just an expansion of the universe of the *Archie* comics. Fittingly, *Riverdale*'s construction is at least somewhat self-aware in its process of translating and adapting the original text, including a fair number of "Easter egg" callbacks and references to the *Archie* comics, which can be caught by long-time fans; additionally, *Riverdale* draws on a frankly impressive number of intertextual references, building the series on a foundation of pop culture pastiche. Jess Wind (2018) focused on this aspect of the show in their presentation at the first annual *Riverdale: Land of Contrasts* conference in the spring of 2018 as the second season was airing on television for the first time; Wind noted that when we begin to examine *Riverdale*'s "dialogue, set dressing, casting, episode titles, production design" we quickly realize that "nearly everything in this show is a nod to something else" (n.p.). Turning a sharp eye to the series reveals references to H.P. Lovecraft, *Les Misérables*, Edgar Allan Poe, ongoing comic book series *The Wicked + The Divine*, as well as a variety of movies and television shows such as *90210*, *The Breakfast Club*, and *Scream*. *Riverdale*'s pastiche is so thick, Wind says, that it becomes impossible to tell whether it is purposeful or banal.

Most importantly for this essay's purpose, *Riverdale* draws on key features of the original comics series, such as the names and appearances of the main characters, as well as some of—but, importantly, not all of—their defining characteristics and relationships. Even so, by ultimately placing these borrowed or translated features in completely new narrative and thematic contexts, the series mimics the structural conventions of fanfiction. In effect, *Riverdale* borrows components from the original text that it deems desirable or usable, placing them in a hypertext on a massive scale, and discards the rest.

Let's focus on that word for a minute: hypertext. Ted Nelson—an American information scientist, sociologist, and theorist—first coined the term in 1965, in a paper largely concerned with information storage and retrieval. In this context, he describes hypertext as

> a body of written or pictorial material interconnected in such a complex way that it could not conveniently be presented or represented on paper. It may contain summaries, or maps of its contents and their interrelations; it may contain annotations, additions and footnotes from scholars who have examined it. [...] Such a system could grow indefinitely, gradually including more and more of the world's written knowledge [p. 96].

More than sixty years later, this definition remains (perhaps shockingly) useful for the purposes of this essay: a description of something that is more than the sum of its parts, and which changes depending upon which pieces are chosen for consumption and in which order they are consumed. Although it is not the main goal of this essay, I argue that *Riverdale* is an excellent example of a massive hypertext: a sprawling narrative with interconnected parts which simultaneously affect and fail to affect its universe. The *Archie* comics are part of this narrative; its self-aware borrowing of elements from other pop culture narratives make *Les Misérables* and *90210,* among others, part of this narrative[3]; fanfiction and other fan-created errata are part of this narrative; spin-off media such as video games and novelizations, should they be produced, are part of this narrative[4]; as Nicholas E. Miller (2018) argues, we may even consider the real lives of *Riverdale*'s actors as a kind of "paratext" that contributes to the overarching narrative as they speak about their characters both formally (in interviews) and informally (through casual, personal social media posts) and thereby increase the content under the umbrella of the hypertext of both *Riverdale* and the Archie universe as a whole. This vast network in its entirety, and not just the show itself, comprises the universe of *Riverdale*—a narrative which has been expanded both by its producers and writers, and by the viewers who consume some or all of its parts.

Perhaps more importantly for my purposes here, I predominantly use the term "hypertext" as a referent for media (such as fanfiction, spin-off shows, and so on) which make up part of this sprawling narrative universe. Interestingly, these hypertexts are, in and of themselves, referents; texts which make use of a kind of narrative shorthand in order to invoke the larger narrative—the central original text, or hypotext—without actually *showing* the larger narrative.[5]

This essay considers the intersection of two key modes of narrative expansion: user-created fanfictions, and interactive (or gamified) fictions such as video games and text-based roleplaying games. In examining these genres of creative work first independently from and then in relation to *Riverdale*, I consider how both categories of media allow the writer/player far more control than what is typically afforded to the narratively-passive television viewers, either by allowing for universe expansion (with alternate or additional narratives, for instance), or by inviting the player to participate in the world by playing out a gamified version of the narrative. This examination uses *Riverdale* as a focal point in exploring the intersections between gamified narratives (such as video games and Choose-Your-Own-Adventure-style books, whether print or digital in nature) and the kind of narrative remediation common in fanfiction. Throughout the research and creation period for *Citizen of Riverdale,* it became increasingly clear to me that gamified narrative and narrative remediation are linked—operations or processes which are separate rather than disparate. The types of video games set in an already-constructed world with an already-familiar cast of characters borrowed from other media—including but not limited to *Citizen of Riverdale,* for instance, or *LEGO Batman,* in an example which invokes not one but two overarching hypertext universes—seems to borrow or adapt the functions, processes, and purposes common in fanfiction. Especially given the *Riverdale* obsession with Gryphons and Gargoyles—a clear parody of *Dungeons & Dragons*—we might likewise trace the function of video games back to their origin in text-based roleplaying games, which, like fanfiction, give the reader/player an option to enter the narrative as both players and as co-creators of meaning.

Ultimately, I link fanfiction and video games using yet another text-based narrative form which places control in the reader's hands—namely, the *Choose Your Own Adventure* (*CYOA*) book series (and its similarly-styled competitors), which I argue serves as a sort of common ground between the hypertext of traditionally textual fanfiction and the hypertext of video games. According to the *CYOA* website, the *CYOA* books first entered the market in 1979, utilizing the same text-instruction-and-participation framework common in *Dungeons & Dragons* and the same reader-controlled narrative construction common in fanfiction.[6] As I argue, *CYOA*-style narratives present a compelling intermediate player in the Venn diagram between fanfiction and gamified versions of original narratives, combining important features from both genres in a similar—yet distinct—narrative form.

Gathering these perhaps-odd bedfellows together in this essay, I interrogate the ways in which these often-disparate forms of fiction (fanfiction, interactive fiction, and gamified narratives) intersect in terms of purpose, form, and function—and how these intersections are palpable or even central to the "text" of *Riverdale*. I close this analysis by returning to the project which sparked these research questions in the first place: an interactive text-only game titled *Citizen of Riverdale* built using Twine, a program self-described as "an open-source tool for telling interactive, nonlinear stories" on its home page (n.p.). The interactive narrative of *Citizen of Riverdale* takes place in the world of the television show without acknowledging the events of the show, thus drawing on an important convention of fanfiction; simultaneously, much as a video game might, it places the player within the narrative and grants them control over how they choose to interact with (and support, or fall in love with, or backstab) the characters of the show. This project, which I undertook before developing the theoretical foundation of this essay, helped reveal to me the ways in which the seemingly disparate subjects of this essay interact or even overlap: *Citizen of Riverdale*, after all, is very much a fanfiction (in the style of "Mary Sue" narratives, in which the author is self-inserted into the narrative, whether subtly or overtly), but also very much a *CYOA*-style gamified narrative—two halves bound together by *Riverdale*'s own history of and complicity in fanfiction-esque pastiche and apocryphal narrative expansion.

Fan Culture and the Co-Creation of Meaning and Narrative

Fanfiction is key to understanding not only other modes of narrative expansion, but the idea of hypertext as a whole; after all, it's logically, logistically impossible to write fanfiction *without* it being a peripheral hypertext to some other, larger narrative. Especially given the show's translation and mediation of the original *Archie* comics source-text, *Riverdale* is prime real estate for a conversation about fanfiction. Just as the producers of *Riverdale* responded to the appeal of rewriting a familiar text into a new context, fanfiction likewise relies and builds upon the appeal of participatory or creative fan culture—namely, the idea that a pre-existing narrative or set of characters can be improved by anyone who cares to take it up, and that even an amateur is capable of co-creating meaning within (and for) a larger narrative.[7] These ideas and their appeal likewise form a central tenet in interactive fictions (including both *CYOA*-style narratives and video games), which invite viewers, readers, and players to enter the narrative and rebuild it in their preferred image. Reader reception theory has long posited that the creation of meaning rests just as much on readers as it does on authors[8]; as Koenitz (2016) writes, interactive narratives put co-creation even more firmly in the hands of readers in a way that "challenges basic assumptions about narrative in the western world—namely about the role of the author and the fixed state of content and structure as the audience takes on an active role and the narratives become malleable" (p. 91). In other words, interactive fictions expect readers to co-create meaning, but also to co-create the narrative itself.

In fanfiction, however, this balance between the original author and the reader tips even further in the reader's favor; the genre of fanfiction, as well as its surrounding community, grants the reader cultural and creative power in contributing character, plot, or thematic developments to the existing narrative. This context, then, places narrative control in the reader's hands much in the way that interactive fiction and video games do. As Maria Lindgren Leavenworth (2015) notes, "fan fictions represent an intermediary stage between print literature and complex, often multimodal, contemporary hypertexts" (p. 40), accomplishing a similar redistribution of narrative control within a more basic textual context than hypertexts (such as interactive fiction, video games, or even the broader conception of the *Riverdale* universe itself as a hypertext) which simultaneously lays the groundwork for these more complex hypertexts to be constructed. These examples describe related but varied processes of narrative expansion, in which the larger narrative—the sprawling hypertext of the universe, comprised of official and unofficial apocryphal media—grows and evolves through the construction or addition of peripheral hypertexts. In other words, these seemingly disparate peripheral hypertexts (including but not limited to fanfiction, interactive fictions, video games as discussed here) surrounding the main narrative (in this case, *Riverdale*) accomplish similar narrative expansions using different processes and frameworks. In this vein, Marie-Laure Ryan (2013) describes fanfiction (and similar fan-created and/or apocryphal works) as part of a major pole of transmedial storytelling[9]: additions to the narrative world which spring up or are demanded once "a certain story enjoys so much popularity or becomes so prominent culturally that it spontaneously generates a variety of either same-medium or cross-media prequels, sequels, fanfiction, and adaptations" (p. 363). In other words, fanfiction is part of the movement of expansion by popular demand—a desire for additional content which is fulfilled either through official channels (when producers of the central text expand or translate the original text into another medium, such as television or video games) or through unofficial channels (fan art, fanfiction, and so on).

As Henry Jenkins (2012) explains, the creation and consumption of fanfiction is a natural extension of the gossip, discussion, and conversation which have always surrounded popular media, since "gossip and fiction writing [both] provide fans with ways to explore more fully those aspects of the primary series that most interest them, aspects often marginal to the central plot but assuming special salience for particular viewers" (p. 85). In other words, by joining a fan community, participating in fan culture, and consuming or producing fan content of their own, consumers are able to spend more time with sections, themes, portions, characters, or specific plot elements that appeal to them directly. Subsequently, they co-create additional meaning around these elements through interpretation and discussion and create peripheral and/or apocryphal meaning by adding their own nodes to the central text.

Writing fanfiction, then, is a way of personalizing and laying claim to a narrative—consuming and building on a static narrative in a way that transforms it, at least a little, into an interactive one. Subsequent readers may well view fanfiction forum interfaces as a *Choose-Your-Own-Adventure*-style set of options and choices, since, as Jenkins (2012) points out, "[f]ans read these stories not so much to relive their own experience … as to explore the range of different uses writers can make of the same materials, to see how familiar stories will be retold and what new elements will be introduced" (p. 181).

Digital interfaces aside, none of this is new; these discussions, as Jenkins (2012) notes, have surrounded popular culture and media in one form or another for centuries. Fan culture has exploded since the 90s for the same reason that interactive digital narratives have become more popular and widespread; the ease and accessibility of digital platforms makes it easier than ever to find and contribute to centralized fan communities, just as they make it easier to find, create, and participate in interactive narratives. As Kirsten Bussière (2023) implies in her essay "Endless Authorship" in this same volume, the proliferation and expansion of digital meeting places for fan creators (and other participants in fandom hypertexts) recalls the formation of the hypertext itself—providing "an easily accessible environment for creators to share their work with a larger audience of people with similar interests [and] extending kinship networks beyond spatial boundaries" (p. 47). It is perhaps no surprise, then, that the processes and frameworks of fanfiction, both narrative and social, are foundational in understanding the ways in which individuals engage with—and seek to expand—the narratives they consume.

The Evolution, Migration, and Growth of Interactive Narratives

With this understanding of fanfiction as a theoretical foundation for (and a tradition of) both hypertext and narrative expansion, we can begin to understand how narrative expansion appears in myriad other forms in our contemporary landscape—including the narrative processes inherent in *Choose Your Own Adventure* (and similarly functioning) novels as well as video games and interactive digital projects such as *Citizen of Riverdale*. The parallels in form and function between the traditional print book *CYOA* novels and digital interactive narratives are unmistakable; in many ways, the *CYOA* novels anticipated or laid a foundation for hypertexts to come, such as those constructed through Twine or presented through video games. Tracing this timeline even further into the future, as this section seeks to do, we can inarguably mark the effects of *CYOA* novels in normalizing and encouraging processes of reader co-creation and narrative expansion and exploration—processes that recall the form and function of video games.

The links between the *Choose Your Own Adventure* series and early text-adventure computer games such as *Zork* seem clear, since, on a foundational level, both are games that use text to build a narrative framework. Less obvious is which came first; *CYOA* began releasing books in 1975 (although author Edward Packard had been working on the idea for several years) while *Zork* was released in 1977. As Grady Hendrix (2011) notes, *Zork* creator David Lebling (2011) had no knowledge of the *CYOA* series until after he'd finished programming his game. "I saw the Choose Your Own Adventure books as being a knock-off," Lebling says. "I saw them … and thought, 'Oh, this is trying to do an adventure game as a book. How strange'" (par. 22). The texts themselves likewise blur the lines between text-based games and traditional novels; as Daniel Kraus (2016) notes, R.L. Stine's 1985 choose-your-own-adventure-style novel, *The Badlands of Hark*, ends each timeline not with the traditional "THE END" but with "GAME OVER" (p. 79), firmly coloring the novel with a feature found predominantly in arcade games rather than following conventions of a traditional fiction or text narrative. As a result, the question of which came first—game narrative or narrative game—has no discernible answer, since *CYOAs*, video games, and even pen-and-paper role-playing games such as *Dungeons & Dragons* are linked and contextualized against one another. Nicholas Tucker, examining the educational value of the *CYOA* series in 1986, writes that "[t]hose who play video-games will be used to such [narrative and structural] devices" employed by the novels (p. 10), reinforcing the long-standing nature of comparisons between the game-narratives and narrative games.

Importantly, however, Tucker's (1986) off-hand comparison of game narrative to narrative game comes ten years after both *CYOA* novels and computer and video games began to hit the market in earnest, and the intervening years muddy the inception (and reception) of both books and games. It is crucial to note, however, that Packard's series of novels had a distinct advantage over their digital counterparts—at least in the beginning. Krystina Madej (2016) notes that text adventure games for computer (notably including Will Crowther's 1975 *Adventure*) were available in the market before either *Zork* or the *CYOA* books, but warns that existence should not be confused with availability: "While text adventure games were already a reality in the computer world at that time," she writes, "computers and game consoles were yet to become a common household presence and the audience for these early games was very limited; print was still sovereign" (p. 28). *CYOA* books, then, were able to accomplish what *Zork* and *Adventure* were not, or, at least, not at first: to put themselves in the hands of millions of users both quickly and cheaply.

This changed, however, as computers became more powerful and less expensive to purchase and the burgeoning computer game industry began to overtake the *CYOA* series in popularity. Notably, this influx of computer games coincided with *CYOA* market saturation, which situated them to inherit the spoils of *CYOA*'s work in gaining both recognition and popularity. What was once *CYOA*'s daring, defining feature—what Hendrix (2011) calls "the tension between narrative and interactivity" (par. 17), and the attempt to balance the two—became its fatal flaw. Readers became dissatisfied with interactive novels much more quickly when it became clear that computers could offer more content, more features, and more interactivity than a print book ever could. As a result, *CYOA* novels gave way to computer games, which could accomplish the same narrative tasks more smoothly and more effectively. Later books in the *CYOA* series were forced to limit the number of endings in order to deliver enough detail and narrative along each path to keep the reader interested, and this, as Christian Swinehart (2011) notes, was "a sure sign that narrative was taking precedence over interactivity. But interactivity wasn't vanishing, it was evolving and books were no longer the optimal medium with which to deliver it"[10] (qtd. in Hendrix, par. 20).

As a result, and despite differences in format and content delivery, we might do well to consider *CYOA* novels, text adventure computer games, and video games as branches growing parallel to one another. The trunk and roots of this metaphorical tree, then, according to Hartmut Koenitz (2016), would be the shared responsibility of co-creation of meaning and narrative—the central tenet of fanfiction. Interactive media expects more than passive consumption from a reader, but an active role in creating the narrative alongside (if still subordinate to) the author. Seemingly disparate types of media are brought together by this key feature: a common blurring of the lines between author and reader, which defines interactive fiction. It's not a question, then, of which came first—print books or digital adventures, *CYOA* or *Zork*—but a question of what these media accomplish as a whole.[11] For the purposes of this essay, it becomes a question of how the function and purpose of interactive fiction relates to the interactivity of fan communities and the creation of hypertext—e.g., *Riverdale* as a whole.

Using These Building Blocks to Make a Game: Citizen of Riverdale *and Other Experiments in Hybridity*

Laying out the ways in which fanfiction overlaps—or even forecasts—the interactive "text" of a role-playing game or video game leads me back to my own digital contribution to the sphere of Riverdale's apocryphal texts. The gamified narrative of *Citizen of Riverdale* situates the player as a newcomer to the community of Riverdale in the version of the town portrayed by the television series, and gives the reader opportunities to meet and interact with the main characters of the show. This construction mimics the show's use of its *Archie* comics source material; it likewise preserves key elements from the original text, but simultaneously re-contextualizes them in an environment which allows a new plot to take place.

38 The Archie/Sabrina Universe

This creative project feels useful to include—not as a case study, per se, but as an experimental, experiential expression of theory turned to creative practice. In other words, to write about the co-creation of narrative is one thing, and to actually co-create is another, even as the two acts operate as sides of the same coin. How, then, might theory be turned into practice? *Citizen of Riverdale* began, as this essay does, with the idea of fan hypertext suggested by the series; unlike this essay, it exists in a much less serious, much less rigorous, non-academic space of fan work and co-creation, taking the form of an interactive, *CYOA*-style fanfiction. The research question at the heart of both this essay and its interactive, non-academic doppelgänger, however, remains the same: *how and why do readers change narratives through interaction and co-creation?* In this section, I examine my own subjective reader response to this question in the context of the theoretical framework of narrative expansion and co-creation set out in the sections above. This by no means stands as an explanation for the process of other fan writers and creators, but, in the style of an autoethnography, demonstrates at least one version of how theory and practice may intertwine in the form of fanfiction and/or interactive fiction. For my own purposes, setting out to write a *CYOA*-style narrative solidified what I, at least, saw as "key features" of the genre—and why and how they prove necessary to a CYOA-style narrative's success.

Like many children of the '90s, I've played my fair share of *Choose Your Own Adventure* (*CYOA*) novels—both the original series published by Bantam (and, later, by Chooseco) as well as the Fighting Fantasy series by Steve Jackson, which relies on more complicated systems and demands the reader not only make choices but draw maps, simulate combat using dice, and keep track of inventory. I have much less experience in creating my own choose-your-own-adventure-style narratives—and yet, as I realized after I had completed and published *Citizen of Riverdale*, I unconsciously mimicked several key components of the genre in its creation—emphasizing how centrally I place these characteristics to the genre of *CYOA*-style narratives, as well as how important I (even unconsciously) believe these characteristics are in inviting the reader to participate in the narrative—which, in this case, I apply both to the stand-alone narrative of *Citizen of Riverdale* as well as the larger hypertext of *Riverdale* as a whole.

The feature I see as most key in both *Citizen of Riverdale* and *Choose Your Own Adventure* stories as a whole is the use of second-person perspective—a feature which felt non-negotiable from the very start of this project. At first, this may seem like a counter-intuitive choice for a narrative project, since second-person perspective is often considered unsuccessful and awkward in literary fiction. David Lebling, one of the programmers behind *Zork*, notes that the use of second-person perspective is infinitely more effective in games and gamified narratives than in literature: "Second-person books, in my experience, have not been all that successful," he explains in an interview for *Slate*. "Second-person games have been pretty successful" (qtd. in Hendrix, par. 17). Perhaps unsurprisingly, *CYOA*-style narratives seek to place the reader at the center of the "game" of its narrative action much like a video game, and as a result have used second-person almost exclusively from their very beginning. This gamble made the series a hard sell, at first, but it soon became apparent that the second-person perspective was a key feature of the books' popularity. For instance, Daniel Kraus (2016), combining a personal retrospective with critical analysis of the series, recalls this feature fondly:

> The second-person point of view, usually an eye-rolling choice in fiction, was immensely pleasurable here, with [the authors] cheekily taking it to you whenever you did something dumb. So unrelentingly dark were "The End" passages ("You cry out for mercy, but you know there will be none") that, after a while, they came to be the affectionate ribbing of a good friend [p. 79].

Perhaps nothing demonstrates the balance between the awkwardness and necessity of this perspective than the title of the very first novel of the series, published in 1979, both before the series was branded as Choose Your Own Adventure and before it was a series: *The Adventures of You on Sugarcane Island*. The syntax of this title barely scans, but despite the choppiness of the phrasing it succeeds at communicating the purpose of the book: to emphasize the role of the reader in the narrative as a protagonist, and subsequently as a co-creator of the narrative itself, rather than a passive and linear consumer of the narrative.

A second key feature of *CYOA* narratives is their avoidance of gendered pronouns or descriptions—another aspect that defies the conventions of traditional fiction.[12] "When you think about the way books work, for the most part the protagonist is a well-defined person," Lebling (2011) notes. "[T]he book is about that well-defined person and it makes sense to say this is a man or a woman. The details are critical to the story" (qtd. in Hendrix, par. 17). The *Choose Your Own Adventure* books (and their similarly-styled competitors) turn this narrative convention on its head; the story only succeeds precisely because their characters have no distinct features, and that, as a result, they become an avatar for the reader.[13] Creating a believable "main character" without attributing a gender was one of my few goals as I began constructing *Citizen of Riverdale*; for the most part, the text refers to the player merely as "you," and, when necessary, as "Casey," which I selected as a suitably gender-neutral name. While *Citizen of Riverdale* offers the reader/player a variety of romantic options, there was no need to limit these options based on the gender of the player, as, given current cultural norms and widespread acceptance surrounding queer sexuality, and especially given the popularity of "slash" fiction in fanfiction communities (which specifically refers to same-sex pairings), it is not unlikely that players may want to pursue same-sex relationships with the characters.

The way I centered these key features—the genderlessness and avatar-like nature of the protagonist which allow, for instance, for possibilities of queerness[14]—made me think about the way in which *CYOA*-style narratives occupy a space between the "Mary Sues" of fanfiction and the character creation (or character selection) component of video games. The result is a genre of fiction which relies on reader participation and play, in a way that is similar—but not exactly parallel—to how video games and fanfiction rely on reader participation and play. Like fanfiction, *Citizen of Riverdale* pulls many of its narrative details from an existing piece of media and invites the writer/reader to imagine themselves within—or with control over—the story. Like video games, *Citizen of Riverdale* lets the reader experience the narrative from within the narrative. In some ways, it is both a fanfiction and a video game, without being precisely or truly either. The safest or most accurate way to describe it, perhaps, is simply as *an expression of narrative expansion*.

Conclusions: Or, Returning to Riverdale

Citizen of Riverdale is a personal example of one of the many ways in which fans participate in a culture of hypertext, co-create the hypertext surrounding popular media, and engage with hypertext as a cultural process or practice. Simultaneously, this project served as a personal reminder of the ways interactive fictions have evolved—or, as Nick Monfort (2015) puts it, migrated (p. xi)—into the digital era. The links between "new" styles of digital or online *CYOA*-style fiction and "traditional" print book *CYOA*-style fiction are undeniable; David J. Missal (2012), who similarly built an interactive narrative as a graduate project, directly links his digital *CYOA*-style story to the foundational and formative print book series he read in his childhood. His version of this project is "designed to provide the same basic experience, while at the same time incorporating contemporary technologies and moving past the out-of-date print medium into a format that is both immediately accessible and wholly interactive in nature" (p. ii). The responsive and interactive features of digital formats allow for the inclusion of images, video, audio, and so on, all of which are not possible in the traditional *CYOA* print book format. As a result, "a work can become a true realization of the old *CYOA* stories, giving the reader actual control over the outcome of the story, even changing it to suit their own desires" (p. iii). And, in a much more obvious way, the digital format remedies a key flaw of print books, namely that "*CYOA* stories lacked the ability to conceal the outcomes of the readers' choices before they made them," since

> [b]ecause they were still laid out like normal books, a reader could take a CYOA and read it from cover to cover, ruining the experience. A digital format, when programmed properly, allows the concealment of anything the author desires, forcing the reader to choose before revealing the outcome. Gone are the days of flipping to the back of a book to read the ending first [p. 2].

Another benefit of digital *CYOA*-style stories is implicit in Missal's project, and in mine: that the production of this genre is no longer limited to physical publishers but is also fairly accessible to interested amateurs; furthermore, because Twine and other similar programs or coding tutorials are freely available online, the barrier to entry is fairly low. These platforms present a natural evolution of print book *CYOA* stories; readers move from co-creating meaning alongside authors in static fiction to co-creating the shape of the narrative in *CYOA* fiction, and finally to co-creating shape, format, and content of the narrative by building their own *CYOA*-style fictions—in ways that would be virtually impossible for fans if their only option in creating a *CYOA*-style narrative was its traditional print book form.

And, as Missal (2012) states, there's no reason to believe this is the end of the line—not in terms of interactivity, in fan or reader participation, or in the possibilities for interactive and digital fiction as a whole; Missal concludes that he "hope[s], in expanding the available modes of content delivery, [...] that one day the work will move beyond something [...] created as an individual and will become a story told by the users as they interact with the piece and add to it" (p. 1). Importantly, Missal evokes the importance and possibilities of co-creation, as I likewise hope to do with both *Citizen of Riverdale* and with this analysis—not only the co-creation of meaning, or of narrative, or of *Riverdale*, but of the shared community which houses fans and producers alike, and which blends and blurs the lines between the two with every passing minute. *Riverdale* invites itself into the world of *Archie* comics, and through this action invites the reader, the player, and the writer into *Riverdale* itself—in an act of co-creation that not only encourages but, in some circumstances, for some fans, demands the construction of apocryphal work.

Which is exactly what finds me on another Thursday night, popcorn freshly popped and a new episode of *Riverdale* on Netflix. I could be yelling at my television screen again, like I always do when I watch a new episode of *Riverdale*.

Instead, I'm working on my next *CYOA*-style fanfiction.

Even in my own modest kingdom within this hypertext universe, Archie and Betty and Jughead and Veronica are still taking on too much responsibility and coming up with idealistic plans to change or save the world. But this time, I'm the one who gets to decide how it turns out—even *if* their shenanigans may well land them in trouble, especially with Casey leading the way. For good or for ill, this little piece of Riverdale is mine to dream about and share: proof that, as the television show demonstrates, narratives are rarely static—and the consumer is not just a delivery point for the hypertext, but a key part in its creation.

Notes

1. Twine is freely available for download or use online at https://twinery.org.
2. *Citizen of Riverdale* is free and, as of this writing, still available to play here: http://www.philome.la/YoDessa/citizen-of-riverdale.
3. As Riley Dueck argued in "Ethel = Barb: A *Riverdale* and *Stranger Things* Crossover Theory" at the "Riverdale: A Land of Contrasts" conference in 2018, *Stranger Things* might also be considered part of the *Riverdale* narrative—if the viewer subscribes to Dueck's conspiracy theory that the two shows take place in alternate (but connected) universes. This paper is still available online and can be accessed here: https://drive.google.com/file/d/1I-jV5TMkUQLmh04XRZtPq7afmVgMzt6R/view.
4. While there are no *Riverdale*-themed video games, there are several small-scale games set in the *Archie* comics universe, including *Archie's Riverdale Run* (announced in 2008 but never released), *Archie: Betty or Veronica* (2013, mobile only) and *Archie: Riverdale Rescue* (2014, initially mobile-only but now available for PC).
5. This is, interestingly, the same mechanism which allowed the publication of *Fifty Shades of Grey*; although the text was originally written and published online as *Twilight* fanfiction in 2009, author E.L. James was able to avoid copyright infringement by further distancing her hypertext (by changing the character names and other defining features, and so on) from the main hypertext of *Twilight*. In this specific case, the peripheral hypertext became so distant from its larger hypertext that it could be separated entirely.
6. As the website also notes, "The series of interactive gamebooks initially had only so-so sales, until some genius in marketing had the idea to "seed" 100,000 books in libraries across the country (thank you, whoever you are!)" ("History of CYOA").
7. This is not to suggest that *Riverdale* is an amateur undertaking, but rather an acknowledgment of the liberties the showrunners and writers have taken with the source material and which inarguably, if only occasionally, seem similar to the sometimes-bizarre inventions of amateur fanfiction writers.
8. We might turn to Jan Radway's *Reading the Romance* (1984) in particular for more on this subject.
9. This fits into a larger discussion of understanding fanfiction (both historically and currently) as a form of transfictionality, which Richard Saint-Gelais (2005) defines as a relationship created when "two (or more) texts ... share elements such as characters, imaginary locations, or fictional worlds" (p. 612). This definition originally applied to secondary works such as sequels, spin-offs, and other hypertexts created by the same author or producer to expand the original text (see the lower right portion of figure 1, which visualizes

the effect of "expansion by the original author" on a hypotext (the original work) by placing a slightly larger area around the original text, expanding outward in every direction equally). Fanfiction similarly fulfils this function by utilizing and reimagining familiar characters and locations in texts *related* to the central, original text—but not *of* the original. The majority of consumers may never access the fanfiction surrounding the hypotext, but for those that participate (either as readers or consumers) in the fanfiction community, these narratives add to an understanding of the central media just as a sequel, an illustrated edition, or any other hypertext might.

10. Although it appears that Hendrix interviewed Swinehart separately for this article, Swinehart has studied and visualized *Choose Your Own Adventure* novels in a project of his own, which is well worth a gander: http://samizdat.cc/cyoa/.

11. Of the sources I consulted, only one offered an explanation for the popularity of the *Choose-Your-Own-Adventure* genre; Tim Bryant links the rise of *CYOA* popularity to a growing sense in consumers that they had little control over their lives, which, somewhat bizarrely, he posits directly stems from the effect of the Cuban Missile Crisis on the political and societal mood of the time. "In an era defined by the unpredictable contingencies of an always threatened and potentially all-consuming war, RPGs forged more optimistic images of self-determination through playful engagement and adaptive choice," Bryant writes (73). "With this investment in self-determination through adaptive choice, RPGs and *CYOA* books challenged the prevalent ethos in U.S. culture of nuclear fatalism by recasting its military tropes into the more manageable and malleable terms of gaming and play" (74). Bryant implies that the *CYOA* books, as well as similarly modelled computer games and RPGs, grant the reader/player a sense of control, "instilling in their readers and players the conviction that they could change the rules of even the most unwinnable situations" (74). This hypothesis ignores or otherwise remains oblivious of the fact that, as Tucker notes, the majority of *CYOA* books were designed to funnel the unwary reader directly to a gruesome end. "To cut to the chase, when you read *CYOAs*, you died. A lot," Tucker writes. "You starved. You drowned. You were swallowed by a snake. You were torn apart by chimpanzees. You were sold for meat. Your entire universe imploded" (78–79). These violent and generally inevitable ends inherently remove control from the reader/player—and the ubiquity of these gruesome conclusions and the player's accompanying lack of control seems to refute Bryant's hypothesis that readers turn to *CYOA* in order to exert control over their own lives in the face of terrifying social and political conditions. Alternately, perhaps even the gruesome, ubiquitous conclusions common in classic *CYOA* novels represent more control to readers than the social, political, or economic conditions of their own lives—a dark thought indeed.

12. The cover images and illustrations which accompany *CYOA* books complicate this somewhat, occasionally showing a figure who ostensibly represents the reader even as the image itself may be quite different from the reader's image in terms of race, age, or gender. These paratextual additions, however, are not technically part of the text itself, which takes pains to avoid *textual* descriptions that may clash with the reader's own self-image.

13. Analyses and histories of *CYOA* alike often state that this makes them relatable to all readers, and while this is largely true, it relies on ableist assumptions; every character or avatar in the series has use of their limbs, lungs, eyes, voice, mind, and so on, which ostensibly excludes or alienates readers who lack (or experience dysfunction with) one or more of these physical characteristics. However, by this same token, we might assume that some *CYOA* novels similarly alienate *all* readers through asking them to play the experience of a shark (*You Are a Shark*) or a cat (*You Are a Cat*) although, judging by sales figures, the idea of becoming a shark or a cat is appealing to readers rather than alienating.

14. This narrative expansion into possibilities of queerness is one of the driving forces behind *Riverdale*'s own addition to the *Archie* comics hypertext, since the show is based at least partially on openly gay showrunner Roberto Aguirre-Sacasa's 2003 play *Archie's Weird Fantasy* which portrays Archie moving to the big city and discovering/publicizing/celebrating his own queer identity (which exists purely in the universe of *Archie's Weird Fantasy* and does not extend to *Riverdale*, as evidenced by Archie's negative reaction when Joaquin kisses him in season three, episode five of the show).

REFERENCES

Bonnstetter, B.E., and Ott, B.L. (2011). "(Re)writing Mary Sue: Écriture féminine and the Performance of Subjectivity." *Text and Performance Quarterly 31*(4), 342–367.

Bussière, K. (2023). "Endless Authorship: Fanfiction, Copyright, and the Extended Archie Universe." In H. McAlpine, R. Sweeney, and J. Wind (Eds.), *The Archie/Sabrina Universe: Essays on the Comics and Their Adaptations* (pp. 45–61). McFarland.

Bryant, T. (2016). "Building the Culture of Contingency: Adaptive Choice in Ludic Literature from Role-Playing Games to *Choose Your Own Adventure* books." In A. Byers and F. Crocco (Eds.), *The Role-Playing Society: Essays on the Cultural Influence of RPGs* (pp. 72–95). McFarland.

Choose Your Own Adventure. (n.d.). "History of CYOA." https://www.cyoa.com/pages/history-of-cyoa.

Dueck, R. (2018, March 11). *Ethel = Barb: A Stranger Things / Riverdale Crossover Theory* [paper presentation]. Riverdale: Land of Contrasts. Abbotsford.

Hendrix, G. (2011, 18 February). "Choose Your Own Adventure: How *The Cave of Time* Taught Us to Love Interactive Entertainment." *Slate*. http://www.slate.com/articles/arts/culturebox/2011/02/choose_your_own_adventure.html.

Interactive Fiction Technology Foundation (2020). Twine landing page. Twinery.org.

Jenkins, H. (2012). *Textual Poachers: Television Fans and Participatory Culture.* Routledge.

Koenitz, H. (2015). "Towards a Specific Theory of Interactive Digital Narrative." In H. Koenitz, G. Ferri, M. Haahr, D. Sezen, and T.İ. Sezen (Eds.), *Interactive Digital Narrative: History, Theory, and Practice* (pp. 91–105). Routledge.

Kraus, D. (2016). "Another Look At: Choose Your Own Adventure Books." *Booklist Reader 112*, 78–79.

Leavenworth, M.L. (2015). "The Paratext of Fan Fiction." *Narrative 23*(1), 40–60.

Madej, K. (2016). *Interactivity, Collaboration, and Authoring in Social Media.* Springer International Publishing.

Missal, D.J. (2012). *Getting There: A Contemporary Choose-Your-Own-Adventure Tale.* ProQuest Dissertations Publishing.

Monfort, N. (2015). "Foreword." In H. Koenitz, G. Ferri, M. Haahr, D. Sezen, and T.İ. Sezen (Eds.), *Interactive Digital Narrative: History, Theory, and Practice* (pp. ix–xiii). Routledge.

Nelson, T.H. (1965). "A File Structure for the Computer, the Changing and the Indeterminate." Proceedings: ACM 20th National Conference, 84–100.

Radway, J.A. (2009). *Reading the Romance: Women, Patriarchy, and Popular Literature.* University of North Carolina Press.

Ryan, M. (2013). "Transmedial Storytelling and Transfictionality." *Poetics Today 34*(3), 361–388.

Saint-Gelais, R. "Transfictionality." In D. Herman, M. Jahn, & M. Ryan (Eds.), *Routledge Encyclopedia of Narrative Theory* (pp. 612–613). Routledge.

Tucker, N. (1986). "Game-Books: The Best-Sellers." *New Society 76* (1221), 10–12.

Wind, J. (2018, March 11). *From Camp to Cringe: Why We Keep Watching* Riverdale [paper presentation]. *Riverdale*: Land of Contrasts. Abbotsford.

Endless Authorship

*Fanfiction, Copyright,
and the Extended Archie Universe*

KIRSTEN BUSSIÈRE

Archie began as a single comic strip in the December 1941 issue of *Pep Comics* and emerged subsequently as a regularly published series in November 1942 (Beaty, 2017, p. 31). Within the first decade of publication, *Archie* comics "sold millions of copies every month" while "many more millions of readers consumed the daily four-panel gag strip" (Beaty, 2017, p. 31). According to the "About Us" section on the Archie Comics website, the franchise recognizes itself as "one of the most successful, longest running brands in the history of the comic industry," and while this statement might be a bit of self-promotion, that does not diminish their success—publishing over two billion comics "in a dozen different foreign languages," to be "distributed all over the world." But who owns Archie? Who owns Jughead, or the rest of the gang for that matter? Of course, Archie Comic Publications, Inc., holds legal ownership of their characters and storylines, but with such a wide readership, fans of the series must have some influence on how their beloved characters are represented as the series progresses.

Archie comics "are read primarily by a preteen" and teenage "audience that is assumed to be interested in the romantic misadventures of the titular hero" (Beaty & Woo, 2016, p.86). As a result, the audience for *Archie* comics is "an especially transitory one, with more or less complete turnover every 4 or 5 years" (Beaty & Woo, 2016, p. 90). Despite this large but limited audience, the presence of *Archie* comics "at supermarket check-out stands" has enabled "even people who have never read an issue" to be able to "identify the central love triangle (Archie-Betty-Veronica) and recognize major supporting characters" (Beaty & Woo, 2016, p. 86). It is also significant to note that the Archie universe extends beyond traditional printed comics into an archival canon encompassing both animated and live-action television series and films. The most recent iteration of *Archie* is the television series, *Riverdale*, which is broadcast on the CW Television Network on Sunday evenings, and subsequently uploaded to Netflix. The series boasts a large following, with 2.3 million people tuning in to their second season premiere on October 11, 2017 (Otterson, 2017, n.p.). This television show has allowed Archie Comics to renew their "cultural significance" and push back against "the long-standing narratives about their outdated politics," which ultimately brings Archie into the hands of a new generation of fans (Miller, 2018, p.205). Between readers and viewers, the *Archie* industry reaches millions of fans on a weekly basis—making the main cast, both in print and onscreen, some of the most recognizable fictional characters in North America to date. And with such a high degree of cultural popularity, fans will undoubtedly produce their own narratives to fill the gaps they see within the canon (which in the context of fandoms refers to officially produced source material). Despite the ubiquity of fan produced texts, they are not accepted by all authors or publishers (Archie Comics included) nor are they completely legal under contemporary copyright law.

In *Authors and Owners*, Mark Rose argues that the "distinguishing characteristic of the modern author" is "proprietorship," in which the "author is conceived as the originator and therefore owner" of the text, and as a result, concepts of creation and possession are deeply connected by the laws of the modern world (1993, p. 1). But it was not always this way; in fact, contemporary conceptions of copyright have only emerged recently. The first instance of copyright law, which was enacted in Britain in the year 1710, was related to three major historical shifts: the invention of the printing press, the conception of literary work as being individually authored, and the capitalist marketplace that emerged in the17th and 18th century (Rose, 1993, pp. 3–4). After this point, authors gained the right to "go to court in pursuit of [their] rights as the proprietor of [their own] works" (Rose, 1993, p. 49). For the first time in history, authors held legal rights that allowed them to dictate the way that their work could be distributed and used.

Founded on the basis that "the unique individual"—in other words, the artist—"creates something original," copyright protects the author's ability to "reap a profit from [their] labors" (Rose, 1993, pp. 2–3). This concept of originality presupposes a sort of artistic genius, in which all ideas within a work, unless otherwise noted as belonging to somebody else, were crafted solely by the individual, as though creation occurs within a vacuum. Copyright thus draws "lines between works" to determine "where one text ends and another begins," implying that one piece of art can be separated completely from all others (Rose, 1993, p. 3). Despite this basic statement of the inherent differences between texts, "current literary thought" is reliant on the idea "that texts permeate and enable one another" (Rose, 1993, p. 3), especially as contemporary stories extend beyond their original form to be absorbed by new narrative media.

In turn, the evolution of digital technology over the last century has profoundly shifted the way that we receive and engage with narrative forms. Online, fans can engage in "discussions about the characters, the episodes, future arcs" and participate in the production and consumption of fanfiction (Busse, 2017, p. 1). These fandoms, as they are popularly referred to, are communities that are "neither well defined nor static, but nevertheless" enable the participants to feel "a strong sense of membership and a feeling of belonging" to others who share a keen interest in "a given film, book, band, or TV series" (Busse, 2017, p. 2). Although the traditional paper-bound book remains popular, the rise of e-literature has created a space for new forms of storytelling to develop—including fanfiction. So, while the print book remains popular, many of the literary paratexts are developed in online spaces. These fan-produced narratives function as what Sara Gwenllian Jones describes as a set of "official secondary texts and tertiary fan-produced texts" that work to "extend and embellish" the source material (2002, p. 84). And although fanfiction originated in the form of print fanzines sold to small audiences "by mail order and at fan conventions" (Jones, 2002, p. 80), in more recent years it has been published almost exclusively online. This movement of fan communities online has allowed the "numbers of [fanfiction] authors and readers" to increase drastically (Jones, 2002, p. 80), since digital technology provides an easily accessible environment for creators to share their work with a larger audience of people with similar interests—extending kinship networks beyond spatial boundaries.

As previously mentioned, fanfiction is not an entirely legal venture despite the lack of legal action pursued against the authors of these narratives. Rebecca Katz argues that while fanfiction is "often assumed to infringe copyright law," its legal position in Canada is "unclear" (2014, p. 73). This confusion likely stems from the fact that most "copyright owners often ignore amateur fanfiction writers, who may not seem like serious 'threats' to rights owners' economic interests" (Katz, 2014, pp. 73–74). That said, the *Canadian Copyright Act*, which is the federal statute that governs copyright law in Canada, has recently undergone changes in order to more appropriately respond to the increase in fan-authored texts being produced and distributed online. In 2012 the Canadian government introduced "new fair dealing categories," including the "user-generated content" section as an attempt to update copyright law with relation to the influx of digital technology (Katz, 2014, p. 74). These provisions are detailed as follows in the "Infringement of Copyright and Moral Rights and Exceptions to Infringement" section of the Copyright Act:

> **Non-commercial user-generated content**
> **29.21 (1)** It is not an infringement of copyright for an individual to use an existing work or other subject-matter or copy of one, which has been published or otherwise made available to the public, in the creation of a new work or other subject-matter in which copyright subsists and for the individual—or, with the individual's authorization, a member of their household—to use the new work or other subject-matter or to authorize an intermediary to disseminate it, if
> **(a)** the use of, or the authorization to disseminate, the new work or other subject-matter is done solely for non-commercial purposes

More simply, works that can be defined as a form of non-commercial user-generated content, including fanfiction, are generally legal so long as the author is not procuring profit from their work, the original work is referenced, and the author of the original work does not experience any negative results stemming from the publication of the secondary content. As a result, Katz asserts that most transformative forms of fanfiction would be protected under Canadian copyright law because the works would "constitute fair use or fair dealing with copyrighted materials: fan fiction [sic] is typically written without intent to profit or to replace first generation texts, but merely comments on, reinterprets, or celebrates popular works" without any adverse impacts on the original author (2014, p. 76).

In the United States of America "copyright protection subsists ... in original works of authorship fixed in any tangible medium of expression," such as "literary works," "musical works, including any accompanying words," "dramatic works, including any accompanying music," "pantomimes and choreographic works," "pictorial, graphic, and sculptural works," "motion pictures and other audiovisual works," "sound recordings," and "architectural works" ("Copyright Law of the United States," 2016, p. 8). Like in Canada, fair use, which serves as a limitation on exclusive authorial rights, allows the use of copyrighted material "for purposes such as criticism, comment, news reporting, teaching (including multiple copies for classroom use), scholarship, or research" ("Copyright Law of the United States," 2016, p. 19). Aaron Schwabach notes that there is "a widespread but incorrect belief that noncommercial [sic] uses are presumptively fair uses" and while "this may reflect the way things often work out in practice" because many copyright owners choose to "overlook noncommercial [sic] fan works," many texts are technically in breach of United States copyright law (2016, p. 63). That said, non-commercial fan produced texts that make use of "considerable transformations of the original texts ... are more likely to be protected as fair use, even if they make use of copyrighted characters or other content" (Schwabach, 2016, p. 69). As such, fanfiction as a cultural phenomenon is only recently, and somewhat unreliably, protected under United States and Canadian law as a form of fair use and fair dealing—some works are legal, while others are not. And even though it is true that many "fan works may infringe on [the creator's] intellectual property rights," it is usually not "financially harmful" (Schwabach, 2016, p. 5). Moreover, "enforcing intellectual property rights" may in fact be more damaging than merely allowing fans to continue to produce fanfiction because it can "can alienate the market for the protected works, with financially disastrous results" (Schwabach, 2016, p. 5).

While very few fan-produced texts are ever subject to any sort of legal action on behalf of the original author or publishing body, many authors and publishers are opposed to fanfiction nonetheless. For example, on the community guidelines page of fanfiction.net, a major online archive and forum of fan-generated content, the site details a number of authors and publishers that have expressed their discontentment with their fictional universes being used for fanfiction—including Archie Comics Publications Incorporated. And although *Archie* encourages fan engagement through the creation of fanart, especially fashion ideas, which they often publish in their comic books. The publishers want to be able to retain power over the way that their characters are represented within textual narratives, and as a result request that fans do not engage in the creation of fanfiction.

Fanfiction is thus what Fiske describes as a form of textual productivity, which means that these narratives are based on elements from within a source text that are then circulated within geek communities (1992, p. 39). Typically unable to "influence the entertainment industry's decisions," fans turn to creating their own media to engage with—acting as what Henry Jenkins terms "poachers" (1992, p. 27). As Jenkins argues, fans of popular culture "assert their own right to form interpretations" and construct their own versions of "cultural canons" (1992, p. 18). And by doing so, fans successfully "imagine alternatives" to the canonical texts, where types of characters who would traditionally be excluded, or who would remain as secondary, are front and center (Duncombe, 2012, para. 1). These forms are "on the margins of the original" and work to bring forward into the universe something wanted by the fan who created it (1992, p. 24). And this ability to "engage transformatively" and rewrite a more inclusive version of their favorite fictional world is particularly important to young Queer people who are typically "alienated by commercially" produced media (Duggan, 2021, p. 3).

As Dessa Bayrock notes in the previous essay, "*Riverdale* itself is already an example of narrative expansion," which means that, perhaps even more than other cultural objects, "the show is particularly suited to rewriting and contextualization" (2023, p. 29). Using three examples from the Archie Comics universe I argue that fanfiction creates a space where fan writers can take on the role of author, and thus provides, for example, a space for persons who identify as LGBTQIA+ to see themselves represented within their favorite stories. Narratives that are often ignored by the official adaptations, like Jughead's potential asexuality, can find an important space in fanfiction communities. And because the producers of *Riverdale* seem to be "at least somewhat self-aware in the process of translating and adapting the original text," as demonstrated by the frequent references to the original *Archie* comics, the "frankly impressive number of intertextual references, building the series on a foundation of pop culture pastiche" (Bayrock, 2023, p. 30), and the use of fan-produced terminology, *Riverdale* fanfiction is unique in the sense that it is likely to go beyond merely allowing individuals to see themselves represented in tertiary, fan-produced texts, to actually influencing the representation on screen.

While the creators of these fan objects are technically "poaching" the work of other authors and creators, it is significant to note that they often earn no monetary income from what they produce but are rather compensated with "prestige" from within the community as well as the opportunity to become authors with the ability to add their own stories to the canon (Fiske, 1992, p. 39). And despite the increased prevalence of fanfiction published and shared within online communities, Jacqueline Lipton notes that "most noncommercial [sic] fanfiction has not become, and is not likely to become, the subject of litigation" (2014, p. 448). And yet, in "Copyright and the Commercialization of Fanfiction," Lipton notes that in the process of creating their "secondary works, fanfiction authors effectively have to engage in a borrowing of copyrightable elements of the original works" (2014, p. 454). Consequently, "it is likely that many fanfiction works would amount to *prima facie* infringements of the reproduction right because, in order for the story to be a successful contribution to the relevant fandom, presumably the author will have to utilize sufficient elements of the original story for readers to identify it as such" (Lipton, 2014, p. 442). For instance, each of the *Archie* fanfictions discussed in this essay makes use of the characters and settings of *Riverdale's* recreation of the Archie Comics extended universe, because without these details their narratives would not be recognized as being a part of this unofficial canon. And yet, the use of these elements, while making the text recognizable as an extension of *Riverdale*, often infringes on the copyright ownership and the requests of Archie Comic Publications, Inc.

Jughead Jones and Asexual Representation

Archive of Our Own, a non-profit open-source repository for fanfiction and other fan-created works, is home to more than 800 entries tagged as being related to *Archie* comics and more than 11,000 entries associated with the television series *Riverdale*. This suggests that despite an extensive canon, parts of the Archie universe, like many other fictional universes, lack what fans desire. For instance, in the comic book series, Jughead Jones is typically defined by two personality traits—"his unappeasable appetite and his utter contempt for romance" (Beaty, 2017, p. 41). While there have been a number of attempts to match Jughead with a romantic partner, these have been largely unsuccessful, and consequently the plot generally circles back to the more traditional image of Jughead as a happy and hungry bachelor, leading a number of fans to believe that Jughead is canonically asexual. This fan theory was officially validated in *Jughead No. 4*, which was written by Chip Zdarsky, illustrated by Erica Henderson, and published February 10, 2016.

In this comic book, Kevin Keller, "the first openly gay character in Archie Comics," tells Jughead that he could not understand his need for more selection romantically, which tacitly demonstrates that Kevin, and perhaps the comic creators, identify Jughead as "not only as asexual but also aromantic" (Miller, 2017, p. 360). Despite the fact that Jughead has been represented as either uninterested in romance or physical intimacy throughout the majority (though not all) of the *Archie* archive, *Riverdale* instead decided to have him pursue relationships with Betty Cooper and Tabitha Tate in the television series. This choice is another instance in which "the sexual becomes the normative," ultimately erasing asexuality as a valid orientation (Miller, 2017, p. 359). As a series that seems to at least attempt to be progressive by featuring a racially and sexually diverse cast of characters, this choice is perhaps a surprising one. Interestingly, the fictional relationship between Betty and Jughead is easily one of the "most popular and controversial 'ships' on Tumblr" and other sites hosting fan communities (Burkhardt, Trott, & Monaghan, 2021, p. 2). Arguably, the intrigue has only been amplified by the relationship and subsequent breakup of the two actors playing those roles (Burkhardt, Trott, & Monaghan, 2021, p. 2). And although there are many members of the fandom who express a particular affinity for Jughead and Betty's relationship—self-proclaimed "Bughead" shippers—there are still a number of fans who have expressed disappointment in the fact that Jughead was represented as heterosexual rather than asexual in the television show. As such, most "'anti–Bughead shipping rhetoric centers on the erasure of asexuality,' both within the fictional world of Riverdale, as well as the world at large" (Burkhardt, Trott, & Monaghan, 2021, p. 2). For instance, on January 26, 2017, a Twitter user going by the name of Shrieking Shannon @Tired said "#Riverdale Hey everyone, I have news for you. JUGHEAD IS ASEXUAL. But apparently @CW_Riverdale wants to contribute to asexual erasure." On the same day, AJ Taylor tweeted "hey @ CW_Riverdale it would be awesome if you kept Jughead asexual like he is in the comics! There needs to be more ace representation on TV!" And more recently, on May 6, 2019, a Twitter user going by the name lucy tweeted "just a friendly reminder that jughead jones was asexual in the comics and that was thrown away when the writers decided they'd have jughead and betty have sex every episode." Even Cole Sprouse, the actor playing Jughead in *Riverdale*, advocated for asexual representation in the series, acknowledging that "[asexual] representation is rare and severely important to people who resonate with it" (De, 2017, n.p.). To date, this element of Jughead's character remains unexplored in favor of the romance between him and Betty, and as a result fans have resorted to writing texts where they can explore Jughead's (a-)sexuality within the *Riverdale* universe.

In "As Much as I Want," a story published on *Archive of our Own* on December 3, 2018, an author writing under the username Elsinor explores Jughead's sexuality in a way that attempts to reconcile the fact that Jughead is asexual despite his ongoing relationship with Betty in *Riverdale*. In this fan-produced text, Jughead is "not interested in anyone [sexually] most of the time," but when he is interested in anyone it is always Betty (Elsinor, 2018, n.p.). Sometimes they engage in sexual activity, most often they do not, "and sometimes [it is] just for her" (Elsinor, 2018, n.p.). This fan work is thus a transformative rewriting of *Riverdale's* Jughead, both aligning his sexuality with the canon of the Zdarsky/Henderson comic book series while still maintaining his relationship with Betty in the television series and portraying a version of Jughead who is asexual but not aromantic. While "models for understanding asexuality vary widely," this reinterpretation of Jughead's character makes sense because "the consensus is that romantic attraction and sexual attraction are not necessarily the same thing for all people, and that not all asexual persons identify as aromantic" (Miller, 2017, p. 360). Without fanfiction, *Riverdale* fans would have to accept the fact that the show positions Jughead as canonically heterosexual—romantically and sexually engaged in a relationship with Betty, a character he traditionally had no interest in within the context of the comics. As a result, "As Much as I Want" is just one example of the way that fans ensure the stories that are vital to them are being told. Fanfiction is therefore a necessary outlet that fans want and need in order to see stories that reflect the diversity of the audience.

Cheryl Blossom and Toni Topaz as Bisexual Icons

Riverdale has strayed from the comic book series in a number of ways and while the work done with Jughead removes an element of diversity, the character changes done to Cheryl Blossom add an additional layer. In the Archie Comics universe, Cheryl is represented as a wealthy teenage girl who is known to flaunt her money and flirt with teenage boys whether or not they are currently in a relationship. While in *Riverdale* Cheryl is still wealthy and flirtatious, she is also depicted as being bisexual and in an ongoing relationship with another bisexual teenage girl, Toni Topaz. To date, there have not been any female characters in the main line of *Archie Comics* who are not heterosexual, so this is a significant moment for the LGBTQIA+ community to have multiple bisexual characters represented in a popular television series. But it is important to note, like most television series, the main characters, Archie, Veronica, Jughead, and Betty, receive the most screen time. Toni and Cheryl, however, are both series regulars, but they are still considered secondary characters, with Toni acting largely as a sidekick to Cheryl's storylines, within the *Riverdale* universe and are not focused on as much—making their relationship subordinate to those of the main characters. Likewise, the series is speckled with regular sex scenes which, while not explicit, make it quite clear that the characters are engaging in intimate activities. For much of the series thus far, apart from a brief stint where almost all of *Riverdale*'s couples were featured in sexually charged montages, Cheryl and Toni's relationship has not been treated in the same way; while they are shown holding hands and kissing, the series does not often give this relationship the same acceptable hyper-sexualization through the type of intimate scenes that the heterosexual couples are allowed. This lack of focus on Cheryl and Toni's sex lives might be a means to avoid upsetting more conservative consumers of the series who are less comfortable with erotic same-sex relationships. And yet, the representation is clearly lacking, and ultimately fails the audience, especially queer viewers, by relegating homosexual relationships to the margins, where they can only be imagined off-screen.

Rectifying this inequality in one example, an *Archive of Our Own* user, writing under the username DeepDownBelow, has authored a slash-fic about Cheryl and Toni's relationship. Slash fiction typically describes the erotic encounters of same-sex characters—shifting the heteronormative standards toward a homoerotic rewriting (Jones, 2002, p. 80). The namesake comes from the "punctuating 'slash'" between the two characters (Jones, 2002, p. 80) here "The Less I Know the Better" is tagged as "F/F," meaning female on female, with the relationship referenced in particular listed as "Cheryl Blossom/Toni Topaz." Slash typically functions to push back against the longstanding cultural "logic" which "dictates that heterosexuality can be assumed while homosexuality must be proved" (Jones, 2002, p. 81). Jones states that the use of the "serialized and segmented" format opens the shows up to fan considerations of "possibilities … for future storylines" that they are invited to enter, experience, and imaginatively engage with (2002, p. 83). This openness for interactivity is furthered by the fact that these stories are often "far removed from the everyday" (2002, p. 85). As such, fans are given opportunities to speculate further about additional plots that could occur—including the writing of new homosexual relationships into the plot or providing further attention to the ones that are already there.

"The Less I Know the Better" functions as the latter, providing an outlet in which fans of Cheryl and Toni are able to focus primarily on their relationship. Unlike "As Much as I Want," DeepDownBelow borrows only the characters from the Archie universe, and transplants them into a different storyline where the characters are twenty-somethings living in Queens, New York. The narrative is currently made up of five chapters, each of which details Cheryl and Toni's sexual relationship and growing friendship, which hints toward the development of a fully-fledged romantic relationship. The story is described as follows:

> When Toni Topaz and Cheryl Blossom first met, it was electric, and they quickly ended up in bed together. Neither wanting a relationship, but neither wanting their fantastic sex life to end, they form an agreement. A no strings attached friends with benefits relationship. One [did not] do relationships; the other was still caught up in the aftermath of one. Will they be able to keep feelings out of it? Or will they not be able to resist the oncoming feelings for the other? [DeepDownBelow, 2018, n.p.].

DeepDownBelow shifts the attention away from the four main characters in *Riverdale* to provide viewers that are disappointed in the lack of representation a space in which they can explore the relationship between Cheryl and Toni in more detail.

Fanfiction thus provides room outside the canon in which fan communities can produce and share the stories that are important to them—essentially rendering themselves as co-authors of the Archie extended universe. The author is then not singular, but with *Archie* it never has been. Rather, since its first edition the comic book series has been collaboratively produced by a number of writers, pencillers, inkers, colorists, letterers, and editors that ensure a comic is up to industry standards before being sent to publishers for printing and distribution. Fanfiction acts merely as an extension of often already-collaborative projects by producing new and diverse stories that fulfill a consumer need that has not yet been fully addressed within the canon. The potential for authorship is thus seemingly endless—by virtue of online communities, it seems that anyone with access to a computer and basic internet is able to contribute to the ever-growing archive that makes up the Archie universe.

Hypertext and Heterosexual, Homosexual, and Skoliosexual Representation

Beyond text only fanfiction, the recent rise of e-literature has created a space for new forms of storytelling to develop, including the hyperlink narrative. Hypertext, as Ted Nelson, who first coined the term, argues, can be best described as "nonsequential writing with reader-controlled links" (qtd. in Douglas, 2001, p. 37) that connect the "fragments of electronic text, known as lexias" (Bell & Ensslin, 2011, p. 311). This primarily digital form thus allows for texts to be composed and read in a manner that defies the tradition of "literary form based on linearity" and challenges traditional "ideas of plot and story" (Landow, 2006, p. 125); furthermore, by allowing readers to determine the plot sequence, these forms further complicate the conception or ideal of the individual author on which copyright law was traditionally based.

Built on Twine, which is an open-source program for creating and sharing interactive stories, Dessa Bayrock's *Citizen of Riverdale*,[1] which was written and produced for the first annual *Riverdale: A Land of Contrasts* conference in advance of this collection, is a recent example of interactive, choose-your-own-adventure styled fanfiction. Functioning as both a choose-your-own-adventure-style narrative as well as fanfiction, *Citizen of Riverdale* opens a number of possible ways for analyzing the impact of digital media on storytelling. As Maria Lindgren Leavenworth argues in her article "The Paratext of Fanfiction," fan produced narratives "represent an intermediary stage between print literature and complex, often multimodal, contemporary hypertexts" (2015, p. 40). Bayrock's *Citizen of Riverdale* goes beyond this intermediary stage to represent a hybrid form, which can be considered equally a mode of fanfiction as well as a hypertext narrative, troubling the questions of authorship and ownership in a number of ways—Bayrock does not have permission to produce this narrative, the audience is participating actively in the construction of the text, and in the context of the conference it was being performed in real-time with audience participation. In traditional print narratives, "the reader's gradual progression from beginning to end follows a carefully scripted route that ensures" they are following the plot in the order intended by the author (Douglas, 2001, p. 40). Hypertext, by contrast, opens up the possibility for a number of non-hierarchical paths that readers can take through the text. And while all these paths have been pre-programmed by the author, "readers have to begin making choices about their interests and the directions in which they wish to pursue them right from" the beginning (Douglas, 2001, p. 40).

Now, that is not to say that there is no authorial intention in hypertext—because of course readers continue to work within the narrative parameters produced by the creator of the text—but rather to say that hypertext provides the reader/player with more options to guide their individual progression through the story. For a story to be considered to be truly interactive, Jane Yellowlees Douglas argues that the "actors in an interaction need to be able to make decisions and take action from a wide range of seemingly endless possibilities" (2001, p. 43), meaning that they must be confronted with a series of choices that impact their progression through the text. As a result, "readers of interactive narratives can proceed only on the basis of choices they make" because of this "absence of a single, clear-cut path" that is typical of hypertext (Douglas, 2001, pp. 42–43). As a result, each reader who engages with the text has the potential to read a different story than anybody else confronted with the same narrative, or even the same reader progressing through the text again, but in a different way than they had previously done.

Douglas argues that "interactive narratives typically represent a spectrum of dialogues between reader and author anticipated in advance by the author" (2001, p. 45). In *Citizen of Riverdale,* all readers begin Bayrock's narrative in the same way: arriving to their new hometown of "Riverdale late at night, packed into the passenger seat of [their] father's tiny red Honda," but from that moment the story shifts to a series of questions that guide the reader's progression through the narrative and toward a variety of potential endings. Readers are encouraged to make decisions by the use of second-person narration, which "features widely across digital, interactive texts" to "create the illusion of being present in a storyworld that is constructed by the reader in creative collaboration with the programmed text" (Bell & Ensslin, 2011, p. 312).

Bayrock thus, from the very beginning of the narrative, implores us to picture ourselves within the text. But, significantly, the main character is not the reader, but rather a non-canonical character presented to the reader with the gender-neutral name, Casey. As in the video game tradition and the *Choose-Your-Own-Adventure* tradition, the text's "you" is actually the "main character, role-played by the reader"—asking for "reader input" while also limiting "the involvement of the reader by preventing" complete identification with the "you" being referred to (Bell & Ensslin, 2011, pp. 312–313). Because *Citizen of Riverdale* does not provide any detailed description of Casey, the reader has the opportunity to determine how they picture the protagonist—opening a number of possibilities in terms of physical appearance as well as the way in which the character is gendered. More simply, Casey can be a male, female, transgender, or genderqueer individual—providing limitless representation. "You" is thus a term that encompasses the "virtual and actual," breaking down the boundaries between the protagonist and the actual reader (Bell & Ensslin, 2011, p. 314) while also placing the reader in the position of author, in the way that they decide which direction to take the narrative as they interact with each lexim.

However, despite this variation there are certain touchstones that each reader will interact with. For instance, at the beginning it does not matter whether or not the reader decides that Casey is hungry, or would rather drive around and get more of a feel for the town, they will eventually end up at Pop's Diner deciding whether they are going to introduce themselves to the "two girls—one dark-haired, one blonde—sharing a milkshake in a corner booth," the "table full of jocks in football jackets" who are "horsing around, pouring salt all over the table," or the "boy staring intently in his laptop" (Bayrock, 2018, n.p.). So, while readers are invited to make choices about the direction the story is headed in, they are confined by the sequencing that Bayrock has imposed on the narrative in order for it to retain a form of logical linearity.

This interactivity represents a sort of gamification of the literary genre: by making decisions about Casey's actions, *Citizen of Riverdale* renders the reader into a player, controlling the avatar to determine the progression of the text. To progress from one section to the next readers must click the blue hyperlinks embedded in the text. Sometimes there is only one hyperlink, meaning that each reader who reaches that specific lexim will inevitably progress to the same one next. Often, however, readers are presented with a series of choices that they are asked to choose between on Casey's behalf. The reader is then, as Bell and Ensslin argue, "integrally involved in the construction of the narrative" (2011, p. 327) and thus integrally involved in the canon.

Hypertext thus promotes a form of co-authorship, in which the way readers engage with the text at hand creates the potential for multiple pathways through the narrative, essentially forming several stories. The hypertext author writes these lexims and connects them through hyperlinks, providing the skeletal structure of the story, but it is the decisions that the reader makes, while functioning as a sort-of author figure, that determines the way that they connect the beginning to the end, creating the potential for endless authorship. In other words, each story is a collaboration. So, if each story is collectively authored by the community of readers, who does it belong to? The original author who wrote the literal text, or the reader who progressed through the plot in a novel way? And what if that original story is fanfiction?

Digital media has allowed the authorship and distribution of fanfiction to grow exponentially. Hypertext fiction is not even particularly popular, and thus, like other forms of fanfiction, it is especially unlikely to infringe on the money-making abilities of the original author. But at the same time, fans of popular culture have the "right to form interpretations" and construct their own versions of "cultural canons" (Jenkins, 1992, p. 18) despite the fact that they do not have legal ownership over them. These forms are "on the margins of the original" and work to bring forward into the universe something wanted by the fan who created it (Jenkins, 1992, p. 24). For instance, readers of Bayrock's narrative are able to romantically engage with the characters in a way that opens up the potential for heterosexual, homosexual, skoliosexual, or other forms of queer partnerships that are not available within the canon. The fan community thus maintains a sort of unlicensed, collective ownership over their narratives of choice. The individual parts of a narrative universe belong primarily to the original author, and then secondly to the fan community, promoting endless iterations of the narrative canon. And, because the authors of fanfiction are not generally making money off of their creations, they are not competing with the original author and instead provide a space for fans to continue engaging with their favorite universes beyond the source material, often bringing further attention and excitement to the original works. Most significantly though, because young people who participate in fandom "are more likely to be queer," fanfiction provides a space for fans, especially those who identify as LGBTQIA+, to write themselves and their experiences into existence (Duggan, 2021, p.4).

The Communal Canon

By way of conclusion, I argue that despite the grey area that fanfiction falls into under contemporary Canadian and American copyright law, it functions as an important element within fan communities that ensures readers are able to see themselves represented within their favorite canons despite the fact that they are unlikely to exert direct influence on the media industry. By engaging with fan narratives, readers are invited into the extended Archie universe, where they can become involved with additional storylines that challenge and undercut the primacy of the corporate canon's comic books, television series, and other related media that falls under the ever-growing umbrella of narratives that makes up the *Archie* publications company. Despite this increased representation, it is highly unlikely that fan-produced narratives would ever be recommodified into the universe to replace the television series, *Riverdale*, in the same way that *Riverdale* cannot replace other media representations of the Archie universe. Instead, their intertextual relationships create a richer universe for fans to engage with—promoting the series rather than taking away from its revenue. Moreover, "the advent of social media" has enabled the "rise of online parasocial relationships between celebrities and fan communities" (Miller, 2018, pp. 207–208). Contemporary fans are thus "more self-consciously visible" than ever before, "interacting with media, producers, artists, and commercial infrastructures" in ways that previously would not have been possible (Busse, 2017, p. 4). As a result, it is perhaps unsurprising that *Riverdale* has explicitly cited fan reaction to its show, using terms from the community and feeding them back into the canon. For example, in "Chapter 20: Tales from the Dark Side," Kevin uses the fan-generated portmanteau couple name for Betty and Jughead when he finds out that they are no longer together, stating, "Hashtag 'Bughead is no more.'" Both the reference to the hashtag, which is one of the ways that fans connect and comment on the show online, as well as the use of the term "Bughead," demonstrates the fact that the relationship between the viewers and producers is inherently symbiotic rather than parasitic, which makes the show especially productive for fanfiction.

The characters and setting that make up the Archie universe are thus familiar cultural artefacts that have been reiterated across genres for decades. As a result, the features, because of their high-recognition value, become adopted by the fans who see themselves as co-owners and co-authors of the texts and their features. In the age of endless authorship, these digital texts are mostly supported by contemporary copyright law, but not always by the original creators, or, in the case of *Archie* comics, the owners of the corporate rights. That said, no matter what the opinion of the technical owner, fanfiction authors produce texts without penalty, pushing forward to a potential return to cultural ownership of literature in which a canon can be added to by any member of a society that wishes to do so. Recent episodes have clearly shown an increased focus on Toni and Cheryl's relationship, which demonstrates that fans can indeed influence how characters are represented. Who knows, maybe Jughead is next? As a result, the digital world opens up opportunities for culturally specific narratives to become the sharead stories of a geek community, thus expanding representation and then possibly pressuring Archie Comics to fix issues of representation within its own shows and comics.

Note

1. Dessa Bayrock discusses her hypertext, choose-your-own adventure story, *Citizen of Riverdale*, in the previous essay, "On Becoming a Citizen of Riverdale: Narrative Expansion Through Fan Fiction, Interactive Fiction, and Other Apocryphal (Hyper)Texts."

References

About Us (n.d.). Retrieved December 1, 2018, from http://archiecomics.com/about-us/.
Bayrock, D. (2018, March). "Citizen of Riverdale." Retrieved December 1, 2018, from http://philome.la/YoDessa/citizen-of-riverdale/play.
Beaty, B. (2017). *Twelve-Cent Archie*. New Brunswick: Rutgers University Press.
Beaty, B., & Woo, B. (n.d.). "An Archie Comic?" In *The Greatest Comic Book of All Time* (pp. 85–95). London: Palgrave Macmillan.
Bell, A., & Ensslin, A. (2011). "'I Know What It Was. You Know What It Was': Second-Person Narration in Hypertext Fiction." *Narrative* 19(3), 311–329.
Burkhardt, E., Trott, V., & Monaghan, W. (2021). "'#Bughead Is Endgame': Civic Meaning-Making in Riverdale Anti-Fandom and Shipping Practices on Tumblr." *Television & New Media*. https://doi.org/10.1177/15274764211022804.
Busse, K. (2017). *Framing Fan Fiction: Literary and Social Practices in Fan Fiction Communities*. Iowa City: University of Iowa Press.
Copyright Act (2017). *Statutes of Canada*, C-42. Canada. Department of Justice. Department of Justice (2018, 10 December). Web. https://laws-lois.justice.gc.ca/eng/acts/c-42/page-9.html#h-26.
De, Elizabeth. (2017, May 25). "Cole Sprouse Says Keeping Jughead Asexual Is 'Severely Important.'" Retrieved December 3, 2018, from https://www.teenvogue.com/story/cole-sprouse-interview-riverdale-jughead-asexual-representation.
Decarlo, D., et al. (1999). *Cheryl Blossom* (No. 25). Pelham, NY: Archie Comics Publications Inc.
DeepDownBelow. (2018, October 10). "The Less I Know the Better." Retrieved December 1, 2018, from https://archiveofourown.org/works/4453841?view_full_work=true.
DeWille, James. (2017, 29 November). "Chapter 20: Tales from the Dark Side." *Riverdale*, The CW Network.
Duggan, J. (2021). "'Worlds ... [of] Contingent Possibilities': Genderqueer and Trans Adolescents Reading Fan Fiction." *Television & New Media*, 15274764211016305.
Duncombe, S. (2012). "Imagining No-Place." *Transformative Works and Cultures* 10.
Elsinor (2018, December 3). "As Much as I Want." Retrieved December 9, 2018, from https://archiveofourown.org/works/16825225?view_adult=true.
Ensslin, A. (2017). "Electronic Fictions." In P. Geyh (Ed.), *The Cambridge Companion to Postmodern American Fiction* (pp. 30–49). Cambridge: Cambridge University Press.
Fiske, J. (1992). "The Cultural Economy of Fandom." In L.A. Louis (Ed.), *The Adoring Audience: Fan Culture and Popular Media* (pp. 30–49). Milton Park, Oxfordshire: Routledge.
Grossman, B., et al. (2013). *B & V Friends Double Double Digest* (No. 237). Pelham, NY: Archie Comics Publications Inc.
Guidelines (n.d.). Retrieved December 1, 2018, from www.fanfiction.net/guidelines/.
Jenkins, H. (1992). "'Get a Life!': Fans, Poachers, Nomads." In *Textual Poachers: Television Fans and Participatory Culture* (pp. 9–49). New York: Routledge.
Jones, S.G. (2002). "The Sex Lives of Cult Television Characters." *Screen* 43(1), 79–90.
Katz, R. (2014). "Fan Fiction and Canadian Copyright Law: Defending Fan Narratives in the Wake of Canada's Copyright Reforms." *Canadian Journal of Law and Technology* 12(1), 73–107.
Landow, G.P. (2006). "Reconfiguring the Author." In *Hypertext 3.0: Critical Theory and New Media in an Era of Globalization* (pp. 125–143). Baltimore: Johns Hopkins University Press.
Leavenworth, M.L. (2015). "The Paratext of Fanfiction." *Narrative* 23(1), 40–60.
Library of Congress (2016). Copyright Law of the United States and Related Laws Contained in Title 17 of the United States Code. Washington, D.C.
Lipton, J.D. (2014). "Copyright and the Commercialization of Fanfiction." *Hous. L. Rev.* 52, 425.
lucy. [HEYUNDERDOG] (2019, May 6). just a friendly reminder that jughead jones was asexual in the comics and that was thrown away when the writers decided they'd have jughead and betty have sex every episode [tweet]. Retrieved from https://twitter.com/HEYYUNDERDOG/status/1125321240066056192.

Miller, N.E. (2017). "Asexuality and Its Discontents: Making the 'Invisible Orientation' Visible in Comics." *Inks: The Journal of the Comics Studies Society 1*(3), 354–376.

Miller, N.E. (2018). "'Now That It's Just Us Girls': Transmedial Feminisms from Archie to Riverdale." *Feminist Media Histories 4*(3), 205–226.

Otterson, J. (2017, October 12). "TV Ratings: 'Riverdale' Season 2 Premiere Scores Series Highs on CW." Retrieved December 4, 2018, from https://variety.com/2017/tv/news/riverdale-season-2-premiere-ratings-cw-1202588201/#!.

Owen, M. (2008). "Illusions of Democracy in Hypertext Fiction." *Genre: Forms of Discourse and Culture 41*(3–4), 177–200.

Rose, M. (1993). *Authors and Owners: The Invention of Copyright*. Cambridge: Harvard University Press.

Schwabach, A. (2016). *Fan Fiction and Copyright: Outsider Works and Intellectual Property Protection*. London: Routledge.

Shrieking Shannon @ Tired [S_O_Sawyer] (2017, January 26). #Riverdale Hey everyone, I have news for you. JUGHEAD IS ASEXUAL. But apparently @CW_Riverdale wants to contribute to asexual erasure [tweet]. Retrieved from https://twitter.com/S_O_Sawyer/status/824648898681704449.

Taylor, AJ [AJabsolute] (2017, January 26). hey @CW_Riverdale it would be awesome if you kept Jughead asexual like he is in the comics! There needs to be more ace representation on TV! [tweet]. Retrieved from https://twitter.com/AJabsolute/status/824558384179318784.

Thomas, B. (2007). "Stuck in a Loop? Dialogue in Hypertext Fiction." *Narrative 15*(3), 357–372.

Yellowlees, D.J. (2001). "What Interactive Narratives Do That Print Narratives Cannot." In *The End of Books—or Books Without End? Reading Interactive Narratives* (pp. 37–62). Ann Arbor: University of Michigan Press.

Zdarsky, C., & Henderson, E. (2016). *Jughead* (No. 4). Pelham, NY: Archie Comics Publications Inc.

Chilling Adventures in Feminism
Sabrina Is Not the Feminist Heroine We Need

Katie Stobbart

Netflix's dark reprise of Sabrina Spellman presented an intriguing premise for a contemporary feminist heroine: a young witch born into a patriarchal society who must resist the constraints of that society and those who are complicit in its misogyny. Lauded by reviewers as "the angry young feminist we're looking for" (Jotanavic, 2018) and "the feminist rage fantasy we need right now" (Toomer, 2018), *Chilling Adventures of Sabrina* (*CAOS*) was to herald a feminist avenger worthy of our times. It has a diverse cast and ample opportunity to explore the intersectional experiences of its characters. It has an outspoken feminist lead (Kiernan Shipka) and several other strong non-male characters. And it has witches, a well-established symbol of female power very popular at the time of its release. The witch has great potential as a vehicle for challenging long-entrenched patriarchal systems of power, with her long history as the othered woman; as the powerful wielder of cures and curses; as the multi-faceted maiden, mother, and crone.

And yet, despite having all the right ingredients for a juicy feminist revenge narrative, *CAOS* fails to actually deliver a feminist heroine. As Megan Henesy writes in "'Leaving My Girlhood Behind': Woke Witches and Feminist Liminality in *Chilling Adventures of Sabrina*," *CAOS* positions itself in contrast to post-feminist narratives of young female power such as *Buffy the Vampire Slayer* and *Charmed*; as we see with heroines such as Buffy, for instance, the "primary interest" of post-feminist heroes " is saving the world, [but] finding 'the right man' comes a close second" (Henesy 2020). In contrast, Henesy writes, Sabrina's thoughts, and those of her friends, are rarely frivolous, and they tend to be eloquent when stating their desires for fairness and equality. In short, these young women are politically "'woke'—and they know it" (Henesy, 2020).

However, I argue that *CAOS* ultimately falls short in demonstrating the power of a contemporary feminist (and anti-post-feminist) heroine, since the show's treatment of non-male characters coats the same old patriarchal patterns in a post-feminist gloss. Rather than providing a milieu for a successful feminist resistance or revenge narrative, the patriarchal society configured by the show deftly defeats any attempts to tear it down. Characters who face intersectional marginalization are sidelined or used as props for white feminism to validate itself. The show hijacks the witch and her coven, attributing her power to a patriarchal devil figure and converting her safe haven into a misogynist religious patriarchal institution. Sabrina is not equipped with the tools or mentors she needs to carry out resistance; the tools she is given instead pave the way forward with good intentions whose outcomes sputter out or subvert her future goals. Sabrina, like *Riverdale*'s Archie, struggles to be the most interesting hero in her own show, let alone the one most equipped to take down the patriarchy. Even held up next to examples from other modern fantasy subgenres onscreen—such as Katniss Everdeen, adapted from Suzanne Collins' fantasy dystopia *The Hunger Games*, or the superhero noir of Netflix's *Jessica Jones*—Sabrina is far from the best at challenging the status quo. Although cast as a feminist hero, both her feminism and heroism are deeply flawed. Is she really a feminist hero at all? Perhaps more importantly: once we consider the many ways in which the show's patriarchal underpinnings begin to solidify by the end of the first season, are we really surprised?

Crones of CAOS

As patriarchal society values beauty and youth among women, we can tell a lot about this show's patriarchal underpinnings by examining how it treats its old or aging women. In the first episode, *CAOS* shows exactly what we can expect for our beloved crones in the story as we are introduced to Mary Wardwell, Sabrina's high school teacher, before and during her impersonation by Lilith (also known as Madam Satan). Wardwell runs into Sabrina and her friends in the first scene of the series, appearing friendly but awkward, and in a rush to get home. Sabrina assumes Wardwell is off to spend a lonely, sad evening at home, and invites her to join them for a social gathering.

"I feel bad for her, living in that house, all alone," Sabrina tells Rosalind, when she asks why she would invite Wardwell to their gathering of youths. Yet despite her initial awkwardness running into her students, Wardwell appears to enjoy her life: she is relatively upbeat as she drives home in the rain, she has fulfilling work and hobbies, and her home seems warm and comfortable. While it is later discovered that she has a suitor, her status as an unmarried older woman at the beginning of the show sets her up as a spinster figure. In itself, this is fine—Wardwell in this light provides us with an opportunity to revise our perceptions of the "spinster" and reclaim the word for empowered older single women. But instead of allowing Wardwell to serve as a positive example of the reclaimed spinster—who lives independently and derives satisfaction in her career and service to the community as its unofficial historian—she is seen by our heroine primarily, if not only, as a lonely old woman with no family. The show then confirms the trope when Wardwell attempts to help an apparent assault victim, resulting in her possession by Lilith. Wardwell is exploited for her single status, under-appreciated by her community, and thrust further into the patriarchal expectations of her gender by the gaze and (mis)perception of those around her. No one observes or assists when she is attacked, or even notices when she comes to work with a radically different appearance and behavior—as a sexier, younger-looking facsimile of herself now that her body is worn as a skin by Madam Satan. What happens to this character is monstrous, and the viewer might indeed read it this way through the framing of the scene. Ultimately, however, Wardwell's death and transformation are necessary for the narrative to move forward; even though this possession could have happened to anyone, it is noteworthy that the spinster was the first on the chopping block. Ultimately, this opening incident serves as a warning for women who fail to adhere to the conventions of a nuclear family—which here places them in a position of risk—as well as for women acting on their own without help, even if helping assault victims: in this case, the Good Samaritan dies.

Wardwell is not the only example of the undesirability of being an older woman in this universe. When Sabrina declines her dark baptism in "Chapter 3: The Trial of Sabrina Spellman" (Maxwell & Seidenglanz, 2018) her aunts Hilda and Zelda are punished for their failure to coerce Sabrina into signing the Book of the Beast. Their punishment is to be stripped of their youth and subjected to ridicule as a result. "We have been stripped of our powers, which means that we will age and rot rapidly until a verdict is reached," Zelda explains to Sabrina, holding up a tooth which has come loose from Hilda's mouth as an example. Zelda then examines herself in a small mirror, preoccupied with looking for early signs of aging. When she goes to Faustus Blackwood—the High Priest of the Church of Satan—asking for a private resolution rather than a public trial, he says, "Poor Zelda: already I see the ravages of age upon you," and pulls a lock of hair from her scalp with mild disgust. Though her initial reaction is to stand briskly and regain her composure, Zelda is particularly miserable as her and her sister's aging visibly escalates. It's important to note that there are no reported health complaints related to this process; these complaints are purely aesthetic; it's the loss of beauty and youth that tortures the Spellman sisters.

The choice of aging as punishment reinforces the outdated idea that youth is an appropriate measure of value, and that losing it decreases one's value in society. Yet in many witchcraft traditions outside of *CAOS*, the Wiccan religion for instance, the crone is a complicated but powerful aspect of the Goddess. "The Crone, also called the Dark Mother, the Old Wise One, or the Hag ... represents Winter, the night, the universal abyss where life rests before rebirth, the gateway to death and reincarnation, the waning moon and the New Moon, and the deepest of Mysteries and prophecies" (Conway, 2001). This powerful old woman in all her aging glory never appears among the aging women of *CAOS*, so we cannot rely on her wisdom to guide its young women in finding their power. Instead, Sabrina is shown that she should want to preserve her youth, and that the way to do so is to submit to Satan and draw her power from him.

Head of the Family

If Sabrina is looking for powerful mentors, she should have to look no further than her own aunts: Zelda and Hilda are powerful witches in their own right and could prove good examples of the kind of fierce spinsters that contemporary feminism should celebrate. And this is not to say they never do—there are many reasons to admire the Spellman sisters. However, though Sabrina's family structure appears on the surface to be unconventionally run by two powerful women, their gender-coded roles manifest into a structure very familiar as a nuclear family that firmly follows the rules of the patriarchy and seldom tolerates deviation from that norm.

Our introduction to Hilda and Zelda is a clear example. Sabrina comes downstairs for breakfast, and in homage to the '50s nuclear family trope, Zelda sits at the dining table reading the newspaper while Hilda performs the role of wife, busying herself with cooking. Zelda offers Sabrina stern guidance on matters of adherence to the social institutions of church and school, and acts as head of the family, whereas Hilda steps in with her expertise when Sabrina needs healing, remedies, food, or to share matters of the heart. Hilda and Zelda even share the typical sleeping arrangement of the unromantic, emotionally divested '50s couple, with a shared room and separate twin beds. The purpose of their union is not childbearing, but child-rearing. There is arguably an element of camp to this subversion of the nuclear family structure in that the patriarchal head of the family is clearly a woman rather than a man—but given how tightly this structure adheres to patriarchal norms in every other sense, I would argue instead that the Spellman family structure reinscribes patriarchal norms with only a single simple edit: if you can't find a stern, religious man to run the family, a stern, religious woman will do in a pinch.

This argument only finds more support as the show continues, and we see Hilda as expressive, openly loving, and submissive to Zelda's position as head of the family. Hilda tends the garden, keeps the house, and follows a typical housewife narrative of yearning for fulfillment by seeking employment outside the house, which is also a serving position. Zelda runs the family business, acquires a position of leadership within the school, and seeks to heighten her status in the church to acquire prestige and power for the family. She is the one to mete out punishment and critique for rule-breaking behavior, and her advice to Sabrina is usually practical, unflinching, and seldom prioritizes emotional and social health. Albeit in a female form, Zelda performs these aspects of the toxic masculine head of household even to brutal extremes, such as temporarily murdering Hilda for sharing her doubts about the Church of Night with Sabrina. Throughout *CAOS*, Zelda is rewarded for male-coded behavior and Hilda is punished for female-coded behavior. As Knight points out for *Nerdist*, Zelda's sororicide is clearly linked to maintaining the patriarchal status quo. "After Hilda was honest with Sabrina about her feelings on the patriarchal structure that guides, constricts, and ultimately rules them, Zelda was quick to let her feelings be known by smashing her loving, nurturing sister over the head and burying her in the garden that Hilda was tending to" (Knight, 2018). Sabrina's family and key mentors are coded as a nuclear family and those roles are reinforced by the structure and plot of the show, which undermines their strength as potentially transgressive or innovative feminist role models. While the show doesn't explicitly heroize or condone Zelda's actions, these actions are inarguably in line with the norms of patriarchal control over others in the household, even if this control necessitates violence.

Some reviewers celebrate *CAOS*'s examples of women's anger, including Zelda's assertiveness in expressing her rage toward Hilda as well as Sabrina's vengeful streak. However, it is important to remember the context of Zelda's rage and violence toward Hilda in this scene, which is a direct result of what Zelda sees as a betrayal and an affront to her authority not only in the house but in the church. In the conversation between Sabrina and Hilda prior to her first being murdered onscreen, Hilda reveals her suppressed anger toward the coven; when Sabrina asks if Hilda has ever regretted her own dark baptism, Hilda waffles, then says darkly that she sometimes fantasizes about going into the forest (a location spiritually significant to the coven) and burning it all down. Likewise, Hilda undermines the patriarchal leadership and courts of the Church of Night when she sides with Sabrina's mother rather than her warlock father on religious matters by formally witnessing Sabrina's Catholic baptism, which took place one day before the Dark Baptism attended by Zelda. Hilda uses the baptismal certificate, representing Sabrina's mother's first and last wishes for her daughter, to help Sabrina escape from her non-consensual contract with the devil devised by her father. This offense merits Hilda's excommunication from the community she belongs to, dealing a major blow to the family's status within the Church of Night. Hilda and Zelda, in this instance, are cast again in their masculine and feminine roles, with Hilda aligned with Sabrina's mother and Zelda with Sabrina's father, as Zelda witnessed his signing Sabrina's name into the Book of the Beast and testified on his behalf. Importantly, when these two sides are forced into a head-to-head confrontation, it is Zelda's patriarchal power which wins.

Zelda's position of power in the household is further affirmed by her role in the church. Interestingly, however, her religious responsibilities as head of the family are rewarded in a way that codes her (within the male-dominated church, as opposed to the female-dominated microcosm of the Spellman household) in a more feminine light; her involvement in the coven's institutions results in the prize of an increasingly close connection to Father Blackwood—one which will eventually turn sexual. In an interview, Miranda Otto (who plays Zelda) elaborates on what she perceives are Zelda's role and aspirations within the Church of Night—namely, that Zelda is prepared to work within patriarchal frameworks in order to achieve her desires.

> "I see Zelda very much as a politician, in some ways," says Otto. "She's part of the party, but she has her own motivations and her own ways that she would like to go with things. But she will toe the party line where she has to, to get where she wants to go, or where she wants Sabrina to go" [as qtd. by Patton, 2018].

Perhaps purposefully, this view of Zelda is perhaps more representative of post-feminism rather than a feminist example of a successful woman. Post-feminism places the onus for success on the individual rather than systemic or community-wide changes:

> In both the postfeminist sensibility and in cultures marked by neoliberalism more generally, languages for talking about structures and culture have been eviscerated. Any remaining power differences between women and men are understood as the outcome of individual choices, not of cultural forces or unfair socio-political systems [Litosseliti et al., 2019].

Although Zelda as a woman aspires to achieve a certain degree of success, she does so as an individual, not acknowledging the system and her privileges within it or how she exacerbates those privileges. This is clear in Otto's interpretation that Zelda will "toe the party line" if it helps her to get what she personally wants. Zelda's potential success does not ultimately change the institution or introduce equality; instead, she succeeds primarily *within* the patriarchal structure of the coven. Zelda, then, is a powerful woman—but she fails when it comes to being a powerful feminist.

"I am home"

Though we might see Zelda's usurping a traditionally masculine role as a feminist enterprise, Zelda's non-maleness undermines her power several times throughout the series. Her methods for acquiring power and status are usually limited to stereotypically feminine pursuits: control over childbirth; sex; stealing a baby. To rise within the Church of Night, she ultimately must marry Faustus Blackwood in season two, which requires her to give up her identity and to entirely commit to the feminine side of the gender binary. When Zelda marries Faustus, she loses rather than gains power. Though her position is technically higher within the church, her relationship to Faustus is one of submissive wife under domineering master. Bespelled, Zelda becomes unrecognizable: she is the biddable, docile stereotype of a woman who is little more than her husband's possession. The viewer is invited to see this as a feminist nightmare—a clear allusion to what we might call Stepford wife-ism.

There is something recognizable about Zelda, however: she echoes '50s-era women and the vision of the past which feminism has, according to post-feminism's implications, already banished. Rebecca Munford and Melanie Waters argue Derrida's hauntology captures such ghosts from feminism's past—just as we see Zelda doing when she becomes the housewife concerned only for her husband's comfort and welfare.

> Derrida's investment in the spectre as a vehicle of nostalgia—for futures that were not realized, or potential that was not fulfilled—speaks, moreover, to post-feminism's idealized formulations of female identities that seem to "ghost" the styles and politics of previous eras [Munford & Waters, 2014].

Zelda's identity is subsumed by this truly haunting visage. As the show builds up to this identity shift, the side character Shirley Jackson becomes more present in the show and threatens Zelda's intentions to marry Faustus. Named for the author of "The Lottery" (1948) and *The Haunting of Hill House* (1959), this allusion is one of the many horror homages within *CAOS*. It's also an unexpected foreshadowing: just as Eleanor in *The Haunting of Hill House* gradually loses her identity, becoming one with the haunted house, Zelda is about to lose her identity and become one with her husband and the housewifely duties that accompany the traditional marriage. Zelda's marriage is, indeed, a haunting, and fits within Munford and Waters' exploration of the housewife as resurrecting the ghosts that haunted earlier waves of feminism.

> The housewife is ... routinely implicated in representations of domesticity which instrumentalize elements of second wave discourses in order to "take into account" women's potential oppression within the home. They do so, however, while simultaneously coding particular styles of (white, middle-class, suburban) domestic femininity as highly desirable [2014].

In her bespelled state, Zelda dresses and acts with a haunting, doll-like kind of beauty. There is a sense of the uncanny in her subservience to Faustus, as she follows his commands without question in a complete reversal of her usual masculine-coded autonomy. She is the weird, patriarchal fantasy of the trophy wife possessing, as a ghost, this otherwise fierce and independent woman. As with Wardwell, *CAOS* hijacks Zelda's free will to transform her into a vision of the patriarchy's will. Her submissiveness to Faustus even trumps her care for her own family. When Hilda asks Zelda if she is worried about Ambrose and Sabrina, who both face potential execution at the hands of the Church of Night, Zelda's only smiling response is "My husband knows best in these matters." This reads as a purposeful punishment for Zelda, and one made to fit her so-called crime: by daring to reach for patriarchal power, she only becomes further subjugated by the system she participates in. Similarly, as Sarah Stang argues later in this collection, Lilith likewise "embodies the misogynistic fear of female power, sexuality, and reproduction—a monstrous woman who serves as a warning to those who might be tempted to transgress patriarchal gender norms" (Stang 2023, p. 85). This shows the unsustainable position of women who seek power within these structures, and demonstrates how power (or even identity) that is granted under such a system can just as easily be taken away.

Zelda's unthinking devotion to her wifely duties is cemented when Faustus asks her to destroy Ambrose's familiar, the one thing that could prove his innocence. He instructs her to find "the mouse in [her] house" and, with unerring accuracy, Zelda locates the mouse and horrifically begins to grind it in the kitchen's meat grinder. Rather than Faustus going himself to dispose of the mouse, Zelda is responsible (as she has been throughout the series) for ensuring her household adheres to the Church of Night's doctrines—but this time, it is also her duty to ensure her house and the creatures allowed to exist within it are a reflection of piety to her husband. "Ladies!" she scolds as the mouse is churned out of the grinder and onto the countertop, "One simply must not keep a mouse in the house. Whatever were you thinking?" Like Shirley Jackson's Eleanor becoming one with the house, Zelda's bespelling has her trapped in this "feminine" affinity to the household and, in Zelda's case, to the institution of marriage. The famous line from *The Haunting of Hill House*, "I am home," signifying the complete subsumption of Eleanor's identity with the house, could be borrowed by Zelda: "I am wife." When Hilda frees her from the spell, she says: "It was torture, being conscious while Faustus made me dance to his infernal tune." She says she was aware "every second. Yet unable to make my own choices." While the subsumption of Zelda's identity into the housewife trope is a torturous experience which supports a feminist viewpoint, this domestic femininity, as Munford and Waters have written, is simultaneously coded as desirable: Zelda in her fugue is youthful, joyfully expressive, and lushly adorned—practically the embodiment of a doll fetish. Luckily Zelda, unlike Mary Wardwell, has a family unit to notice her odd behavior.

The Unbreakable Patriarchy

Is the patriarchal spell over Greendale even breakable? Is it possible for Sabrina as the show's heroine to make a meaningful difference? Post-feminism suggests the work of forging an equitable world is done, but feminism is a position requiring movement. In the world of *CAOS*, such movement seems unlikely, or even impossible. Instead, *CAOS* merely cheerleads ineffectual performances of feminist ideas with no actual impact on the world's inequity and injustice.

One of the most surprising elements in a purportedly feminist franchise was to have *CAOS*'s witchcraft constructed as a deeply patriarchal system mirroring Christianity. The modern coven is usually a group of witches uniting in practice and—particularly as witchcraft continues to intersect with a contemporary focus on care—support. In contrast, *CAOS*'s coven, the Church of Night, is more akin to a religious boarding school whose practices are blatantly unequitable and which encourages a fierce and even life-threatening sense of competition among its students (see Ly & Nguyen, 2018).

Many feminists are reclaiming witchcraft practices as a way to reconnect to natural patterns, prioritize self-care and relationships, integrate non-secular spirituality and ritual into their lives, and radically resist the capitalist patriarchy (Bennet, 2019). As Jessica Bennet writes for the *New York Times*, witches are suddenly everywhere, from podcasts and panels to colleagues at work giving tarot readings (2019). The rise of mainstream witchcraft sees many women reclaiming the word "witch" as something more than either fantastical Hollywood sorcery or a name for a woman that rhymes with and sometimes stands in for the word "bitch." "Witches have long been linked to women's issues, which are front and center in the present political moment," writes Bennet. She cites Pam Grossman, the author of *Waking the Witch: Reflections on Women, Power, and Magic*: "Witches reflect our fears and our fantasies about women with power" (2019). Our current moment in feminism is intertwined with a reclamation of the witch identity, as well as a focus on women's trauma with empowering social movements like #MeToo and increasingly public call-outs for high-profile perpetrators of sexual assault, including but certainly not limited to Donald Trump when he served as president of the United States. It makes sense, then, that women are increasingly drawn back to the power of the witch.

CAOS takes this form of community associated with women's belonging, sharing, and power, and turns it into a hierarchical patriarchal institution, with both the church and the school featuring men in the highest positions of power where they command and enforce rules for behavior and controlling (women's) access to these institutions. The High Priest is a man; the three judges in the witch court present as male; the Anti-Pope is a man; Satan himself is male. Within *CAOS*'s narrative logic, all female witches derive their power, whether literal magic power or social capital, from men.

In the second episode, after Sabrina enlists the "weird sisters'" help to get revenge against the football players who bullied Theo, she is surprisingly open with Prudence—the leader of the weird sisters, and Sabrina's sometimes-rival—about her doubts about going through with her dark baptism, saying that "on some level, I'd be giving up my freedom."

> PRUDENCE: You are. In exchange for power. An even exchange.
> SABRINA: But I want both. I want freedom and power.
> PRUDENCE: (Laughs) He'll never give you that—the Dark Lord. The thought of you, of any of us, having both terrifies him.
> SABRINA: Why is that?
> PRUDENCE: He's a man, isn't he?

This summates the underlying logic of the power dynamics in the show. While women do hold relative positions of power and are able to use magic, women are never in charge. The exchange between Sabrina and Prudence could be read as a direct critique of this reality, but pointing out the inequality of women compared to men in institutional structures is no longer revolutionary—or really a critique. Sabrina's struggle is not new; her realization that men will always seek to keep control over her power is one that women have been having for decades, if not centuries. What should be a powerful moment is undercut by the fact that the power structures of the show are simply replicating—and thereby enforcing—the tired traditional patriarchal hierarchy common in the majority of mass media. Madam Satan occasionally flaunts her power over Faustus Blackwood, but she does so by asserting stereotypes of men relying on brute force and women using coercion to achieve their goals—and, ultimately, she is accountable to Satan. When she fails to convince Sabrina to complete the dark baptism, the demoness cowers in fear of punishment from Satan, and then kisses his hoofed feet when she gains his forgiveness. Meanwhile, Zelda takes power for herself by investing in the status rules set out by the institution; by emulating male-coded behavior; by having sex with the High Priest; and by exerting control over his and his wife's reproduction and desire to have a son. Then, eventually, she marries him. Even after all these efforts, when the marriage falls apart due to Blackwood's departure, so does her bid for power in the Church of Night.

A further example of the church's blatant patriarchal structure and Sabrina's ineffective attempts to challenge it are the two manifestos, presented by Faustus and Sabrina, respectively, both of which seek to dictate the moral underpinnings of the society. At one of the Sons of Satan club's meetings, Faustus presents his manifesto or New Testament, which formalizes the subjugation of women and humans (the perceived weaker counterpart to the strong, masculine institution). His five facets of Judas are:

1. The sons of Satan are heirs of the Earth; take what thou wilt as is your right—by fire, blood, or deceit.
2. Mortals are the swine of the Earth; we must not lay with them.
3. The Sons of Satan are the swineherds of [mortal] man.
4. As Lilith served Satan, so must witches serve warlocks.
5. Warlocks shall claim dominion of the Church of Night just as their father rules over Hell [Barry & Pillai, 2019].

In contrast, Sabrina seeks out her father's manifesto, which essentially states the opposite, professing equality among witches and humans, and reverence for women.

1. As mortals are the godspawn of the Earth, so witches are the hellspawn. They share a common home and destiny.
2. Not only may witchkind lay with, love with, and live amongst the mortals, it is their sacred prerogative.
3. As Lilith was mother of demons, so all witches must be revered as the matriarchs of the Church of Night.
4. Magic is the Dark Lord's gift to witches. It can and should be used for pleasure, for gain, and to satiate the senses.
5. Only the true union of mortals and their witch brethren will bring the era of the Morning Star [Barry & Pillai, 2019].

Spellman's tenets are also missing some key features, which can be summated in a popular aphorism of diverse inclusion: "Nothing about us, without us." The tenets, written by a privileged white man, have no apparent consultative input from any of the people they affect. Both sets of tenets infer heterosexuality, neither allows for men to be anything but iron-fisted, and neither has any language promoting equity among its followers. Perhaps mortals have no desire to "lay with, love with, and live amongst" these Satan-worshipping witches. Perhaps witches would rather be matriarchs of a less fraught gathering of like-minded individuals, or not to be part of the Church of Night at all. Furthermore, we must remember that Sabrina's desire is to stop Faustus from "regressing" the Church of Night, which is not the same as reforming it. At best, her and her compatriots' efforts momentarily undermine or throw wrenches into the system. There appears to be little hope or endeavor of dismantling it in favor of a more equitable institution.

Another entire essay could be written on men's behavior and the limitations placed upon them by this patriarchal coven. I have focused on non-men and how these institutions affect them because it is unclear whether *CAOS* has made its patriarchs so, well, patriarchal, in order to give the non-men of the show something to rebel against, or if at least some of their behavior is due to entrenched expectations of male-coded performance of gender in the show-makers. Regardless, the patriarchal structure of (in particular) the Church of Night and Academy of Unseen Arts is rendered so powerfully patriarchal that the non-patriarchal and/or feminist factions of the show have little to no power to challenge it. These institutions bear little resemblance to the witchy traditions and present-day practices of the craft that tend to celebrate and empower women, equity, and community. Instead, it resists having women in power and enforces a patriarchal hierarchy, often using scenarios in which women are exploited as a key way to create tension and narrative drama. While we may read the Church of Night as an overly dramatic version of a patriarchal villain designed to highlight the righteous struggle of feminists against sexist institutions, it is difficult to ignore the fact that, throughout the show, this feminist struggle is continually and consistently painted as the dramatic and ineffectual whining of a teenager raging against the rules a parental-like higher power has put in place for her own good, and which are not for her to understand.

The Lamb and the Lottery

One such scenario is the Feast of Feasts (Ly & Nguyen, 2018), which takes place concurrently with human Thanksgiving. In preparation for the Feast of Feasts, lamb entrails are hung on the front door of 14 coven families, an act ironically reminiscent of the story of Passover: a sacrificial lamb's blood marked on the doors to be passed over by God when he strikes down every firstborn child of the Egyptians. The Feast of Feasts is similarly marked, with a twist befitting *CAOS*'s horror genre, as a ritual of cultural survival. In this case, it memorializes the sacrifice of a witch who killed herself so her coven would have food throughout a hard winter in the woods that threatened their survival.

The Feast of Feasts has one woman from each of the 14 selected families enter a lottery using straws to determine who will be "queen" for the ritual. The patriarchal unfairness of this lottery is clear to Sabrina as well as to the show's viewers; not only are the families selected, but then those families select specifically a woman from their household. Though, as Sabrina points out, there is no longer a need for the ritual as people are no longer starving, the Feast of Feasts is considered a sacred holiday and will go forward despite her objections. "The Feast of Feasts is happening, and like it or not, we are participating," Zelda declares. The patriarchal nature of the lottery is reinforced by the allusion to Shirley Jackson's famous short story "The Lottery." In that story, Whittier argues, the lottery is also inherently patriarchal despite an outward appearance of randomness.

> The ritual of the lottery itself, like the society it seems to preserve, is patriarchal. Men—Mr. Summers and Mr. Graves—conduct it; a head of household, typically male, selects the first ballot; members of the selected household draw in inverse order of their chronological positions in the family hierarchy except where age breaks down before gender and the wife draws before her husband, who thus becomes "first and last" in the scheme. Men have choice; women choose only when they are already at risk in the lottery pattern. Furthermore, marriage, the patriarchal purchase and renaming of women, preempts blood, so that any married daughter draws her lot within her husband's clan, not her mother's; she moves from man (father) to man (husband) [Whitter, 1991].

As in "The Lottery," the participants in the Feast of Feasts draw lots from a box, and the marked lot signifies which woman will be selected. Whittier points out the inversion of democracy in Jackson's lottery. But in both lotteries, the goals of feminism are also thwarted by the inversion of the democratic process. In "The Lottery," the lottery "inverts the democratic ceremony of voting: individuals draw rather than enter 'ballots'; they do not choose, but are chosen; and election to high office is replaced by selection for death" (Whittier, 1991). It's notable that *CAOS*'s fictional Greendale is situated in Massachusetts, near the site of the Salem witch trials; New England is also linked in this colonial history of hanging witches, and the barbarism of the two rituals resulting in death have similar misogynist qualities.

The Hunger Games' ceremony known as "the Reaping" likewise bears a resemblance to *CAOS*'s Feast of Feasts, as well as to Jackson's "The

Lottery." The Reaping loses the Passover metaphor and displays a gender balance among its randomly selected tributes, but otherwise both rituals feature a teenager being selected for a kind of twisted honor: like the naming of a queen among witches in *CAOS*, Katniss and her fellow tributes are treated as champions, and live in luxury until the final, brutal part of the entertainment-as-ceremony-as-ritual in which tributes are ultimately sacrificed in order to ensure the survival of their communities. It's also of note that the name "Hunger Games" implies the ritual's direct link to the survival of the 12 (formerly 13) districts. While Katniss volunteers as tribute to spare her younger sister Prim from being chosen, Sabrina volunteers to spare her aunt Zelda and with the intent of ending the ritual; similarly, while Katniss' goal at the beginning is survival, ending the ritual becomes her raison d'être over the course of the series.

> By volunteering to take her sister's place, an act that Katniss regards as a death sentence, she unwittingly performs what will be construed as her first act of heroism and defiance of the Capitol's rules. Although "volunteering" is often seen in two of the other districts—which supply luxury goods and military personnel to the Capitol, and where being a tribute is considered more an honour than a punishment—Katniss is the first in her district to ever volunteer, and the act is read not only as selfless but also as a direct but subtle challenge to the Capitol's bid to pit residents and districts against each other [Ruthven, 2017].

Like Katniss, Sabrina also volunteers for her lottery as an act of rebellion against the system that runs it. Unlike Katniss, she is not as focused on saving her family member but is more concerned with challenging her aunt's belief in the lottery's continuation—if it was her own niece who was selected as tribute, would Zelda capitulate to Sabrina's view of the lottery as an outdated, barbaric tradition?

Of course, Sabrina is not selected as queen—rather, she serves as handmaiden to Prudence in the time leading up to the Feast of Feasts. Prudence, like the tributes of District One and Two in *The Hunger Games* and like the sacrificial virgins of history, views her selection as a great honor, and basks in luxury until, at the ceremony, she learns that the lottery was rigged from the beginning by Constance Blackwood, who viewed Prudence's claim to her husband's name as a threat to her own children's succession. And ultimately, Sabrina fails in her crusade to prevent the Feast of Feasts from occurring. In Prudence's stead, Mildred—a witch who was disappointed not to have been chosen—steps forward to the altar and slits her own throat as the offering. The coven then descends upon her body, tearing it apart and eating it with crude utensils and, in some cases, their bare hands. This echoes the barbarism of both the stoning in "The Lottery" (which is further echoed with an unrelated ritual stoning of symbolic poppets later in the episode by two other characters) and in *The Hunger Games*' deadly cornucopia and the bloodbath that follows.

Yet, a key difference between "The Lottery" and these contemporary versions is the survival of their heroines. Sabrina and Prudence both live; Katniss moves on to further challenge the dystopian society and to see the end of the Hunger Games. Notably, this is not the end of the Feast of Feasts, as Mildred offers herself before Faustus Blackwood can finish saying that "this year..." there would be no feast. There is no suggestion that the ritual won't continue in future years, and the feast ended up taking place anyway, with a woman volunteer. This ritual and Sabrina's failure to effectively challenge it is just one example of the unbreakable quality of *CAOS*'s patriarchy.

"Other" Heroes

Despite Sabrina's burgeoning magical power throughout the first two seasons of *CAOS*, her actions are ultimately impotent. Although the show seeks to cast Sabrina as the feminist hero of the show, there are certainly stronger potential candidates for young feminist heroines within *CAOS*'s own cast of characters. Consider Prudence, who, during the Feast of Feasts and perhaps when the third season begins, is the Harry Potter to Sabrina's Neville Longbottom: a magical orphan selected for a potentially fatal role in the continuation of their community. This role could easily have gone to the other character—to Sabrina, or to Neville—but, meaningfully, did not.

Although both are complicit in the patriarchal Church of Night, Sabrina is naive where Prudence is wiser to the ways of the world she inhabits. Where Sabrina follows the trope of the virgin slowly building up to her first time with a long-term suitor, Prudence is sexually liberated. Additionally, as a Black teenager, Prudence is better situated to understand concerns of intersectionality within contemporary feminism, where the theory of intersectionality makes space for the "intersecting" nature of a person's identity—and subjugation or privilege subsequently granted to them—on the basis of race, class, gender, ability and so on (Crenshaw, 2017). Centering Prudence through this lens would provide ample room to explore the marginalization of not just women but witches of color, an opportunity the show failed to take. Like Sabrina, Prudence also has a strong connection to the leadership of the Church of Night, and from a narrative standpoint, Prudence is also a greater figure of interest as the head of the weird sisters, whose prophetic triad offers an image of the witch at the peak of her power, like the triple goddess or the three fates holding the threads of destiny. Despite ostensibly drawing her power from

Satan, Prudence and her orphan sisters seem to carry this "other" (both alternative and non-normative) power that unites them as well as even delivering prophecies, such as the one they receive in a dream in Season 2, "Chapter 5: Blackwood."

Citing several examples of how the experiences of people of color could have been included in *CAOS*'s history of witchcraft, from the witch of color who contributed to the start of the witch trials panic in Salem, to witchcraft's intersection with historical colonization and slavery, to the more modern outlawing of witchcraft religions practiced by people of color, Jess Joho argues that *CAOS*'s white savior feminism ignores important aspects of witches' history "to resurrect the same old specters of white women victims" (Joho, 2018). What can Sabrina offer that hasn't already been offered by the ghosts of white feminist saviors past?

Prudence's is not the only narrative to be sidelined that might have provided a more prevalent, more fulfilling intersectional feminist story in the show. As Joho argues, "*CAOS* sidelines most character arcs that aren't about straight or white people, and even edges into racist stereotypes, like the Wise Old Black Magical Character that is Roz's grandmother" (2018). The problem with *CAOS*'s attempt at feminism has also been remarked by other reviewers:

> The show emphasizes Sabrina's moral perfection so heavily that it sidelines its supporting cast and makes them irrelevant, save for the role they play in reaffirming Sabrina's wokeness. As if terrified of having Sabrina be perceived as an ignorant white girl, the show tries so desperately to absolve her of the pitfalls of white feminism that it ends up furiously reinforcing them instead [Xandra J., 2018].

Sabrina's schoolfriends Roz and Theo both have potentially exciting story arcs that show prospective alternatives to the power offered by Satan, yet this potential is patently ignored by Sabrina. She is always their "helper," not their magical colleague, and the supernatural conflicts her friends face are of little notice to her until their knowledge or experience directly benefits her own ventures and capacity to prove herself as a feminist heroine who protects the marginalized.

> [Theo] and the football players are reduced to a simple binary of victim and victimizer, and divested of any meaningful personhood. They are not here to grow, learn, be humbled, challenged, or empowered; they exist solely as tools for the woke witch to establish and cement her wokeness. And any politics that seeks to validate the perfection of its most privileged advocates first and foremost is not a good politics [Xandra J., 2018].

Sabrina, then, rather than the righteous feminist avenger that has been suggested by promotions and many reviews, is a poor-weather friend who seldom participates in the conflicts her friends endure beyond interventions to save them from what, often, her own actions have wrought.

Vengeful Young Feminists

Though we should not set aside the dream of greater diversity in our feminist heroes, an analysis of Sabrina as potentially "the angry young feminist we're looking for" should compare Sabrina with her contemporaries: other young, feminist, fantasy heroines who strive to dismantle the patriarchy, such as Katniss Everdeen and Netflix's Jessica Jones. Both are more successful intersectional feminist heroines in similar genres (fantasy dystopia and superhero noir to *CAOS*'s magical horror). Despite their presentation as white, cisgender, and heterosexual, each has a more layered experience of marginalization: Katniss through her experiences with abject poverty and Jessica with domestic psychological and sexual abuse at the hands—or rather, mind—of the Netflix series' patriarchal villain Kilgrave.

> Having survived the trauma of abduction and violence, Jessica Jones now operates as a big city private detective who brings something extra to the job. Krysten Ritter plays Jones as a loner who, having faced the darker complexities of superhuman ontology, refuses to politely follow the rules, displaying none of the glamorous female superhero clichés [Green, 2019].

The traumatic origins of both Katniss Everdeen and Jessica Jones provide them each with a logic that informs their use of violence as necessary to dismantling the patriarchy. For instance, Shana MacDonald outlines the productivity of Jessica's actions when she initially chooses not to run from but to challenge Kilgrave to protect more potential victims:

> In not fleeing, she turns to fight against Kilgrave and get in his way, a decision that both names a problem and poses a problem. She names Kilgrave's abuses; she becomes a problem due to her non-compliance; and his misogyny becomes her problem once again as she feels compelled to prevent his abuse of other women. This is the snap that turns her into a vigilante and compels her into violent actions, all of which stem from her own trauma and rage [MacDonald, 2019].

Meanwhile, Katniss is forced into violence by the dystopian patriarchy run by President Snow. First, she hunts for survival; then, she uses those survivalist skills to survive the Hunger Games; then, she rises beyond the concerns of her own and her friends' survival to rebel against the powers that be as a renegade political figure known as the Mockingjay, a name inspired by the imitation of birdsong she uses to communicate solidarity with her allies, and likely for the implication that her continued existence mocks the society she rebels against.

> Her growth throughout the trilogy, from one who "confronts the tyranny" of her country's government for personal reasons to one with more politically engaged and community-focussed motives, is crucial for understanding her role as materialising a third-wave feminist politics. Katniss resists the dystopian postfeminist and neo-liberal demands for individualism in favour of affective bonds and community action [Ruthven, 2017].

Jessica and Katniss are both positioned as transgressive figures within their patriarchal environment, pushing against the status quo and dipping into the "darker," more aggressive aspects of their power to do so. The idea of a "bad girl" who justifies her violence as a response to violent or sexual trauma that she herself has endured is a trope all too often informed by misogynistic logic, but both Katniss and Jessica add complexity to this narrative structure in how they use their new-found power to overturn the patriarchal structures which haunt and ultimately dominate them.

CAOS would have us believe that Sabrina is cut from a similar cloth: Sabrina sticks up for her transgender friend Theo; she starts a feminist club at school; she starts a book club to help her soon-to-be-blind friend Roz; she frequently touts feminist-sounding aphorisms. However, Sabrina's use of violence often amounts to rather childish assaults: petty acts of vengeance against those who have wronged her friends. She sets spiders on her principal when he won't help her and her friends; she tricks the football players into playing out a homoerotic scenario in the mines. Her actions that are supposedly carried out in the name of fighting against the patriarchy don't accomplish much: the club (ironically named WICCA), which Sabrina starts while Principal Hawthorne is away, is co-opted by Madam Satan and then presumably fizzles out; the football players continue being football players and likely continue their behavior off-screen.

The other inferred justification for Sabrina's darker acts is that she is a witch, and that's just what witches do. It's an argument that ironically resembles "boys will be boys" and, similarly, Sabrina carelessly disregards any responsibility to the welfare of the wider community beyond her circle of friends, despite big shows of performative allyship such as storming into Principal Hawthorne's office to lecture him, or starting a club without any intention of following through as its leader (since, at the time, Sabrina expected to leave school within the next few days). Sabrina's social position and lack of understanding for intersecting marginalization also undermines *CAOS*'s ability to respond to the feminism of our time, whereas many aspects of *The Hunger Games*—e.g., its exaggerated capitalist hinterland/metropolis body politic, its highly performative reality game show style—and *Jessica Jones* with its #MeToo-appropriate plotline provide us with opportunities to engage productively with the inequities of the real, contemporary world.

> Now, in the #MeToo era, the Trump era and post–Weinstein, Jessica Jones exists as an even more dynamic vehicle for exploring how women—even women with the status of superhero—deal with the aftermath of abuse, how revenge sits uneasily with a moral code and how women, more than men, need extreme strength to avoid being haunted by their past [Doyle, 2019].

Conversely, *CAOS*'s first episode horrifically punishes a woman for rescuing an apparent sexual assault victim; later fails to end with any certainty a ritual in which past "queens" have been raped by their high priests as par for the course; and has its so-called feminist heroine use her witch allies and powers to sexually assault four male mortal students. *CAOS* doesn't right its patriarchal wrongs; it perpetuates them with mild or temporary, if any, protest, and our so-called feminist heroine is too motivated by her own self-interest to challenge it with any efficacy.

Imagine if Sabrina, or any of its prominent characters, were cast as a killjoy like Jones or a rebellious Mockingjay rather than as the sweet sixteen ingenue with a savior complex and a latent Betty-like "dark side" characteristic of the Archie franchise. Far from the feminism we're looking for, Sabrina is more of a post-feminist heroine who speaks of equality but is firmly rooted in the past with her eyes fixed on her own success within the Church of Night, almost purely on her father's behalf.

The Dark Lord's Sword

In the first season, Sabrina is presented to us as the strong female lead, the righteously angry young feminist carving her way through a patriarchal world, and yet the finale has her becoming part of the patriarchal structure and losing her position of power by signing Satan's Book of the Beast. She loses her freedom, and she transforms her identity and appearance to match her new status as a witch initiate.

One interpretation of Sabrina's signing the Book of the Beast positions her as a woman making a choice that will allow her to come into her own power. However, she never gives informed consent for this choice. Over the course of the season, Sabrina is led in a Gothic fashion through dark threshold after threshold by Madam Satan until she is given an ultimatum. Her desire to safeguard the mortal half of her life is exploited and manipulated so she believes the only way to do so is to sign her free will away to Satan. This, though, would have us believe her will was never free to begin with. Multiple characters reiterate that she ultimately has no choice in signing the book, and she proves them right. Every time she is offered a choice, it is not a path she forges for herself but one that leads her toward the future imagined for her by the patriarchal structures of her household, her church, and her school.

The second season has Sabrina walk even further down that garden path, with her becoming "the Dark Lord's sword" in Season Two, "Chapter 17: The Missionaries." Like an avenging Messiah, Sabrina rises from the dead after she is struck by three of the angels' bolts, resurrects her fellow witches, and sets the angels on fire. Later, she heals her fatally wounded cousin Ambrose with a touch, as well as Roz's blindness, stating that she no longer needs spells. It becomes clear that not only has Sabrina signed the Book of the Beast, but that, as the second season draws to a close, she has embraced the role of literal savior, appearing to unthinkingly accept the hellish power from the very entity she has supposedly set out to resist. "I am the Dark Lord's sword," she proclaims in a demonic voice, only the whites of her eyes showing as she slaughters the angels wearing a crown of thorns.

Sabrina assumes that it is her half-mortal nature that enables her to tap into such extraordinary powers, and supposes that is the reason her father wanted witches and mortals to mate. "I think that's why I came back: to spread his gospel," she says, despite all evidence suggesting that this miraculous power comes from the devil. She begins to hold Jesus-like gatherings to spread the word. Then, although she has not seemingly accepted the connection between her newfound powers and Satan, she uses her ability to conjure up an image of the devil and have him speak. The fact that this is the way she takes down Blackwood, who is subsequently relieved of the Anti-Pope title at Satan's behest, reduces her success to trickery. As far as we know, she is not successful in using her own power, but is a conduit for the devil's power and image.

As the second season draws to a close, it's even clearer that Sabrina's extraordinary and miraculous powers are likely drawn from the devil, as she is revealed to be the literal daughter of Satan. Finally, at the end of "Chapter 18" she sees the mural on the doors to hell in the mines and concludes: "It means I am the herald of Hell; I *am* evil." When Sabrina confides in Harvey despairingly that she is a pawn of the devil yet again, she fails to recognize that she has *always* acted as the devil's pawn, even when she claimed a position of resistance. Her actions, coerced or otherwise, always lead her closer to this supposed destiny. Season one has her signing the Book of the Beast. Season two has her becoming Satan's herald and realizing she is his daughter. Season three, presumably, will see Sabrina becoming Hell's Queen, exactly what Satan desires for her.

Not the Heroine We Need

Despite many reviews stating the contrary, Sabrina is far from the contemporary feminist heroine, or the feminist revenge fantasy, who might herald meaningful resistance to patriarchal structures—both on and off screen. If anything, *CAOS* portrays a brand of post-feminism that confuses it with its intersectional counterpart. There are no institutional resources for Sabrina to draw on as a potential heroine; her role models are just as implicated in and punished by the patriarchal figures and systems in the show; and Sabrina herself is not a strong force for change, either in comparison to her canonical peers or her contemporaries outside the *CAOS* universe.

At time of writing, the third season of *CAOS* was mere weeks from being released. As seasons three and four have since been aired, there are many avenues of further discourse left to explore. Will the key resistance plot for Sabrina in the third season revolve around saving her boyfriend, Nick Scratch? What does it mean that some part of her true father, Satan, is embodied within her boyfriend? When she says in the season three trailer that "Hell is under new management" does she mean Madam Satan's or her own? There are a few teasers implying Sabrina *will* accept her supposed destiny as Queen of Hell; yet it remains to be seen if Sabrina's queendom will have her defeating both Satan and the challenger Prince Caliban, or if it means she works in conjunction with one of the show's patriarchal villains to claim dominion over Hell. We can also expect to see the return or resurrection of one of our ghosts, Mary Wardwell, and examine what the patriarchy may have in store not just for its heroine but for its spinsters.

Despite considerable evidence in support of the continued status quo, Sabrina and her friends do have the opportunity to turn things around. As the plot continues to thicken, boil, and bubble in the *CAOS* cauldron, we might keep our fingers crossed that all this patriarchal bullshit is just a backdrop for the feminist revolution to come. But we shouldn't hold our breath.

REFERENCES

Aguierre-Sacasa, R., & Toland Krieger, L. (2018, 26 October). Chapter One: October Country, in Warner Bros. Television, *Chilling Adventures of Sabrina*.

Aguierre-Sacasa, R., & Toland Krieger, L. (2018, 26 October). Chapter Two: The Dark Baptism, in Warner Bros. Television, *Chilling Adventures of Sabrina*.

Barry, M., & Pillai, A. (2019, 5 April). Chapter Sixteen: Blackwood, in Warner Bros. Television, *Chilling Adventures of Sabrina*.

Bennett, J. (2019). "When Did Everybody Become a Witch?" *New York Times*. Retrieved from https://www.nytimes.com/2019/10/24/books/peak-witch.html

Boylan, B. (2006). "'I Am Home': The Feminist Implications of Identity Loss in Haunted House Narratives." *Articulāte* 11, Article 4.
Conway, D. (2001). *WICCA: The Complete Craft*. Berkeley: Crossing Press.
Crenshaw, K. (2017). *On Intersectionality: Essential Writings*. New York: The New Press.
Doyle, J. (2018). "Jessica Jones Is Back and It's Still a Fierce Feminist Thriller." *The Globe and Mail*. Retrieved from https://www.theglobeandmail.com/arts/television/netflixs-jessica-jones-is-back-and-its-still-a-fierce-feminist-thriller/article38253336/.
Green, S. (2019). "Fantasy, Gender, and Power in Jessica Jones." *Continuum: Journal of Media & Cultural Studies* 33(2), 173–184.
Hedtke, C., Calhoon Bring, L., & Negret, A. (2019, 5 April). Chapter Eighteen: The Miracles of Sabrina Spellman, in Warner Bros. Television, *Chilling Adventures of Sabrina*.
Joho, J. (2018). "The Problem with *Sabrina*'s Intersectional Feminist Witchcraft." *Mashable*. Retrieved from https://mashable.com/article/chilling-adventures-of-sabrina-intersectional-feminism/#_WtYHPVyJOqp.
Knight, R. (2018). "8 Most shocking *Chilling Adventures of Sabrina* Moments." *Nerdist*. Retrieved from https://nerdist.com/article/chilling-adventures-of-sabrina-most-shocking-moments/.
Litosseliti, L., R. Gill, & L. Garcia Favaro (2019). "Postfeminism as a Critical Tool for Gender and Language Study." *Gender & Language* 30, no. 1, 1–22.
Ly, O., & Nguyen, V. (2018, 26 October). Chapter Seven: Feast of Feasts, in Warner Bros. Television, *Chilling Adventures of Sabrina*.
MacDonald, S. (2019). "Refusing to Smile for the Patriarchy: Jessica Jones as Feminist Killjoy." *Journal of the Fantastic in the Arts* 30, no. 1, 68–84.
Maxwell, R., & Seidenglanz, R. (2018, 26 October). Chapter Three: The Trial of Sabrina Spellman, in Warner Bros. Television, *Chilling Adventures of Sabrina*.
Munford, R., & Waters, M. (2014). "Chapter 1: Postfeminism or Ghost Feminism?" and "Chapter 3: Haunted Housewives and the Postfeminist Mystique." *Feminism & Popular Culture: Investigating the Postfeminist Mystique*. New Brunswick: Rutgers University Press.
Patton, R. (2018). "How Zelda & Hilda on *The Chilling Adventures of Sabrina* Are Challenging the Church of Night from Within." *Bustle*. Retrieved from https://www.bustle.com/p/how-zelda-hilda-on-the-chilling-adventures-of-sabrina-are-challenging-the-church-of-night-from-within-12967123.
Ruthven, A. (2017). "The Contemporary Postfeminist Dystopia: Disruptions and Hopeful Gestures in Suzanne Collins' *The Hunger Games*." *Feminist Review* 116, no. 1, 47–62.
Thorland, D., & Seidenglanz, R. (2019, 5 April). Chapter Seventeen: The Missionaries, in Warner Bros. Television, *Chilling Adventures of Sabrina*.
Toomer, J. (2018). "*Chilling Adventures of Sabrina* Is the Feminist Revenge Fantasy We Need Right Now." *SyFy Wire*. Retrieved from https://www.syfy.com/syfywire/chilling-adventures-of-sabrina-is-the-feminist-revenge-fantasy-we-need-right-now.
Whittier, G. (1991). "'The Lottery' as Misogynist Parable." *Women's Studies* 18, no. 4, 353–366.
Xandra J. (2018). "Why I Stopped Watching Netflix's *The Chilling Adventures of Sabrina* During the First Episode." *Medium*. Retrieved from http://medium.com/@XandraJ/why-i-stopped-watching-netflixs-the-chilling-adventures-of-sabrina-during-the-first-episode-1aeaa61a24ce.

"When will the world learn? Women should be in charge of everything"
Lilith as Villain, Victim, and Feminist in Chilling Adventures of Sabrina

Sarah Stang

In *Chilling Adventures of Sabrina* (*CAOS*), Netflix's dark, violent, and decidedly "feminist" adaptation of the *Sabrina the Teenage Witch* comics, Lilith is a central character, featured in every episode of the first three seasons. During the first two seasons, Lilith poses as Sabrina's teacher and fellow witch, becoming her mentor while secretly working to corrupt the young half-mortal, half-witch and lead her down an evil path so she will become more susceptible to Lucifer's influence. Lilith serves Lucifer as his loyal follower and lover, believing that he will make her his queen in return for her service, though he ultimately betrays her. In the third season, Lilith serves as Sabrina's guide and mentor, this time without ulterior motives, becoming a maternal figure in several ways. Although this season sees Lilith disempowered, she remains one of the strongest feminist voices as well as a complex central character who oscillates between antagonist and ally. This essay is a close reading of *CAOS*'s Lilith as an attempted feminist reclamation of the mythological demoness. Many fans, critics, and scholars have hailed *CAOS* as a feminist adaptation of the source material (e.g., Henesy, 2020), while others have questioned its apparent feminism as superficial or actually postfeminist (e.g., Brüning, 2021), yet much of that writing has focused on Sabrina's character and only briefly discussed Lilith. To address that gap, this essay conducts a close reading of *CAOS*'s Lilith in relation to her historical/mythological context as well as her presence in popular culture to unpack whether the show's take on the demoness can be considered a feminist reclamation. As I demonstrate, like many of the show's characters, Lilith's portrayal is complicated and at times contradictory. In this sense, as was discussed in the previous essay, *CAOS*'s apparent feminist bent is not as clear as it seems, yet I argue that the show's centralization and attempted redemption of Lilith is important to consider given her history as a mythological monstrous woman and an icon of Jewish feminism.

In Jewish mythology, as in *CAOS*, Lilith was Adam's first wife, who was created at the same time as he was, before Eve was made (Schwartz, 2004, p. 216). Lilith refused to submit to Adam as her husband or to lay beneath him during intercourse, so she fled the Garden of Eden and supposedly became an evil, dangerous, sexually predatory "demon of the night," or "night hag" (Schwartz, 2004, p. 216). She has become the primary demoness in Jewish mythology—the Queen of Demons—and was likely based on the Babylonian night demon *Lilitu*, a succubus who seduced men in their sleep (Schwartz, 2004, pp. 216–218). She is also associated with infant mortality as a child-murdering witch as well as being the mother of demons and monsters. In this sense, Lilith is a character who embodies the misogynistic fear of female power, sexuality, and reproduction—a monstrous woman who serves as a warning to those who might be tempted to transgress patriarchal gender norms. Indeed, J.J. Cohen (1996) has argued that the monster polices the borders of what is permissible, and that "the woman who oversteps the boundaries of her gender role risks becoming a Scylla, Weird Sister, Lilith, ... or Gorgon" (p. 9). With the understanding that Lilith is a kind of female monster, this essay compares *CAOS*'s Lilith to the original mythological figure and analyzes her as an example of feminist film theorist Barbara Creed's monstrous-feminine (1986; 1993).

Lilith has always been a complicated figure for feminist readings of mythology and art, yet her continued appearance in popular media—such as *True Blood, Supernatural, Shadowhunters*, as well as *CAOS*—suggests she remains a fascinating figure in our cultural imagination. As I discuss in this essay, *CAOS*'s approach to reclaiming Lilith is to gradually transform her from villain to victim to feminist ally. While her portrayal is problematic in several ways—such as the continued reliance on the trope of the seductive, manipulative, and deadly witch/demon/*femme fatale*—I argue that this interpretation of Lilith functions as an important intervention into and subversion of the misogynistic legacy of one of the world's oldest female monsters.

The Monstrous-Feminine

As a tool of oppression, the figure of the monster polices the borders of what is permissible, and to step outside of social norms risks either "attack by some monstrous border patrol or (worse) to become monstrous oneself" (Cohen, 1996, p. 12). This is particularly true for women: not only are women often the victims of monstrous aggression in popular culture, but they are also commonly portrayed *as* the monsters. In her book *The Monstrous-Feminine: Film, Feminism, Psychoanalysis* (1993), feminist film theorist Barbara Creed uses the psychoanalytical concept of the abject to analyze female monstrosity in film. According to feminist philosopher Julia Kristeva (1982), the abject is that which is considered disturbing, revolting, and threatening to normative concepts of selfhood and identity because it challenges the borders we have established between human and animal, culture and nature, self and other. This involves bodily fluids, excretions, transformations, physical hybridity, perceived bodily impurity, and, most importantly, female sexual and reproductive functions. Kristeva demonstrates that the patriarchal fear of female physicality, fecundity, and potency has resulted in women's bodies being both strictly controlled and reviled as abject.

Using the abject as a conceptual framework for analyzing female monstrosity, Creed observes that "all human societies have a conception of the monstrous-feminine, of what it is about woman that is shocking, terrifying, horrific, abject" (1986, p. 44). Importantly, she argues that the monstrous-feminine in mythology, art, and popular culture encompasses more than just female versions of male monsters, as "the reasons why the monstrous-feminine horrifies her audience are quite different from the reasons why the male monster horrifies his audience" (1993, p. 3). Rather, Creed found that the female monster is terrifying because of her physicality, her ability to reproduce on her own, and the emasculating (castrating and/or penetrating) threat she poses to men. Accordingly, as Creed observes, "the feminine is not per se a monstrous sign; rather, it is constructed as such within a patriarchal discourse which reveals a great deal about male desires and fears" (1986, p. 70). In other words, these female monsters threaten to take phallic power from men and claim it for themselves, thereby posing an immediate and terrifying challenge to patriarchy. *The Monstrous-Feminine* (1993) remains one of the most thorough studies of female monstrosity in film and serves as a central foundation for much of the feminist teratology—the study of monsters—that followed.

In her application of the abject to the monstrous-feminine in film, Creed discusses several mythological female monsters, especially those who are associated with monstrous reproduction. This is because abject symbolism relates primarily to female reproductive processes and body parts, especially menstrual blood, the "engulfing" vagina, and the "oceanic" womb. Western mythology is full of monstrous mothers, from Lilith, the mother of demons in Jewish mythology; to Tiamat, the primordial goddess of chaos and creation in Babylonian mythology; to the goddess Echidna, the half serpent mother of monsters in Greek mythology. Western literature is similarly preoccupied with monstrous mothers, with Grendel's mother in *Beowulf* serving as a particularly obvious and early example—she is not even named, she is defined by her role as monster and mother of a monster. The emphasis on mythology here is important, as Jane Ussher (2006) has noted:

> Mythology, because of its rich symbolism, and its exaggerated lore, is easy to dismiss [... as] merely fictions that have no impact on the lives of women. However, this is not the case. Representations reflect and construct the regimes of truth within which women become "woman" [p. 3].

Mythology is also a tool for policing normative behavior and can therefore be understood as a form of cultural discourse connected to regimes of power (see Foucault, 1976/1990). Portrayals of monstrous women drawn from mythology and remediated in contemporary popular culture are therefore important to consider because they shape how women have been and continue to be treated within our societies. As Samantha Langsdale and Elizabeth Rae Coody (2020) state in their introduction to *Monstrous Women in Comics*, "cultural definitions of women as 'less than human' can allow and justify monstrous treatment of them" (p. ii). Similarly, in her book *Unbecoming Female Monsters*, Cristina Santos (2016) argues that phallocentric discourses, like mythology or popular culture, exercise dominance over the female body by depicting women "who fail to accept their predefined roles within their culture and society as monstrous" (p. xv). Like all women in a patriarchal society, female monsters are placed into certain archetypal categories based on their age and behavior: the beautiful virgin becomes the siren; the sexually promiscuous woman becomes the seductive succubus or vampire; the dominant, single, or stepmother becomes the reproductive monster or the fairy tale witch; the post-menopausal woman becomes the hag, witch, or crone (p. xvii). As I will demonstrate, Lilith, as one of the earliest female monsters and the prototypical *femme fatale*—a character archetype which was popularized in the cinematic film noir genre but encompasses any kind of dangerous, deceptive, seductive, self-serving woman who tempts and uses the male protagonist for her own gain (Doane, 1991)—occupies several of those categories.

A History of Lilith

Although scholars have debated her roots, the general consensus is that Lilith first appeared in ancient Sumerian, Assyrian, and Mesopotamian writings, in which she was described as a wind spirit or night demon named *Lilitu*, whose name derives from the proto–Semitic *layil* ("night"), but is also connected to the word for "storm" (Carvalho, 2009, p. 21). This spirit/demon was a kind of succubus who seduced men in their sleep (Schwartz, 2004, pp. 216–218). The succubus is a demonic woman who seduces and destroys men through sexual activity and has been linked with both Lilith and vampirism more generally. The name of this monster is derived from the Latin *succubare* ("to lie under") and she is often depicted as a beautiful young woman with animal aspects, like bird claws, a serpentine tail, or bat-like wings (Davidson, 2012, p. 40). Other scholars have connected Lilith with one of the Babylonian deity Anu's daughters, Lamashtu (Fernandes, 2015, p. 733), a malevolent demon goddess who would torment women during pregnancy and childbirth and kidnap and devour newborn babies. According to Siegmund Hurwitz (1992), Lilith is associated with both Lamashtu and Ishtar or Inanna, the Mesopotamian goddess of love, desire, beauty, and fertility as well as the Queen of Heaven. In this sense, Hurwitz argues that Lilith has two aspects: a "Lamashtu aspect" which is responsible for torturing pregnant women and devouring babies and an "Ishtar aspect" which is that of a seductress or succubus who preys on men (1992, pp. 34–62). Her association with the divine is important, as feminist scholars have long noted the slippage between goddess and monster as mythology gets reinterpreted and interwoven into folktales, literature, and media. In some cases, this has been a systematic, purposeful transformation in order to disempower goddesses—usually connected to the earth and fertility and so representative of life and death itself—since powerful women signify a threat to patriarchal society and so must be made monstrous and evil (Caputi, 2004, pp. 315–341). Indeed, as Jane Caputi (2004) has argued in her book *Goddesses and Monsters*, patriarchal rewritings of myths "recast goddess as devil, monster, and whore" (p. 13). Lilith, as demoness and succubus, occupies all three of those misogynistic categories.

In ancient Jewish scripture, a "lilith" or "lilit" is mentioned in a list of beasts in Isaiah 34:14, listed alongside beasts such as wolves and goats. While this word is likely a reference to a nocturnal bird like a screech owl, its translation as "demon of the night," "ghost hag," or "night hag" also suggests its connection to the Mesopotamian *Lilitu* or Lamashtu. While referring to a screech owl as a night demon/hag perhaps makes sense, it also invokes the misogynistic and ageist term "hag" as well as the trope of a woman's voice being described as a "screech" or "shriek" and being framed as deadly or at least unsettling. The most famous example of this trope is the banshee, a female spirit from Irish folklore that shrieks or wails to signal death. Terms like "screech," "shriek," "scream," and "wail" are often used to refer to female voices, whereas, as Michel Chion has noted in *The Voice in Cinema* (1999), a man's cry is often called a shout rather than a scream, suggesting aggressive power or primal marking of territory. The man's shout is therefore voluntary, calculated, and purposeful, whereas "the woman's cry is rather more like the shout of a human subject ... in the face of death" (Chion, p. 78). The woman's scream, then, reveals either her weakness and fear if she is a victim—she cannot act, she can only utter a non-linguistic, involuntary scream—or, if she is monstrous, it signals her threatening, animalistic nature.

The Latin Vulgate Book of Isaiah 34:14 instead translates her name as *lamia* but this word comes from the same Mesopotamian root word. In this sense, both Lilith and the lamia can be understood as the same creature, usually described as a succubus or sexually aggressive vampire who eats children and drinks the blood of men. Interestingly, in Greek mythology, Lamia was the name of a beautiful woman who became a child-eating monster after her own children were killed by the goddess Hera in a jealous rage. The lamia later became a category of evil female monsters with half-woman, half-serpent bodies who seduce young men and feed on their flesh (Skene, 2016, p. 369). Again, this suggests the conflation of a child-eating monster with a seductive monster who preys on men. Perhaps this is because both activities point to transgressive female behavior—rather than submitting to a man and bearing his children as a "good" woman should, these monstrous women completely subvert their normative gender roles. In any case, Lamia/the lamia, like Lilith, is envisioned as a succubus—an evil or demonic female incarnation of lust—who leads men astray and uses her sexual powers to drain or destroy them while also tormenting other women by kidnapping and devouring their babies. In this sense, she is a monster in terms of her relationship with sexuality and reproduction—both aspects of female existence that are highly policed within patriarchal society and closely associated with Creed's concept of the monstrous-feminine.

While Lilith as a character, as opposed to a screech owl, is not mentioned in canonical Abrahamic scripture, she is associated with Jewish and early Christian mythology and folklore. While likely adapted from the previously discussed Sumerian and Mesopotamian writings, the Jewish (and later Christian) demoness Lilith also stems from certain non-canonical interpretations of the Jewish creation myth, which is told twice in Genesis. The first version implies that the first man and woman were created by God at the same time, out of the same earth or dust, but the second, more elaborate version instead states that the man, Adam, was created first. This second version describes the first woman being created from Adam's rib, to be his helper and companion (Genesis 2:22). Although common understanding of scripture is that these are simply two different versions of the same story, the differences are important for feminist considerations of this text and the ongoing cultural consequences of the misogyny inherent in the second version. Whereas the first version suggests an egalitarian creation similar to most of the world's creation myths, the second version has the first woman made only as an afterthought to keep the first man company and serve him. Not only is she made from his flesh, instead of the earth itself, Adam is the one who gets to name her, choosing the name Eve, just as he was tasked with naming all the animals. The second version therefore implies that woman is made for man, is derived from him, is named by him, and so belongs to him. It also places Eve at the same level as animals—like them, she is a lesser being over which Adam is given dominion.

An alternative reading of this dual creation story is that the first version is the first creation story, in which God created the first man and woman at the same time, to be equals. This is interpreted as the story of Lilith's creation alongside Adam, thereby implying that Lilith was the first woman, she was made at the same time as the first man and out of the same substance, and she was named by God just as Adam was. This interpretation was solidified in Jewish folklore through the satirical medieval text the *Alphabet of ben Sirach*, in which Lilith's backstory is elaborated. According to this text, as soon as God created Lilith, she and Adam immediately began to fight:

> She said, "I will not lie below," and he said, "I will not lie beneath you, but only on top. For you are fit only to be in the bottom position, while I am to be the superior one." Lilith responded, "We are equal to each other inasmuch as we were both created from the earth." But they would not listen to one another. When Lilith saw this, she pronounced the Ineffable Name and flew away into the air. Adam stood in prayer before his Creator: "Sovereign of the universe!" he said, "the woman you gave me has run away." At once, the Holy One, blessed be He, sent these three angels to bring her back. Said the Holy One to Adam, "If she agrees to come back, what is made is good. If not, she must permit one hundred of her children to die every day" [qtd. in Ellens, 2011, p. 151].

Lilith decided that the price of her children's lives was worth her freedom, and so every day one hundred demons perish. Interestingly, the account does not describe the process by which Lilith transforms from a human woman into a demon, yet her children are demonic. This suggests that her refusal to return to Eden and submit to Adam was enough to classify her as demonic, meaning that disobedient women are automatically framed as evil within this misogynistic worldview. It also does not indicate how she produces so many demonic children, so it appears that after fleeing into the desert she began to reproduce parthenogenetically—a common ability of the monstrous-feminine and an important aspect that renders her particularly threatening within a patriarchal worldview. In later writing she was depicted as the wife of Samael, an evil archangel or great demon whose attributes and behavior resemble the later Christian notion of Satan. While Samael may have fathered those countless demonic children, it is Lilith who is referred to as the mother of demons and whose role as creator of monstrosities is centralized. In this sense, she embodies the monstrous-feminine as both a maternal monster and a sexually liberated, seductive monster, though her association with succubi is somewhat odd given that the term *succubare* means "to lie under" and yet Lilith refused to do so.

As Diana Carvalho (2009) has demonstrated, in iconography found on various ancient objects, Lilith is associated with both the owl (or other night birds) and the serpent. The image of Lilith as a half-serpent woman not only recalls the lamia I previously discussed but also connects her to other serpent-women hybrid monsters and goddesses, such as Medusa from Greek mythology. Medusa was originally a beautiful woman who was raped by the god Poseidon in Athena's temple and was then punished by Athena for her own rape by being made monstrous. Like Lilith, Medusa is a figure who represents female transgression, the unfair treatment of women, and rage against misogynistic norms and societal structures. The association of Lilith with the serpent continued in Medieval Christian folklore and art, in which she is commonly portrayed as the very serpent that tempted Eve to eat the forbidden fruit in the Garden of Eden (Fernandes, 2015, p. 733).

Since the early Middle Ages, Lilith has been the most prominent and detested demoness in Jewish mythology, depicted as the Queen of Hell, the wife of the demon Samael, and the mother of all demons and monsters. Christian mythology similarly constructed her as an incarnation of evil, temptation, and lust, a depiction which influenced European art and literature. For example, Mephistopheles in Goethe's *Faust* also describes Lilith as "Adam's wife, his first" and warns: "Beware of her / Her beauty's one boast is her dangerous hair / When Lilith winds it tight around young men / She doesn't soon let go of them again" (1808/2014, 1.4206–4211). In the mid–19th century Dante Gabriel Rossetti painted *Lady Lilith*, a portrait of a beautiful woman combing out her hair and gazing at her reflection in the mirror. Rossetti wrote an accompanying sonnet that again refers to her as Adam's first wife, "the witch he loved before the gift of Eve," and describes her as a seductive, deceptive, dangerous, spider-like figure (Rossetti, 1868).

In more contemporary popular culture, especially in the dark fantasy genre, Lilith continues to be associated with monstrous motherhood, vampirism, the succubus, witchcraft, feminine evil—i.e., the *femme fatale*—as well as being described as Adam's first wife. For example, in C.S. Lewis' *The Lion, the Witch, and the Wardrobe*, the villainous White Witch is descended from Lilith. In Neil Gaiman's *Lucifer* series of graphic novels, as well as its television adaptation, Lilith is Adam's first wife and the mother of all demons, though her role is minor and she never appears in the show. In *Supernatural*, Lilith was the first human to ever serve Lucifer, and so became the first demon. Although she is extremely powerful, her death is required to release Lucifer from the seals that were binding him. Later, she is revived by God and forced to serve him, meaning her existence in that narrative is limited to serving and sacrificing herself for powerful male figures. In *True Blood*, Lilith is the first vampire and a central antagonist, and in *Shadowhunters* she is the first woman and a demon, as she was cast into Hell by God for her disobedience. In these television appearances, Lilith's role as Adam's ex-wife, violent antagonist, and mother of demons/vampires adheres to the character's mythology and historical cultural positioning. Importantly, at no point is she shown with much sympathy or room for redemption, and, like any other villain, she is defeated by the heroic protagonists or their allies. *CAOS*'s portrayal of Lilith follows the trend set by these shows in that she is the central antagonist of the first season, as well as a demoness, the first woman, a witch, and an evil *femme fatale*. However, unlike these previous works, *CAOS* centralizes Lilith as a character, as she appears in every episode in the first three seasons. In addition, although she often interacts with or acts in relation to either Lucifer or Sabrina, Lilith has her own character development, her own plotlines, and her own thoughts, feelings, and desires. Most importantly, instead of killing her off, the show's writers grant her a chance at redemption.

Sabrina's *Lilith*

In *CAOS* as in Jewish mythology, Lilith was the first woman, Adam's first wife, who refused to submit to him and so was expelled by God from the Garden of Eden. While the mythological figure fled into the desert, becoming a demoness, succubus, child-eater, mother of demons and monsters, and the wife of the demon Samael, the show's version of Lilith found the fallen archangel Lucifer Morningstar, helped nurse him to health, and became his lover and devoted servant, as well as the world's first witch. She gives herself the title "Madam Satan" in his honor and introduces herself in "Chapter 10: The Witching Hour" as "the Mother of Demons, the Dawn of Doom, Satan's concubine…. First Wife to Adam, saved from despair by a fallen angel" (Aguirre-Sacasa, Maxwell, & Seidenglanz, 2018). Instead of marrying Samael and mothering a host of demons, Lilith finds comfort in the arms of a fallen Lucifer, an important departure from the source material, since Jewish tradition does not centralize Lucifer as a personification of evil in the way Christianity does. Although she refers to herself as the mother of demons in the aforementioned quote, this is not mentioned again and instead she seems to be simply one demon among many, albeit a powerful and favored one. Lilith desperately wishes to be officially recognized by Lucifer and to reign over Hell by his side, a reward she was promised in return for her obedience and service. This service includes her task of posing as Sabrina's teacher and mentor, Mary Wardwell, in order to lure her toward the darkness so she may be more easily manipulated by Lucifer. Although she claims to obey her Dark Lord, Lilith is threatened by Sabrina, whom she sees as a rival for Lucifer's favor.

As previously mentioned, throughout the Middle Ages Lilith "was often represented, in painting and in sculpture, as the serpent who led Eve into sin" (Fernandes, 2015, p. 733). In this sense, she has been understood as a corrupting influence even for women, convincing Eve to disobey both her God and her husband—the two male authority figures who held dominion over her. This imagery of a female demoness persuading an innocent, naïve, younger woman to commit a sinful or evil act is paralleled in *CAOS*. Although Sabrina is no Eve, Lilith tempts her toward the darkness while also viewing her as a rival, a potential replacement: she fears that Lucifer will love Sabrina more and will make her the Queen of Hell instead of giving that title to Lilith as promised. Although Sabrina is Lucifer's daughter rather than his lover, the distinction is blurred: the witches in the world of *CAOS* are encouraged to offer themselves up to their Dark Lord as lovers, Lucifer's attitude toward Sabrina when he appears in the flesh in season two is easily read as incestuous, and Lilith's consuming envy positions Sabrina as a rival for Lucifer's affections and attention. That Lucifer ends up trapped in the body of Sabrina's boyfriend also supports the interpretation that the show is positioning him as a father-lover while also presenting him as a lord or god-like figure and the symbolic embodiment of the patriarchy.

Due to this complicated dynamic, Lilith's relationship with Sabrina can be read as maternal: like the wicked fairy tale stepmother, Lilith pretends to love, guide, and mentor Sabrina while secretly burning with envy for her success, youth, beauty, and, most importantly, her close relationship with her father. This positions her as a bad or monstrous mother, which is a common aspect of the monstrous-feminine and a clear reference to the mythological Lilith—the mother of demons who allowed one hundred of her children to die every day in exchange for her freedom. It is also important that Lilith is a witch because, as Erin Harrington (2018) has argued, the figure of the fairy-tale witch (or hag/crone) cannot be divorced from a kind of monstrous motherhood, as often these "wicked, withered presentation[s] of feminine evil" are presented in opposition to the youthful beauty of their daughters or daughter figures (p. 255). Indeed, witches are often presented as a threat to younger women in contemporary adaptations of well-known fairy tales. For example, in Disney's *Snow White*, the Evil Queen seeks to murder her own daughter-figure once she starts to become more beautiful than her; in *Cinderella*, Lady Tremaine is positioned as the villain, envious of her daughter-figure's grace and beauty; Mother Gothel in *Tangled* literally sucks the magic out of her daughter-figure's hair to maintain her own youth; and Ursula in *The Little Mermaid* steals the younger woman's voice and tries to marry her lover.

While Lilith is not as close to Sabrina as her aunts, she is one of the titular character's three main mother-figures/female mentors though she is the only one who does not have Sabrina's best interests at heart, at least until the third season, as will be discussed later. She does, however, push Sabrina toward feminist activism—encouraging her and declaring that "women should be in charge of everything" (Aguirre-Sacasa & Krieger, 2018). This push does result in Sabrina using her powers for evil, such as traumatizing her arachnophobic principal with a swarm of spiders in "Chapter 1: October Country" and terrorizing some high school bullies in "Chapter 2: The Dark Baptism," thereby pushing her further along the Path of Night and making her more susceptible to Lucifer's influence. Although she has ulterior motives, her actions do in fact make Lilith a positive role model for Sabrina, at least in some ways. For example, she pushes for gender equality on the basketball team, stating that "there shall be absolutely no gender discrimination at Baxter High under my regime" (Aguirre-Sacasa & Sullivan, 2019).

In addition to her twisted maternal role, Lilith is also portrayed as deceptive, two-faced, manipulative, vengeful, remorseless, and desperate for Lucifer's attention and approval. Lilith is overtly sexual, using her sexuality to manipulate and even devour mortal men—she literally consumes Principal Hawthorne after revealing her true identity to him (Aguirre-Sacasa, Maxwell, & Seidenglanz, 2018)—a trope that recalls her beginnings as a vampiric succubus and the world's first *femme fatale*. She is also easily enraged, killing her familiar for even suggesting that Satan is grooming Sabrina, not Lilith, to reign at his side (Aguirre-Sacasa, Maxwell, & Seidenglanz, 2018). Transformation, deception, vengeance, sexual predation, and violence are all aspects that point to the monstrous-feminine—attributes or behaviors that have been associated with transgressive, monstrous, or "bad" women, thereby revealing masculine fears regarding feminine (sexual) power. Although she kills her familiar for his suggestion, Lilith has the same doubts about her Dark Lord. Indeed, the show reveals that Lucifer tricked her, manipulated her, and used her. Lilith is therefore positioned as both a villain and a victim—rejected and vilified by her first husband and her God and now betrayed by Lucifer, the man she turned to for comfort after being cast out from Eden. The first time, Lilith was replaced by another woman, one made from Adam's flesh to ensure her obedience to him—a superior version only because she was willing to obey and submit, at least at first. The second time, she sees Sabrina as her replacement, again a superior version because she is Lucifer's own flesh and blood (just as Eve was Adam's flesh and blood).

In this sense, the show relies on the trite, stereotypical, and ultimately misogynistic trope of a female villain who is both sexually manipulative and a bad mother. The first season's seemingly uncritical use of these tropes undermines the feminist ideology that *CAOS* ostensibly incorporates into its narrative. As a demon, succubus, and (almost literal) fallen woman, Lilith is a perfect scapegoat as well as a model for the monstrous-feminine. These problematic aspects of stereotypical female villainy can themselves be traced back to Lilith and so could be interpreted as the show's writers staying true to the source material. As Nylah Burton (2018) observes of *CAOS*'s Lilith, "the Lilith on the show is not much different than the Lilith that Jewish feminists have rejected for years. She is sultry and seductive, using her body to make men her prey so that she can literally eat them" (para. 8). She goes on to argue that "the show tries to be subversive and feminist, but there is no subversion in ... a patriarchal and misogynistic portrayal of Lilith" (para. 8). Indeed, as was argued in Katie Stobbart's essay in this collection, *CAOS*'s supposed feminism leaves much to be desired, since "the show's treatment of non-male characters coats the same old patriarchal patterns in a post-feminist gloss" (p. 63). However, just as Jewish feminists have re-interpreted and reclaimed Lilith as "a female symbol for autonomy, sexual choice, and control of one's own destiny" (Rivlin, 1998, p. 392), her portrayal in *CAOS* can be read as empowering, to an extent.

Cristina Santos' (2016) exploration of the witch is particularly interesting for an analysis of Lilith as a feminist figure, as she demonstrates that although the fairy tale witch is associated with old age and child-eating, witchcraft is also associated with "carnal lust" (p. xix). In this sense, the witch is, like Lilith, possessed of multiple aspects. Santos argues that the witch, as an old and threatening woman, embodies a sexual freedom:

because she is post-menopausal and so infertile, she can seek sexual intercourse for pleasure without the risk of pregnancy (p. 91). Woman therefore becomes dangerous and monstrous "when the patriarchal desire to harness her sexuality and reproductive powers is denied" (p. 91). Although the association of female sexuality with villainy is a harmful trope in general, the portrayal of Lilith as sexually liberated and seductive fits in with her historical portrayal while also offering the possibility of reading her use of her own sexuality as a weapon against the patriarchy as a feminist aspect of *Sabrina*'s (and Lilith's) story. However, Lilith's backstory in *CAOS* remains problematic—Lilith was rejected by Adam and God and immediately rebounded into the arms of Lucifer, obeying and serving him even though she refused to do so with her first husband. Although this could suggest that she loved Lucifer in a way that she never loved Adam, it still frames her as desperate to please a man, to have him love her in return, and to be made his queen. Lucifer is manipulative and deceptive in a way that Adam might not have been, but a character as sly, intelligent, and savvy as Lilith seems to be should not have taken millennia to realize that she was being used. In this way, *Sabrina*'s Lilith is a disempowered version of the legendary demoness, though she does eventually empower herself once Lucifer betrays her, helping Sabrina and the other witches to trick, defeat, and trap Lucifer, and finally proclaiming herself the Queen of Hell. This narrative, as well as the parallel realization Zelda has about Faustus—the misogynistic, power-hungry leader of the coven—suggests that women cannot (or will not) be empowered by men. In other words, powerful men will never share their power, they will only use and manipulate women into remaining obedient daughters or wives. Rather, women must work together to overthrow male gods, lords, husbands, fathers—in other words, the patriarchy—and empower themselves and other women. However, as was discussed in the previous essay and will be addressed below, this feminist collectivism is undermined by the show's post-feminist leanings in the form of powerful women leaders and mentors, like Lilith, who care primarily about their own power and prestige and seek to rule rather than dismantle patriarchal power structures.

CAOS presents both Faustus and Lucifer in a multifaceted role—father, lord, and lover—thereby aligning them thematically as well as positioning them both as villainous representatives of patriarchal, paternal misogyny. In this sense, the female characters' rejection of and rebellion against Faustus and Lucifer has been read as their rejection of the patriarchy itself (Frost, 2019; Toomer, 2018; Vandervalk, 2019). This rejection is cemented when the witches then decide to transform their coven, The Church of Night, into a matriarchal institution and when Lilith decides to proclaim herself Queen of Hell. *CAOS*'s attempt at a feminist narrative is by no means subtle, and Lilith's rehabilitation is central to that narrative. It is important to remember that the mythological figure of Lilith was the first one to reject the patriarchy and misogyny—she turned against her God and her husband, both of whom wanted to control and dominate her—and claim power for herself. Although in some versions of her myth she married Samael, she is considered the Queen of Hell and the mother of demons and monsters, living on as a central figure in the Judeo-Christian cultural imagination. Although she is presented as both a wicked mother/stepmother and a seductive and deceptive *femme fatale*, when Lilith realizes that Lucifer never intended to make her his queen, she begins her path toward a kind of feminist redemption. Her understanding that she had been used and discarded by yet another powerful male figure leads her to help Sabrina defeat her father, and the witches' victory over Lucifer allows Lilith to finally proclaim herself Queen of Hell, thereby taking power for herself. After she crowns herself, she reminds Sabrina of her own power and freedom as a woman and a witch, imploring her to "never give up either again" (Aguirre-Sacasa & Seidenglanz, 2019). While she is advising Sabrina in this scene, her words might also be a reminder to herself to never give up her own power and freedom—what she has worked so hard to achieve—and to never again fall victim to narcissistic, authoritative, and treacherous men. Although her concern is with her own power rather than with dismantling oppressive hierarchies, Lilith's transition from villain (evil demoness) to victim (used and betrayed by men) to queen makes her a compelling character for a feminist reading and reclamation, which is particularly important given contemporary Jewish interpretations of the demoness as a feminist icon.

From Empowerment to Humiliation

If the show had ended after season two, with Lilith crowned queen, this reading of the mythological demoness as feminist icon would also end here. However, this analysis is complicated in the very first episode of season three, with Lilith presented as a cruel, narcissistic, capricious, and violent monarch. She tortures Sabrina's boyfriend Nick, in whose body Lucifer is trapped, and keeps him chained up, half naked, to her throne (Aguirre-Sacasa & Seidenglanz, 2020). She initially recoils at the discovery that Sabrina and her companions have entered Hell to rescue Nick, and sends demons to attack, torture, and kill them. Her fear of being usurped by Sabrina seems to overcome whatever warm, protective feelings she had developed for the young woman. Indeed, her fear of losing her throne drives her, as she agrees to release Nick to Sabrina only in exchange for the latter's public endorsement of Lilith as queen. In this sense, Lilith's feminist redemption is tainted by her competitiveness, cruelty, and hunger for power. Although she did help her fellow witches, once she gained power within the same violent patriarchal hierarchy that had always oppressed her, she is driven by the fear that her power is fragile and easily threatened by the younger woman who has a more legitimate claim to Lucifer's throne.

Meanwhile, the newly matriarchal coven led by Zelda begins to pray to Lilith as their new goddess, given Lucifer's defeat and imprisonment. Although this could be read as reaffirming Lilith's feminist empowerment, the prayer itself once again positions her as the monstrous-feminine: "Hail Lilith, full of disgrace. Cursed are you amongst women. And cursed is the fruit of thy womb" (Aguirre-Sacasa & Seidenglanz, 2020). Not only does the prayer refer to her as "Lilith, Mother of Night," it also ends with a repetition of "praise Madam Satan." Lilith is therefore framed as a disgraced, cursed, reproductive monster while still being associated with her abusive, cruel, and violent husband-figure, Lucifer, even though she turned against him, betrayed him, and fears his return. Lilith does not seem to mind this, however, as she is both surprised and exulted at being the object of worship. Unfortunately, her position as goddess-queen is short-lived. Regardless of Sabrina's lack of interest in the throne of Hell and initial willingness to declare Lilith queen, by the end of the first episode of season three Lilith loses her crown to Sabrina and instead serves as her regent. While Sabrina does not want to rule Hell, the other demons see her as the only legitimate heir since she is Lucifer's daughter. Lilith, on the other hand, has no legitimate claim and so to keep another demon from usurping the throne and waging war on Earth, Sabrina declares herself queen and embraces the name Morningstar. Although Lilith had always loathed the thought of Sabrina being crowned Queen of Hell instead of her, she seems to take her disempowerment in stride. Lilith embraces her role as Sabrina's regent, once again becoming a supportive, guiding, and maternal figure for the young witch, although this time without the ulterior motive of serving Lucifer and leading her down the Path of Night. As she states, "I shall reign by your side, Sabrina, forever and a glorious day" (Barry & Benjamin, 2020).

Her positioning as feminist ally was somewhat ambiguous in the second season, as her motivations for helping the other women and challenging patriarchal power structures were clearly tied to her own safety and empowerment. In the third season she is solidified as an ally, working tirelessly to help Sabrina keep the throne even though the young witch is not overly dedicated to the role. By supporting the younger woman, Lilith is also helping to keep a power-hungry male demon from taking control of

Hell and managing to retain a modicum of power for herself. However, given the empowerment Lilith had experienced at the end of the second season—getting out of an abusive relationship and claiming power for herself instead of waiting for someone else to crown her—her almost immediate relegation to a supportive, secondary role is both disappointing and undermines the reading of Lilith as a feminist icon. In addition, while much of the third season portrays Lilith as a commanding, wise, and capable figure, even if only as regent, Lucifer's escape from his imprisonment in Nick's body makes her frightened and desperate. In her fear of Lucifer's vengeance, Lilith seeks safety with the coven, but Zelda turns her away because not only can she not be trusted as "the ultimate wild card," Lilith was also useless as a goddess—she failed to supply them with any kind of power (Conkel & Goi, 2020). Lilith was therefore not powerful enough to replace Lucifer as an object of worship, nor was she worthy of keeping his throne.

The undermining of Lilith's character does not end with her short-lived and ultimately mediocre performance as queen and goddess. Like many misogynistic portrayals of *femme fatale* women, Lilith uses sexual and reproductive manipulation in a desperate attempt to save herself (see Doane, 1991). After escaping from Nick's body, Lucifer ends up trapped within Faustus—thereby combining both patriarchal and misogynistic male threats into one form. Knowing that Lucifer intends to kill her, Lilith puts him to sleep and convinces the Faustus part of him to impregnate her. When Lucifer awakens and threatens Lilith, she saves herself by revealing that she is with his child—his *male* child, no less—and so he grants her a stay of execution until she gives birth (Bring & Macneill, 2020). At the end of the third season, Lilith is once again in a kind of violent, abusive, manipulative relationship with Lucifer, though as she states to Sabrina, "don't mistake survival or codependency for love. We are very much not together" (Bring & Macneill, 2020). From that point on, however, Lilith is almost always shown standing reluctantly by Lucifer's side, at least when she is not helping Sabrina.

The coven turns to the more potent goddess Hecate for their power, and Lilith is left pregnant with her enemy's son, awaiting an inevitable murder at his hands, and forced to prepare his daughter for her official coronation—disempowered, humiliated, and certainly no longer a feminist icon. Ordered by Lucifer in her last act as regent to "prepare our young queen," she bows her head to Sabrina, clearly resigned to suffer this humiliation (Aguirre-Sacasa, King, & Seidenglanz, 2020). She still embodies a feminist maternal/mentor role for Sabrina, reminding her that "every queen must be made battle-ready, every girl must prepare for war. Gird your loins, let nothing touch you. Let no man hold power over you. And when they cry out for mercy, the Morningstar must show them none" (Aguirre-Sacasa, King, & Seidenglanz, 2020). This is a clear parallel to her last words to Sabrina at the end of the second season, in which she reminded her to never give up her power, and is perhaps advice she wished she had been given as a young woman. However, the fact that Lilith's last words in season three are "behold the Queen.... Sabrina Morningstar" (Aguirre-Sacasa, King, & Seidenglanz, 2020) underscores the disempowerment Lilith has suffered: having to recognize Sabrina as Queen of Hell when she so desperately wanted that title for herself means that all her fears from the first season have come true. Although she advised Sabrina never to give up her power at the end of season two, Lilith ends up having to give up her own power in season three.

The Rehabilitation and Reclamation of Lilith

Lilith is the archetypical *femme fatale* in that she is beautiful, seductive, manipulative, and deadly, and it is worth repeating that she became a sexualized, vampiric, child-murdering monster because *she refused to submit to a man*. This association between disobedient, willful, or powerful women and monstrosity speaks to the underlying patriarchal fear of women, which is why it is unsurprising that, as Creed (1986) observed, "classical mythology was populated with gendered monsters, many of which were female" (p. 2). Many of the most well-known female monsters in contemporary popular culture are drawn from classical mythology and religious folklore and have been remixed and remediated across cultural objects, including *CAOS*. However, unlike other works that simply present Lilith as a villain to be confronted and defeated by the protagonists, *CAOS* appears to recognize Lilith's positioning within Jewish feminist thought, at least to an extent. Lilith's centrality for Jewish feminism is underscored by the fact that the first Jewish feminist journal, founded in 1976, is called *Lilith*.

Feminist scholars have reinterpreted Lilith and Eve as the two aspects of woman within Jewish thought—the dangerous, wanton, evil woman who disobeys, deceives, and seduces versus the good woman who obeys, submits, and bears (man's) children. However, whether Lilith or Eve, the first woman is portrayed as a problem: Eve gave into temptation, disobeyed God's commands, and got herself and the first man, Adam, cast out of the Garden of Eden, an Earthly paradise. So even though Eve is the "good" woman, she is still the one who unleashes suffering and pain upon the world. Similarly, in Greek mythology, the story of Pandora, the first woman, communicates a particularly negative view of women. Pandora was created as an explicit punishment for mankind, made by a male god after male humans already existed. She was endowed with both beauty and cunning, was insatiably curious, and was single-handedly responsible for releasing all evil and sorrow into the world. The misogynistic association of women with evil, corruption, deception, and chaos—in the forms of Lilith, Eve, and Pandora—therefore stems from antiquity, and was repeated by respected scholars and philosophers whose work has shaped Western thought. For example, in his book *The Gender Knot: Unraveling Our Patriarchal Legacy*, Allan Johnson (2005) noted that the ancient Greek mathematician and philosopher Pythagoras identified the "evil principle" as that which "created chaos, darkness, and woman" (p. 63). This association has been propagated within mythology and folklore across cultures, and it is important to remember that many of these ancient stories were written by men in order to justify the oppression of women, to blame mankind's sexual temptations and sins on "bad" women like Lilith, and to uphold misogynistic and patriarchal social systems via religious practices. In this sense, Lilith, like most mythological female monsters as well as the *femme fatale* archetype in general, is used as a tool to police female gender roles, sexuality, and reproductive processes.

However, when read through a feminist lens, Lilith becomes an important figure for gender equality. In the first issue of *Lilith*, Aviva Cantor Zuckoff (1976) explained the publication's name:

> Lilith is a *powerful* female.... By acknowledging Lilith's revolt and even in telling of her vengeful activities, myth-makers also acknowledge Lilith's power. Even if we accept Lilith's vengeful activities ... we can regard them as having originated in self-defense against male domination and as a consequence of having to fight on alone, century after century, for her independence. What men are saying, really is that Lilith "fights dirty." But this is a meaningless concept designed to keep women from developing and utilizing their strength to fight, period. Lilith, it must be emphasized, is a fighter and a fighter in a good cause [para. 10; emphasis in original].

Other traditions have also embraced Lilith, accepting her as both a sexualized *femme fatale* and an empowered, rebellious feminist. For Occultist and Wiccan traditions, Lilith is a central figure and her reclamation is part of larger efforts to resist oppressive patriarchy, so her prominent role in *CAOS*, as a tale of witchcraft, is appropriate. Although she begins as a villain designed with all the worst misogynistic tropes in mind, Lilith's transition from victimized villain to feminist ally, and her (admittedly short-lived) victory when she proclaims herself Queen of Hell, speaks to her potential as a redeemed, empowered, and reclaimed feminist figure. Season three's disempowerment of Lilith and the show's general reliance on tired tropes of monstrous and manipulative femininity mean that the feminist reclamation of Lilith remains *in potentia* in *CAOS*. Although Sabrina is now the Queen of Hell, as we have seen, that title tends to change hands relatively often. Most importantly, Lilith's monstrosity, villainy, and ambiguity in *CAOS* do not preclude that potential redemption and reclamation, especially when we consider that, within a patriarchal worldview, women are always already ambiguous, abject, evil, and monstrous. As Rosi Braidotti (1994) has observed in her book *Nomadic Subjects*:

> Woman, as a sign of difference, is monstrous. If we define the monster as a bodily entity that is anomalous and deviant vis-à-vis the norm, then we can argue that the female body shares with the monster the privilege of bringing out a unique blend of fascination and horror [p. 81].

By embracing her own power and monstrousness, Lilith uses the tools at her disposal to fight for that good cause that Zuckoff mentioned—gender equality—even if things do not always go her way and she must sometimes support other women at the expense of her own empowerment. Indeed, for feminist scholars like Deborah Covino, the abject, evil, and monstrous woman is subversive and liberating: she "immers[es] herself in the significances of the flesh, becoming willfully monstrous as she defies the symbolic order" (2004, p. 29). Lilith embraces her own monstrosity and empowers herself and, occasionally, other women while defying and rejecting patriarchal rule, even if she does not work to dismantle patriarchal power structures and falls into several problematic tropes of the monstrous-feminine. Perhaps most importantly, she is centralized in the show's narrative and given space to tell her own story and enact her own agency—in this sense, *CAOS's* Lilith is a noteworthy, albeit complicated and at times problematic, representation of the mythological demoness.

REFERENCES

Aguirre-Sacasa, R., & King, D. (Writers), & Seidenglanz, R. (Director) (2020). Chapter Twenty-Eight: Sabrina Is Legend [television series episode]. In L.T. Krieger, J. Goldwater, S. Schechter, R. Aguirre-Sacasa, & G. Berlanti (executive producers), *Chilling Adventures of Sabrina*. Warner Bros. Television; Berlanti Productions; Archie Comics.

Aguirre-Sacasa, R. (Writer), & Krieger, L.T. (Director) (2018). Chapter One: October Country [television series episode]. In L.T. Krieger, J. Goldwater, S. Schechter, R. Aguirre-Sacasa, & G. Berlanti (executive producers), *Chilling Adventures of Sabrina*. Warner Bros. Television; Berlanti Productions; Archie Comics.

Aguirre-Sacasa, R., & Maxwell, R. (Writers), & Seidenglanz, R. (Director) (2018). Chapter Ten: The Witching Hour [television series episode]. In L.T. Krieger, J. Goldwater, S. Schechter, R. Aguirre-Sacasa, & G. Berlanti (executive producers), *Chilling Adventures of Sabrina*. Warner Bros. Television; Berlanti Productions; Archie Comics.

Aguirre-Sacasa, R. (Writer), & Seidenglanz, R. (Director) (2019). Chapter Twenty: The Mephisto Waltz [television series episode]. In L.T. Krieger, J. Goldwater, S. Schechter,

R. Aguirre-Sacasa, & G. Berlanti (executive producers), *Chilling Adventures of Sabrina*. Warner Bros. Television; Berlanti Productions; Archie Comics.
Aguirre-Sacasa, R. (Writer), & Seidenglanz, R. (Director) (2020). Chapter Twenty-One: The Hellbound Heart [television series episode]. In L.T. Krieger, J. Goldwater, S. Schechter, R. Aguirre-Sacasa, & G. Berlanti (executive producers), *Chilling Adventures of Sabrina*. Warner Bros. Television; Berlanti Productions; Archie Comics.
Aguirre-Sacasa, R. (Writer), & Sullivan, K. (Director) (2019). Chapter Twelve: The Epiphany [television series episode]. In L.T. Krieger, J. Goldwater, S. Schechter, R. Aguirre-Sacasa, & G. Berlanti (executive producers), *Chilling Adventures of Sabrina*. Warner Bros. Television; Berlanti Productions; Archie Comics.
Barry, M. (Writer), & Benjamin, R. (Director) (2020). Chapter Twenty-Five: The Devil Within [television series episode]. In L.T. Krieger, J. Goldwater, S. Schechter, R. Aguirre-Sacasa, & G. Berlanti (executive producers), *Chilling Adventures of Sabrina*. Warner Bros. Television; Berlanti Productions; Archie Comics.
Braidotti, R. (1994). *Nomadic Subjects: Embodiment and Sexual Difference in Contemporary Feminist Theory*. Columbia University Press.
Bring, L.C. (Writer), & Macneill, C.W. (Director). (2020). Chapter Twenty-Seven: The Judas Kiss [television series episode]. In L.T. Krieger, J. Goldwater, S. Schechter, R. Aguirre-Sacasa, & G. Berlanti (executive producers), *Chilling Adventures of Sabrina*. Warner Bros. Television; Berlanti Productions; Archie Comics.
Brüning, K. (2021). "'I'm neither a slut, nor am I gonna be shamed': Sexual Violence, Feminist Anger, and Teen TV's New Heroine. *Television & New Media*. https://doi.org/10.1177/15274764211015307.
Burton, N. (2018, November 9). "'Chilling Adventures of Sabrina' Got This Jewish Feminist Demon Totally Wrong." *Alma*. https://www.heyalma.com/chilling-adventures-of-sabrina-got-this-jewish-feminist-demon-totally-wrong/.
Caputi, J. (2004). *Goddesses and Monsters: Women, Myth, Power, and Popular Culture*. University of Wisconsin Press.
Carvalho, D. (2009). Woman Has Two Faces: Re-Examining Eve and Lilith in Jewish Feminist Thought." Master's Thesis, University of Denver. https://digitalcommons.du.edu/etd/115/.
Chion, M. (1999). *The Voice in Cinema*. Columbia University Press.
Cohen, J.J. (1996). *Monster Theory: Reading Culture*. University of Minnesota Press.
Conkel, J. (Writer), & Goi, M. (Director). (2020). Chapter Twenty-Six: All of Them Witches [television series episode]. In L.T. Krieger, J. Goldwater, S. Schechter, R. Aguirre-Sacasa, & G. Berlanti (executive producers), *Chilling Adventures of Sabrina*. Warner Bros. Television; Berlanti Productions; Archie Comics.
Covino, D.C. (2004). *Amending the Abject Body: Aesthetic Makeovers in Medicine and Culture*. SUNY Press.
Creed, B. (1986). "Horror and the Monstrous-Feminine: An Imaginary Abjection." *Screen* 27(1), 44–70.
Creed, B. (1993). *The Monstrous-Feminine: Film, Feminism, Psychoanalysis*. Routledge.
Davidson, J.P. (2012). *Early Modern Supernatural: The Dark side of European Culture, 1400–1700*. Praeger.
Doane, M.A. (1991). *Femmes Fatales: Feminism, Film Theory, Psychoanalysis*. Routledge.
Ellens, J.H. (Ed.). (2011). *Explaining Evil, Vol. 1: Definitions and Development*. Praeger.
Fernandes, M. (2015). "Lilith: From Powerful Goddess to Evil Queen." In A.N. Pena (Ed.), *Revisitar o mito: Myths Revisited* (pp. 733–741). Húmus.
Foucault, M. (1976/1990). *The History of Sexuality*. Trans. R.J. Hurley. Vintage.
Frost, N. (2019, April 3). In "The Chilling Adventures of Sabrina" Season 2, Even Magic Can't Fix Toxic Masculinity." *Quartz*. https://qz.com/quartzy/1585208/season-2-of-sabrina-has-a-new-focus-on-gender-and-equality/.
Goethe (1808/2014). *Faust: A Tragedy; Parts One and Two*. Trans. M. Greenberg. Yale University Press.
Harrington, E. (2018). *Women, Monstrosity and Horror Film: Gynaehorror*. Routledge.
Henesy, M. (2020). "'Leaving My Girlhood Behind': Woke Witches and Feminist Liminality in *Chilling Adventures of Sabrina*." *Feminist Media Studies* 21(7), 1143–1157.

Hurwitz, S. (1992). *Lilith—the First Eve: Historical and Psychological Aspects of the Dark Feminine*. Daimon Verlag.

Johnson, A. (2005). *The Gender Knot: Unraveling Our Patriarchal Legacy*. Temple University Press.

Kristeva, J. (1982). *Powers of Horror: An Essay on Abjection*. Trans. L.S. Roudiez. Columbia University Press.

Langsdale, S., & Coody, E.R. (Eds.). (2020). *Monstrous Women in Comics*. University Press of Mississippi.

Rivlin, L. (1998). "Afterword: Lilith Lives." In E. Dame, L. Rivlin, & H. Wenkart (Eds.), *Which Lilith? Feminist Writers Re-Create the World's First Woman* (pp. 389–393). Rowman & Littlefield.

Rossetti, D.G. (1868). *Lady Lilith*. Delaware Art Museum. http://www.rossettiarchive.org/docs/s205.rap.html.

Santos, C. (2017). *Unbecoming Female Monsters: Witches, Vampires, and Virgins*. Lexington Books.

Schwartz, H. (2004). *Tree of Souls: The Mythology of Judaism*. Oxford University Press.

Skene, B. (2016). "Lamia." In J.A. Weinstock (ed.), *The Ashgate Encyclopedia of Literary and Cinematic Monsters* (pp. 369–370). Routledge.

Toomer, J. (2018, November 2). "Chilling Adventures of Sabrina Is the Feminist Revenge Fantasy We Need Right Now." *SyFy Wire*. https://www.syfy.com/syfywire/chilling-adventures-of-sabrina-is-the-feminist-revenge-fantasy-we-need-right-now.

Ussher, J.M. (2006). *Managing the Monstrous Feminine: Regulating the Reproductive Body*. Routledge.

Vandervalk, K. (2019, April 9). "Casual Righteousness: The Feminist Evolution of Teen Dramas." *Bitch Media*. https://www.bitchmedia.org/article/feminist-evolution-teen-dramas.

Zuckoff, A.C. (1976, Fall). "The Lilith Question." *Lilith Magazine*. https://www.lilith.org/articles/the-lilith-question/.

"Put your cape away"

Riverdale's #MeToo Moment

MELISSA WEHLER

In one of the most shocking moments in the *Riverdale* series, viewers watched helplessly as Cheryl Blossom is drugged, sexually assaulted, and nearly raped by episode newcomer, Nick St. Clair. Veronica Lodge and the Pussycats watch as Nick leads a barely standing Cheryl out of the gala. They immediately leave the stage, track him down, and manage to pull Nick off Cheryl just as he is undressing himself. The Pussycats proceed to violently attack Nick, kicking and punching him until they ultimately render him unconscious. Cheryl is whisked out of the room and into the arms of the women who saved her. Archie Andrews, the usual champion of the series, shows up too late for his normal heroics, and Cheryl tells him, "You can put your cape away. The Pussycats already saved me" (Allen & Pressman, 2017). The episode, "Chapter 18: When a Stranger Calls," aired on November 8, 2017, a little less than a month after Alyssa Milano's now-famous tweet: "If you've been sexually harassed or assaulted write 'me too' as a reply to this tweet" (2017). The tweet brought Tarana Burke's #MeToo Movement into the public spotlight, and it exploded over social media in the weeks leading up to the episode. While this uncanny timing could not have been predicted by the showrunners, the episode speaks to the cultural zeitgeist that set the stage for #MeToo. It is impossible then to read the episode without seeing it as a product of this climate, specifically, and fourth-wave feminism's approach to sexual violence and harassment, generally.

Set against the landscape of fourth-wave feminism and the #MeToo Movement, this episode illustrates how the *Riverdale* series offers a nuanced analysis of the cultural conditions that created fourth-wave feminism and the #MeToo Movement. In particular, the series depicts the repercussions of sexual assault on individuals and communities, the politics of covering-up sexual assault and silencing survivors, and the ways that women are often called upon to right such wrongs themselves. It offers a complex view of survivorship and justice where no character truly functions as a moral paradigm and no institution offers real or lasting resolutions. To understand the way the series engages in these conversations, this essay analyzes episodes that incorporate conversations from fourth-wave feminism and the #MeToo Movement and traces their themes and story arcs to understand the impact of these conversations on the characters. In this reading, *Riverdale* is situated as an important artifact of the #MeToo era that provides commentary on the era's principle issues, co-opts language from fourth-wave feminism and #MeToo debates, and depicts the complicated nature of justice, resolution, and closure when it comes to sexual misconduct.

Fourth-Wave Feminism and the #MeToo Era

As a social and political movement, #MeToo encapsulates the ideals of fourth-wave feminism and uses tools like social media as the primary mechanism for its activism and organization. Fourth-wave feminism emerged as a recognizable movement in 2008 as feminists started to use social media as a platform for activism with #MeToo creator, Tarana Burke, at its forefront. In 2006, Burke had created a page on MySpace, an early social media platform, to promote the #MeToo Movement (Ohlheiser, 2017). On October 15, 2017, Alyssa Milano would use this same hashtag and spark a global conversation about the abuses of persons in power and the pervasive problem of sexual misconduct. It is impossible to deny the cultural, social, and political impact of the movement: "Within 24 hours, 500,000 people responded on Twitter, and the hashtag #MeToo appeared on Facebook 12 million times," and "by the end of January 2018, more than 150 high-profile men had been publicly accused" (Hillstrom, 2019, pp. 53–54). Moreover, #MeToo's focus on issues of sexual misconduct was informed by the work that fourth-wave feminists, like Burke, were already doing and also informed the ways that fourth-wave feminism would subsequently frame their movement.

In the time between Burke's initial #MeToo campaign in 2006 and Milano's tweet in 2017, three critical changes had taken place in the social and political landscape. First, fourth-wave feminism emerged as an identifiable wave of feminism with its own political and social agenda, politics, philosophies, and activism. Because of the nature of social movements, it is difficult to declare a specific time when the movement began. However, Jessica Valenti, founder and editor of the feminist blog *Feministing*, said in

2009 that she did not see herself as a third-wave feminist "because it never seems very accurate to me. I know people who are considered third-wave feminists who are 20 years older than me" and that if there was a fourth wave it was "online" (Solomon & Valenti, 2009). Valenti's *Feministing* is an early example of the way that fourth-wave feminists would use the internet to define and refine their movement. Like Valenti, Laura Bates also used the internet to galvanize fourth-wave feminism through *The Everyday Sexism Project* in 2012. The function of the website is to collect the personal stories of sexism and to catalog the ways sexism is often overlooked and normalized despite being so widespread and toxic. A year later, K. Cochrane (2013) announced the arrival of the fourth wave by featuring its emerging voices. In *All the Rebel Women*, Cochrane collects "rebels" like Bates who were wielding the internet to raise their collective voices about harassment, rape culture, and slut-shaming. Later, Nicola Rivers (2017) and Prudence Chamberlain (2017) outlined fourth-wave feminism's relationship to the preceding waves and helped to solidify its platform. The movement quickly began to be defined as focused on online activism, female empowerment, and intersectionality (Munro, 2013). A second important change was the arrival of social media as one of the most dominant forms of media. Social media was already being wielded as a tool for activism and political organization. #ArabSpring, #BlackLivesMatter, and #BringBackOurGirls were viral social media campaigns that had brought attention, awareness, and action to political and social movements in the United States and abroad. Sites like *Feministing* and *The Everyday Sexism Project* also focused on the same issue that would be at the heart of #MeToo: bringing attention to the pervasiveness of sexual misconduct. A third important change was that the political landscape in the United States had shifted dramatically from the presidency of Barack Obama to Donald Trump. Indeed, when analyzing #MeToo, many critics identify the 2016 election of Donald Trump as one of the catalysts for the success of the movement:

> When voters elected him president despite [sexual assault] allegations, some observers predicted that the apparent lack of public concern would make women reluctant to come forward with such complaints in the future. Instead, the idea that powerful men could take advantage of their positions to abuse women generated a sense of outrage that seemed to imbue more women with the courage to make public disclosures [Hillstrom, 2018, p. 50].

Coupled with the emergence of fourth-wave feminism and its use of social media, the election of Donald Trump contributed to the cultural zeitgeist that allowed the #MeToo Movement to flourish. Thus, when *Riverdale* debuted on January 26, 2017, it entered a cultural, political, and social landscape that was already engaged in conversations about sexual misconduct, and it was about to find itself at the epicenter of #MeToo in its second season.

Riverdale *Foreshadows* #MeToo

In its first season, *Riverdale* draws on familiar, mainstream narratives around sexual harassment and demonstrates their damaging impact on individual women and communities of women. The episode "Chapter 3: Body Double" is *Riverdale*'s first attempt at tackling some of the everyday sexual harassment that their viewers face, especially their teenage target audience. In the episode, characters Veronica Lodge and Betty Cooper confront Chuck Clayton, captain of the football team and "Riverdale High's resident golden boy," who has spread rumors about Veronica following their date (Lawrence & Krieger, 2017). Veronica and Betty discover that this is far from an isolated incident and that members of the football team have been keeping "score" in a "playbook" where they record tallies of their sexual exploits (Lawrence & Krieger, 2017). The playbook of sexual exploits is a popular trope in teenage drama, and as Cheryl says, "reeks of suburban legend" (Lawrence & Krieger, 2017). In this case, however, the playbook is indeed real and offers a vehicle for the series to explore other very real issues facing *Riverdale*'s teenage audience.

The crux of the episode comes when Veronica finds out that she is being slut-shamed online, and it illustrates the toll slut-shaming takes on individuals who experience it. In the episode, we learn that Veronica and Ethel Muggs have been slut-shamed, a type of harassment and bullying tactic used to depict an individual, especially a woman, as promiscuous to publicly shame and humiliate them (Sweeney, 2017, pp. 1579–1580). Slut-shaming has been a central issue in fourth-wave feminism, and feminists have used it to call out the double standards for men and women when it comes to sex and sexuality (Friedman, O'Reilly, Teekah, & Scholz, 2015, p. 3). In the episode, the consequences for slut-shaming are clear: Veronica is depicted as personally and emotionally devastated. She cries as she reads a thread of derogatory comments about herself on social media. The portrayal of online harassment in this episode and its impact on survivors mirrors the real, lived experiences of *Riverdale*'s viewers who have been the target of this kind of harassment and bullying. A Pew Research Center poll found

> 21% of women ages 18 to 29 report being sexually harassed online […] roughly half (53%) of young women ages 18 to 29 say that someone has sent them explicit images they did not ask for. […] 35% of women who have experienced any type of online harassment describe their most recent incident as either extremely or very upsetting ["Online Harassment 2017," 2017].

Borrowing from the real world of its viewers, *Riverdale* illustrates the trauma of online harassment through characters like Veronica and Ethel.

But slut-shaming does not just impact the individual being shamed. The audience learns that this behavior has impacted an entire community of women who have become social outcasts at the school. Ethel, for instance, has had the words "Sloppy seconds" written on her locker, a phrase commonly used to demean someone who has engaged in sexual activity, and she says, "They are ruining our lives, but to them, it's just a game" (Lawrence & Krieger, 2017). Chuck and his real-world counterparts wield slut-shaming as a weapon, empowering themselves while simultaneously deflecting the attention from their own sexual harassment. To reinforce this point, Veronica references Steubenville and Glen Ridge by name during the episode. In the 2012 Steubenville rape case, a sixteen-year-old woman was raped by two high school football players who documented it on social media (Pennington & Birthisel, 2016). In the 1989 Glen Ridge case, a seventeen-year-old girl was raped and sexually assaulted by members of the football team (Lefkowitz, 1997). While Chuck's behavior does not rise to the same level of sexual predation as these examples, Veronica's point—and the writers' point—is that high schools can often create an environment where certain persons, like football players, are given privileged positions that they weaponize against others, particularly women, and expect not to experience consequences.

The episode also establishes another foundational principle of fourth-wave feminism and the later #MeToo Movement: women believing the survivors of sexual misconduct, supporting them through their trauma, and fighting for their assailants to be brought to justice. Betty gathers the women to share their accounts and talk about how slut-shaming has impacted them. She tells Veronica "this story is bigger than we thought," saying that she "started asking around, to see if what happened to you happened to anyone else, and if anyone would go on record" (Lawrence & Krieger, 2017). Ethel agrees to go on the record with Betty describing how "one day last year, Chuck and I talked in the library for 10 minutes. I helped him with a Pre-Calc problem, and nothing happened. But the next day, he started telling people that I let him do stuff to me. Like, sex stuff" (Lawrence & Krieger, 2017). Betty reassures her that what happened to her was "horrible" and when Cheryl tries to discredit Ethel's account, Veronica cuts her off, saying, "I'm not lying about what happened to me. And Ethel's not lying. And proof or no proof, book or no book, I am going scorched earth on these privileged, despicable miscreants. You wanna get caught in that backdraft, Cheryl? Call me, or any of these beautiful, young, strong, intelligent women 'slut' one more time…" (Lawrence & Krieger, 2017). Veronica and Betty's defense of other women helps them to form a coalition whose collective action is greater than their individual efforts.

Forming a coalition of women would later be at the foundation of #MeToo where much like these characters, women found strength in numbers. #BelieveWomen and #BelieveSurvivors would become a rallying cry for feminists who offered public support to survivors while also demanding public accountability for perpetrators. These hashtags began trending during the Brett Kavanaugh Supreme Court hearings. Kavanaugh had been accused of sexual harassment and assault by Dr. Christine Blasey Ford, a former classmate. Speaking about the hearings and the hashtags, Burke said, "'Believe women' or 'believe survivors' is not just like, 'Believe us at all costs, don't investigate,' you know, 'If I say it, it's true.' It is—let's start with a premise that people aren't lying and at least give them the respect of interrogating what they're saying" (Ostby, Mic Staff, & Burke, 2018). In this scene, Veronica and Betty co-opt the language of fourth-wave feminism, believe the survivors of sexual harassment, and support them in their trauma.

And while the creators could have allowed this moment to stand as an idealized culmination of feminist cooperation, they decide instead to interject a dose of harsh reality in the form of Cheryl Blossom. Upon hearing the accusations, Cheryl refuses to believe the women's accounts—even calling them "sluts" herself—and repeats a common refrain in sexual misconduct cases: "boys will be boys" (Lawrence & Krieger, 2017). In this moment, Cheryl functions as a fictional representation for the all-too-real conversations that usually accompany sexual assault allegations. Speaking about then-Supreme Court nominee Kavanaugh, culture critic Garber (2018) identifies that normalizing sexual misconduct is at the heart of the "boys will be boys" rhetoric: "Once again, in much of the public discussion, the empathy settles on the man accused. There but for the grace, etc.: If youthful indiscretions like that are allowed to affect the fate of a basketball-coaching, soup-kitchen-volunteering, daughter-nurturing, carpool-driving Supreme Court nominee, whose fortunes wouldn't be affected?" As Garber notes, Cheryl's parroting of this phrase seeks to normalize the actions of the football team to offer a defense of her beloved brother.

Cheryl's rebuke of her classmates embodies the ways that critics of #MeToo use victim-blaming to redirect the focus from the perpetrator's actions to the actions and non-actions of the survivors. Her rebuke also illustrates the very real fear survivors have of not being believed when they do disclose their allegations (Teng, 2018, February 15). Cheryl—who eventually does believe the women's accounts—will come to depend on this same network of female support when she faces her own #MeToo moment in season two. It sheds light on why survivors of sexual misconduct are reluctant to come forward, and it also reinforces the problems with schools and society allowing "boys to be boys" at the expense of girls being allowed to be girls.

When Chuck refuses to correct the rumors or apologize for spreading them, Veronica and Betty create their own justice—a theme that will be repeated later in the series when Cheryl Blossom needs rescuing from Nick St. Clair. Shockingly, Veronica and Betty drug and torture Chuck—Betty nearly drowns him—until he confesses and apologizes on video. The scene is certainly a mixed resolution for viewers. On one hand, Veronica and Betty manufacture a resolution that would otherwise be denied to Veronica and the other women. Chuck is unrepentant at the beginning of the scene, and indeed, only seems to change his mind once Betty applies physical force. Other characters, such as Ethel, not only approve of these tactics but celebrate their success. Chuck's comeuppance appears to be acceptable in the logic of the series and certainly speaks to viewers like Ethel who are glad to see the bully being bullied. On the other hand, Veronica and Betty's tactics completely undermine what is framed as their victory. First, the use of drugs, physical restraint, and torture are shocking. Veronica and Betty do not just become the very bully they are punishing, they actually prove to be much worse. Second, while the scene is framed as feminist, it problematically relies on racist imagery and stereotypes as K. Griffiths (2017) rightfully points out: "the pro-feminist message of the episode took on an uncomfortable racial coding when Chuck is chained up in a hot tub by the white Betty and white-passing Veronica, the former of whom threatens to boil him alive while calling him 'good boy.'" Third, their "victory" is also short-lived: Chuck immediately recants his confession and calls them "crazy" (Lawrence & Krieger, 2017). For viewers, the implication is that while this kind of vigilante justice may produce short-term results, it is a damaging and unsustainable long-term strategy.

Betty and Veronica's short-term solution to the "Chucks" of their world is the direct result of a complete breakdown of the so-called protective institutions that have failed the characters involved, forcing them into increasingly lose-lose situations. First, because the principal did not believe Ethel who actually did come forward, Chuck and the football team are emboldened to continue terrorizing the women of Riverdale. This also had a chilling impact on the other survivors who do not report the football players' actions out of fear of players and the non-action of the principal. They only report their harassment and assaults to Betty—and all of them decline to go on record. Because of the non-action of the school officials, Chuck eventually ensnares Veronica and later Betty, which results in some consequences for Chuck and the football team, but at a serious cost to both Veronica and Betty. Second, Chuck has been immersed in social and cultural institutions that reward men who aggressively pursue sexual conquests and condone his slut-shaming. His real comeuppance is not that he is tortured but that he is kicked off the football team where he was able to draw cultural capital and social power. Finally, for their part, Veronica and Betty are largely rewarded for their role in Chuck's drugging and torture by the same institutions that should have been the ones to intervene. They are problematically referred to as "avenging angels" and lightly chided by Veronica's mother to not "take matters into your own hands" (Lawrence & Krieger, 2017). Betty obtains and burns the playbook, and the episode ends with Cheryl praising Ethel who has come forward to corroborate Betty's story, saying "Hashtag JusticeForEthel," a direct reference to social media activism. Veronica and Betty are the heroes of the story according to the episode, but the "Dark Betty" that was unleashed that night has consequences for seasons to come, and Veronica learns to work around the justice system rather than with it, which will play out in the episode with Nick St. Clair to disastrous effect.

A Stranger in Riverdale

Throughout the first season, the series' creators establish several core themes that were readdressed during one of the most climactic and consequential episodes of the second season. "Chapter 18: When a Stranger Calls" ominously refers to two "strangers" featured in the episode. One of the "strangers" is Nick St. Clair whose family has come to call on their friends, the Lodges. Interestingly, the other stranger in the episode, the Black Hood serial killer, is depicted as a parallel but somehow no-less-threatening foil to the seemingly polished playboy. Through the character of Nick St. Clair, the series engages with conversations at the heart of fourth-wave feminism and the #MeToo era: the prevalence of sexual predators. Nick employs common tactics used by sexual predators to coerce someone into sexual activity and displays some of their common psychological characteristics, including "well-polished social skills, overriding desire for self-gratification, narcissism, and lack of remorse" (Mitchell & Glamb, 2012, p. 608). Introduced as a "ghost from [Veronica's] bad girl past," Veronica describes him as an "outrageous flirt" (Allen & Pressman, 2017). Veronica's characterization of him as a "flirt" reinforces that what he does is harmless fun, but Nick does more than just flirt with the women of Riverdale—he attempts to sexually assault and rape them. Nick's flirtatious disguise may be less obvious than the Black Hood's costume, but this "stranger" is just as sinister.

Like other sexual predators, Nick wears his playboy persona to operate in the open, mask his real intentions, and lure his would-be victims into a false sense of security. He wields sex as a weapon, using increasingly violent tactics to maintain and sustain his social and cultural capital. He starts with rhetorical arguments that seek to manipulate and pressure his victims, graduates to the use of mind-altering drugs to lower his victims' inhibitions, and then finally resorts to physical aggression and violence. First, Nick attempts to verbally manipulate Veronica into sex. After their hotel party winds down, Nick and Veronica are left alone where Nick attempts to seduce her. She tells him that she is sorry if he "got the wrong idea" about her interest in him and reminds him that Archie Andrews is her boyfriend (Allen & Pressman, 2017). In this exchange, Veronica articulates the language of consent by telling Nick that he has misinterpreted her behavior and physically removes his hand from her thigh. Nick, however, brushes off this rejection and continues to apply pressure, saying, "Oh, come on, Vee. You barely looked at that hayseed yokel all night," referring to Archie, and describes her as "all over [him]" (Allen & Pressman, 2017). This rhetorical tactic frames Veronica as the one who initiated the sexual contact, and therefore, is now beholden to see it through. Sexual consent, however, is reversible, meaning that even if she had initiated the sexual activity—which she did not—that does not mean that she cannot change her mind and revoke her previous consent. At this point, Nick becomes aggressive and begins to grab Veronica's hands and dress. Again, Veronica reinforces her refusal, saying, "Nick, we're friends, we're old friends" (Allen & Pressman, 2017), emphasizing and repeating that their relationship is platonic and not sexual. When Nick tries to forcibly kiss her, Veronica pushes him off of her and tells him to stop. Nick, rebuked for the final time, slut-shames her, saying, "Same old Veronica, huh? You flirt and you tease, but in the end, you think you're better than me" (Allen & Pressman, 2017). Nick's accusations and escalating use of physical force borrows the characteristics of power-assertive rapists: "The power-assertive rapist is narcissistic and self-centered; he has a poor appreciation for the rights of others. This kind of rapist has undergone defective socialization, resulting in poor impulse control. The power-assertive rapist exploits any vulnerability and is willing to use force to achieve sexual domination" (Baker, 2012). Nick's inability to leverage his power over Veronica in this scene leaves him more desperate and more dangerous, demonstrating how precarious it can be for women during and after such encounters.

Like in the first season, a character's sexual misconduct is followed up with an apology that functions as a means to an end rather than an acknowledgment of wrongdoing. The day after his failed assault, Nick appears contrite and comes to Veronica for forgiveness. He admits he "crossed a line" and offers an explanation: "it's not an excuse, but over the last three months, I've been in and out of rehab. It's been … a struggle" (Allen & Pressman, 2017). Veronica corrects him saying that he had "obliterated the line," however, after glancing over at her father and remembering that she is supposed to be securing his parents' investment, she forgives Nick: "Last night was messy, but we've all been there. So, why don't we start over with two glasses of ginger ale" (Allen & Pressman, 2017). Much like Chuck's apology, Nick's apology is insincere, given only under duress, and is simply a means to an end. Chuck's and Nick's non-apology apologies echo the rhetorical approach and tone of the men accused during the #MeToo reckoning who were more sorry to be caught than sorry about their offenses. Men like Charlie Rose, Louis C.K., and Kevin Spacey all offered non-apology apologies where they blamed not knowing enough about consent, not understanding the power dynamics of sex and celebrity, and like Nick, abusing alcohol and controlled substances (Silva, 2017). These non-apology apologies helped these men to address the issue in public without having to actually admit to their actions and face consequences for them.

Nick also manipulates his would-be victims by leveraging his social and economic privileges. Veronica relents to Nick's pressure to take the party drug because her father has ordered her to show Nick a "good time" to get the wealthy St. Clair family to invest in their Southside project (Allen & Pressman, 2017). Nick clearly interprets "father's orders" to include sexual favors, and indeed, later in the episode, this interpretation is reinforced by Veronica's father when he says that her "charm offensive is paying off" (Allen & Pressman, 2017). In this exchange, Nick uses his social and economic privileges to remind Veronica of his power over her and her family. Veronica is also reminded that she is likewise beholden to the power of her father who has put her in such a precarious situation. Later, Nick again attempts to apply pressure by leveraging his socio-economic privileges and suggesting a *quid pro quo*: sexual favors in exchange for his help in securing funding for her family's project. He reminds her that he has the "power to implode this pathetic deal your criminal father's so desperately trying to make happen. So unless you want that to go away, I'd be thinking of ways you might start showing me some appreciation. If you need help, I can suggest a couple" (Allen & Pressman, 2017). As he threatens her, he reinforces his dominance by running his hands through her hair. In both instances, Nick tries to coerce sexual favors and disregards the need for active and enthusiastic consent.

Nick's predatory tactics rapidly escalate throughout the episode, transforming him from a sexual predator into a rapist. Moments after his faux apology to Veronica, viewers watch Nick drop a small pill into

Cheryl's champagne glass, and the next time we see Cheryl, she is stumbling over the dance floor. Nick asks her if she is feeling well, knowing that he has drugged her. He takes the increasingly unconscious Cheryl back to his hotel room where he starts undressing and climbs on top of her. Ariana Romero (2017), a pop-culture critic, argues that Nick "doesn't want to share anything with Cheryl—he wants to use her like a plaything" and compares Nick's handling of Cheryl's body to a "little boy dragging his toy home from the park" (Romero 2017). Once Cheryl is unconscious in his room, he "throws Cheryl on his bed, he splays her out like a broken doll, again turning her from person to living sex toy" (Romero 2017). Nick does not attempt any real advances with Cheryl—who appears to be interested in him romantically and perhaps sexually—before he drugs her. This seemingly inexplicable action demonstrates that he is more interested in power than he is in sex, a quality of power-assertive rapists. He does not risk being rejected by Cheryl as he was by Veronica and can control the situation entirely—or so he believes.

While Nick is a "stranger" in Riverdale, Riverdale is no stranger to men like Nick. The women of Riverdale have already held a potential sexual predator accountable through collective action. With the support of the other survivors, Betty, Veronica, and Ethel use a combination of support, reporting, and violence to ensure that Chuck faces the consequences of his actions. Over two seasons, these women have become adept at manufacturing swift, violent justice for one another through their any-means-necessary approach. This savvy community of female survivors works outside the institutions that routinely fail them and have no issue working in a morally and legally gray area. Veronica and the Pussycats arrive in time to thwart Nick's attempted rape of Cheryl and deliver an immediate, physical reckoning for the character. Romero (2017) describes this scene as

> something you wish would happen to any and all sexual assaulters and harassers, attempted or guilty. And with what's going on in Hollywood right now with sexual predators finally getting pushed into the spotlight and some even facing the consequences of their actions, the timing couldn't be more perfect.

Much like Betty's handling of Chuck, the scene certainly plays to a desire to see actual retribution carried out on a character that was created to be hated. After all, viewers have watched—and possibly experienced—institutions fail to protect women from the Chucks and Nicks of the world. The audience is also watching this scene against the backdrop of #MeToo where powerful men in almost every industry were being outed as sexual predators after years—and sometimes, decades—of abuse. While many of these men were forced to resign from their positions, few of them were formally charged, and those cheering on Veronica and the Pussycats reasonably fear that outside of this moment, Nick may never face any formal justice much like his real-world counterparts.

Characters like Nick and Chuck embody socially conferred privileges when it comes to sexual predation. Chuck is caught before his behavior escalates to sexual assault and rape. Chuck shares Nick's gender and social status privileges, but he does not have Nick's race and socio-economic class privileges. Day (2018) remarks on the racial inequality when it comes to race and public accountability for one's actions:

> In this country, in short, black boys can never simply be "boys." Consider 14-year-old Emmett Till, lynched by a vicious white mob over allegations involving sexual assault of a white woman in 1955 in Mississippi. Worse, it took decades for white political leaders to decry his lynching.

Nick's gender, race, status, and socio-economic class allow him more social and cultural capital and certainly save him from the public naming and shaming that Chuck goes through when he is removed from the football team. Nick's ability to use his privileges to operate in the shadows parallels many of the accounts of #MeToo. Harvey Weinstein, Matt Lauer, Louis C.K., and Charlie Rose sexually harassed and assaulted women, and despite widespread knowledge of their actions, were shielded by their privileges and the "boys will be boys" rhetoric (Usborne, 2018, August 5). Because of their privilege, these men were allowed to continue their behavior until the public reckoning of the #MeToo Movement. In Riverdale, the #MeToo politics play out along the same gender, social status, race, and socio-economic class lines for both the perpetrators and the survivors.

Surviving Surviving

"Chapter 18: When a Stranger Calls" also illustrates the aftermath of sexual assault for its survivors and the importance of women telling their accounts to other supportive women. The Pussycats take Cheryl back to Veronica's room where Betty and Archie join them. Cheryl experiences the entire spectrum of emotion as she works through her trauma. First, she experiences shock—"If you hadn't come when you did…"—and then anger—"I want to press charges. I want Nick to pay. To suffer. To burn in hell" (Allen & Pressman, 2017). Through all of it, Josie and Veronica surround her on the bed, enfolding her in their arms and allowing her space and time to cry. Archie tries to assume his mantel as resident superhero, but Cheryl has already been rescued by the women who have now cocooned her in Veronica's bedroom.

The world outside of Veronica's bedroom is a much less supportive space where survivor accounts are approached with skepticism and antagonism. When Betty and Veronica were helping survivors to tell their stories about the playbook, it was Cheryl who played the doubting, accusing foil. Now, when Cheryl herself is assaulted, Cheryl's mother, Penelope, offers a damning, dissenting voice in the aftermath of Cheryl's attempted rape. Penelope, sitting opposite Veronica's parents, reiterates the "boys will be boys" victim-blaming rhetoric: "I just wish you'd stopped her from talking to Sheriff Keller. Lord knows what Cheryl did or said to the St. Clair boy to provoke him" (Aguirre-Sacasa & Kiley, 2017). Importantly, Cheryl's mother has not spoken to her daughter about the assault and immediately jumps to the conclusion that Cheryl's account is either exaggerated or outright false. Hearing Penelope's initial reaction to the news also helps to contextualize Cheryl's previous skepticism about the football team's sexual harassment and bullying. Her mother has steeped her in the rhetoric of victim-blaming, slut-shaming, and self-hatred that allows her to make excuses for sexual predators. Penelope is not interested in pressing formal charges and is upset that the police have been contacted. She is embarrassed about the "situation," victim-and slut-shames her daughter, and asks for "discretion" before uttering the most damning summation of a sexual assault: "After all, nothing really happened to Cheryl" (Aguirre-Sacasa & Kiley, 2017). Penelope's summation has a chilling effect on Cheryl who immediately brushes off both her mother's dismissal and her own feelings about the assault, saying that making a statement to the police was just a "momentary lapse in sanity" (Aguirre-Sacasa & Kiley, 2017). Without her mother's support, Cheryl, like many survivors, is forced into silence (Teng, 2018, February 15), and the next we see her, she tells Betty she's "compartmentalizing" (Aguirre-Sacasa & Kiley, 2017). The contrast between Cheryl's friends and her mother demonstrate the critical role women play when it comes to supporting or sabotaging survivors.

When Cheryl has a run-in with Nick, she learns how powerful belief—and doubt—truly are. Nick initially pretends to not really know her by mispronouncing her name. This subtle rhetorical move helps Nick to communicate that Cheryl was nothing to him—not even worthy of the most basic courtesy. Cheryl, in disbelief, says, "You roofied me. You tried to rape me" (Aguirre-Sacasa & Kiley, 2017). Playing dumb, Nick says, "I don't think that's what happened," calls her "a desperate tart from a truck-stop town," and tells her to "not distort reality to cover your morning-after shame. You were high, half-naked and begging for it" (Aguirre-Sacasa & Kiley, 2017). Nick gaslights Cheryl and reasserts his power over her. He demeans her by calling her names, and like he did with Veronica, suggests that she is at fault for what happened between them. When the gaslighting does not seem to work, he asserts another kind of power: money. Nick reveals that Penelope has taken the St. Clairs' hush money that will ensure, as Nick says, that she is "not gonna be saying anything about that night to anyone" (Aguirre-Sacasa & Kiley, 2017). Nick uses hush money as a weapon against Cheryl to stop her from pressing charges much like his real-world counterpart Harvey Weinstein (Harris, 2019 June 14). Cheryl confronts her mother about taking the hush money, saying, "You'll defend daddy even after he murdered your son. But you won't stand up for me, not even against my would-be rapist" and pleads with her to "care about me more" (Aguirre-Sacasa & Kiley, 2017). Belief, as Cheryl learns here, is not a matter of fact but one of opinion that can be bought, sold, won, and lost. Cheryl can only speak her truth but cannot make others believe it.

In raising the question of belief, the series also addresses another serious hurdle for sexual assault survivors: whether they will report their assault. First, Veronica grapples with her own decision to stay silent about her assault and the attenuating guilt she feels. She tells the group that she feels "so sick" about what happened to Cheryl, saying, "Nick's a monster. And there's no way he hasn't done this before. Probably right under my nose" (Allen & Pressman, 2017). Veronica, of course, has first-hand knowledge of his predatory nature given his attempt to assault her after the party. She expresses guilt and sees herself as responsible for Nick's actions because she did not come forward. Of course, Nick's actions are his own, and even if Veronica had come forward, there is no guarantee that she could have stopped him from attempting to rape Cheryl let alone anyone else, and in perpetuity. Later, Veronica tells Cheryl her own #MeToo story, saying, "It's not just you. He's done it to other girls, I mean, hell, he even tried to do it to me. The night before the open house" (Allen & Pressman, 2017). Cheryl presses Veronica, asking if she had reported it to anyone, and she tells Cheryl she did not. Like many survivors of sexual assault, Veronica worries about what disclosing the assault will do to her and her family: "Along with feeling the shame of such subjugation, a survivor experiences shock that such a violation could be trafficked along the channels of a personal or professional connection. [...] He or she often chooses to not speak about the harm they suffer from, much less ask for help. Thus, support and aid for survivors of person-to-person traumas are often delayed, or worse, never delivered, because such survivors frequently hide their own suffering" (Teng, 2018, February 15). She is fearful—and rightly so—that her father would hurt or possibly kill Nick if he were to find out, and she does not want "his blood on my dad's hands or on mine" (Aguirre-Sacasa & Kiley, 2017). Veronica also fears retaliation from the powerful St. Clair family, and indeed, Nick tells Cheryl to "tell that bitch Veronica she's lucky I'm not pressing changes" (Aguirre-Sacasa & Kiley, 2017). Cheryl takes exception to Veronica's seeming double-standard, saying, "And yet you were happy to fill them in on my after-dark-drama, weren't you? Well, I won't be a puppet for your thirst for vengeance. You want justice? You go after Nick in court, Veronica" (Allen & Pressman, 2017). Cheryl believes Veronica is using her as a weapon against Nick, while Veronica views Cheryl as someone who can stop Nick and keep him from assaulting someone else.

The relationship between the two characters in this scene mirrors one of the most important criticisms of #MeToo. Because it is social and public, observers worried that disclosing a sexual assault or witnessing the disclosure of sexual assaults could further traumatize survivors (LaMotte, 2017; McClurg, 2018). Aida Manduley, therapist and sexuality educator, notes that her clients "feel that it's inescapable […] and I am concerned with the victims of sexual trauma and violence who are saying to me 'I can't get away from the trigger, it's everywhere'" (LaMotte, 2017). Veronica confronts the realities of her own assault. She discloses it for the first time and talks about the guilt she feels for not disclosing it. In this highly vulnerable moment, she relives her trauma through Cheryl's story. Cheryl, still working through her own feelings about her assault, is herself forced to re-experience it through Veronica's disclosure. She has also had to face the initial rejection of her mother and is feeling betrayed by Veronica for not reporting. And while the consequences should be for Nick to face, viewers see that the pressure and the stakes are actually highest for Veronica and Cheryl.

Like real-life sexual assault survivors, Veronica and Cheryl are called upon to tell their stories to an audience that is unlikely to be receptive of them or their trauma. In a study about the cultural stigma around sexual assault stories, researchers found "whether endings were positive or negative, sexual violence stories were perceived as hard to tell and unlikely to be told. Similarly, even when story endings were positive, participants judged narrators of sexual violence stories as less likeable than narrators of other types of trauma stories" (Delker, Salton, McLean, Syed, 2020). Viewers watch Veronica and Cheryl articulate their individual and collective fear of being stigmatized by their friends, family, and community.

Ultimately, for both Veronica and Cheryl, disclosing their assaults does not result in real justice but rather in the same self-manufactured justice first explored in season one. Much like Chuck, Nick operates in a privileged sphere of society that seems to make him immune to the typical sanctions for sexual predators, so the Core Four—with the help of Veronica's parents—take it into their own hands to become his judge, jury, and executioner. First, he suffers several broken bones after a car accident that the series heavily implies was orchestrated by the Lodges as retaliation for the assaults. Second, Archie later finds Nick recovering from his car accident, attempts to extort him for more money for Cheryl, and physically assaults him on Veronica's behalf. Third, when Nick returns in a later episode, viewers learn that his father is "this close to disowning [him]," believing Nick will "never have the guts to be in the family business" (Aguirre-Sacasa & Phang, 2018). If Veronica and Cheryl kept silent, it is very unlikely that Nick would have even faced these consequences—as short-lived and short-sighted as they are. *Riverdale* shows viewers just how fraught navigating these waters can be for survivors and how accessing real justice—even with the characters' social standing, their financial means, and a friendly police department—does not always result in prison sentences.

Alternative avenues to justice, however, do not have a lasting impact, and while Veronica notes that "Karma is a bitch" when it comes to Nick's accident, alternative justice also results in some karmic justice for the Core Four (Aguirre-Sacasa & Kiley, 2017). First, none of the witnesses can testify against Nick because the drugs are still in their system, meaning that they would have a "credibility problem" on the witness stand, ensuring that Nick never truly faces justice (Aguirre-Sacasa & Kiley, 2017). Second, Southside High is raided to look for the Jingle Jangle that Nick had procured and further provokes an already looming gang war. Third, Betty gives the Black Hood serial killer Nick's name as his next target, and while he did not murder Nick St. Clair, Betty had to face the fact that she could have played a role in killing another person. Fourth, Nick returns to Riverdale later, kidnapping Archie and holding him for ransom. With these rippling repercussions, the series goes out of its way to reinforce once again that short-term vendettas do not provide actionable solutions for sexual assault survivors or help to establish a culture of accountability for sexual predators.

The Reality of Riverdale

As a series, *Riverdale* deliberately and seriously tackles the issues of sexual misconduct as it wrestles with a reality that has been fundamentally shaped by fourth-wave feminism and the #MeToo Movement. In episodes like "Chapter 3: Body Double" and "Chapter 18: When a Stranger Calls," the series depicts the realities of sexual crimes, predators, and survivors that reflect the very real social and cultural conversations happening around it. And just as the series engages with these conversations, so too do its creators and actors. Following the airing of "Chapter 18: When a Stranger Calls," Madelaine Petsch, the actress who plays Cheryl Blossom, released a public service announcement about sexual assault and date rape. She spoke about the episode and the public service announcement on her YouTube channel. Petsch (2017) described how this episode and the sexual assault depicted impacted her: "when I read what happened to Cheryl—I won't spoil anything—but I cried for like an hour and a half." In the video, she provides viewers with information about reporting sexual assault and resources for survivors, saying, "know that you're not alone. I feel like that's a huge message a lot of people could have used including myself and knowing that you're not alone and that people genuinely care is really important" (Petsch, 2017, November 8). A month before, Petsch had self-disclosed in a tweet that she was also a survivor of sexual assault using #MeToo (Petsch, 2017, October 19). Petsch has also actively discussed #MeToo and her own perspective on its importance:

> I joined the #MeToo Movement. I think what people don't understand is that #MeToo doesn't necessarily only relate to the industry, it relates to any kind of sexual assault [...] The #MeToo Movement was huge and incredibly empowering for women to be able to stand up and be like, "That happened to me, as well." It connected this whole group of women from all over the world together in this kind of beautiful way. I mean, it's sad that that happened, but, at the same time, it's like, the fact that we can own that is *huge* [Iverson, 2019].

In addition to Petsch, several of the other women from the series have reported their own #MeToo accounts. Camila Mendes, the actor who plays Veronica Lodge, gave an account of being drugged and sexually assaulted in a story that certainly echoes Cheryl Blossom's assault (Kercher, 2019). Lili Reinhart, the actor who plays Betty, wrote about her own experience "where a man in a position of power over me, used that said power to try and take advantage of me" much like what Nick attempts with Veronica (Reinhart, 2017). While some storylines on *Riverdale* can sometimes veer into the unbelievable, its #MeToo moments, as these accounts attest, are all too real.

References

Aguirre-Sacasa, R. (Writer), & Kiley, M. (Director) (2017, November 15). Chapter 19: Death Proof [television series episode]. In R. Aguirre-Sacasa (Producer), *Riverdale*. Burbank, CA: Warner Bros. Entertainment, Inc.

Aguirre-Sacasa, R. (Writer), & Phang, J. (Director) (2018, April 25). Chapter 32: Prisoners. [television series episode]. In R. Aguirre-Sacasa (Producer), *Riverdale*. Burbank, CA: Warner Bros. Entertainment, Inc.

Allen, A. (Writer), & Pressman, Ellen S. (Director) (2017, November 8). Chapter 18: When a Stranger Calls [television series episode]. In R. Aguirre-Sacasa (Producer), *Riverdale*. Burbank, CA: Warner Bros. Entertainment, Inc.

Arnstrong, K., & Miller, T.C. (2015, December 16). "Unbelievable Story of Rape." *The Marshall Project*. Retrieved from https://www.themarshallproject.org/2015/12/16/an-unbelievable-story-of-rape.

Baker, T.E. (2012). Rapist Profiles. In *Encyclopedia of Trauma: An Interdisciplinary Guide*. Thousand Oaks, CA: SAGE.

Bates, L. (2012). The Everyday Sexism Project. http://everydaysexism.com/.

Chamberlain, P. (2017). *The Feminist Fourth Wave: Affective Temporality*. Cham, Switzerland: Palgrave Macmillan. doi:10.1007/978-3-319-53682-8.

Day, K. (2018, September 28). "White Boys Will Be Boys: Kavanaugh, #MeToo and Race." *Religious News Service*. https://religionnews.com/2018/09/28/white-boys-will-be-boys-kavanaugh-and-race/.

Delker, B.C., Salton, R., McLean, K.C., & Syed, M. (2020). "Who Has to Tell Their Trauma Story and How Hard Will It Be? Influence of Cultural Stigma and Narrative Redemption on the Storying of Sexual Violence." *PloS One* 15(6), e0234201. https://doi.org/10.1371/journal.pone.0234201.

Friedman, M., A. O'Reilly, A. Teekah, & E.J. Scholz. (2015). Introduction. In A. O'Reilly, M. Friedman, A. Teekah, & E.J. Scholz (Eds.), *This Is What a Feminist Slut Looks Like: Perspectives on the SlutWalk Movement*. Ontario: Demeter Press.

Garber, M. (2018, September 17). "Brett Kavanaugh and the Revealing Logic of 'Boys Will Be Boys.'" *The Atlantic*. https://www.theatlantic.com/entertainment/archive/2018/09/brett-kavanaugh-and-the-revealing-logic-of-boys-will-be-boys/570415/.

Griffiths, K. (2017, April 6). "We Need to Talk about 'Riverdale's' Diversity Problem." *Bustle*. https://www.bustle.com/p/riverdale-.has-a-huge-representation-problem-despite-its-amazingly-diverse-cast-49201

Hillstrom, L.C. (2019). *The #MeToo Movement*. Santa Barbara, CA: ABC-CLIO.

Iversen, K. (2019, August 5). "Madelaine's Madelaine." *Nylon*. Retrieved from https://nylon.com/madelaine-petsch-nylon-august-2019-cover.

Kercher, S. (2019, September 9). "Camila Mendes Is Flying High." *Women's Health*. Retrieved from https://www.womenshealthmag.com/life/a28800294/camila-mendes-riverdale-self-care-interview/.

Koblin, J. (2019, October 17). "Netflix's Top 10 Original Movies and TV Shows, According to Netflix." *New York Times*. Retrieved from https://www.nytimes.com/2019/10/17/business/media/netflix-top-ten-movies-tv-shows.html.

LaMotte, S. (2017, October 19). "For Some, #MeToo Sexual Assault Stories Trigger Trauma Not Empowerment." CNN. Retrieved from https://www.cnn.com/2017/10/19/health/me-too-sexual-assault-stories-trigger-trauma/index.html.

Lawrence, Y.E. (Writer) & Krieger, L.T. (Director) (2017, February 9). Chapter 3: Body Double. [television series episode]. In R. Aguirre-Sacasa (Producer), *Riverdale*. Burbank, CA: Warner Bros. Entertainment, Inc.

Lefkowitz, B. (1997). *Our Guys: The Glen Ridge Rape and the Secret Life of the Perfect Suburb*. Berkeley: University of California Press.

McClurg, L. (2018, January 23). "What Happens When #MeToo Stories Reignite Old Trauma." KQED. Retrieved from https://www.kqed.org/futureofyou/438664/what-happens-when-metoo-stories-reignite-old-trauma.

Milano, A. [@Alyssa_Milano] (2017, October 15). "If you've been sexually harassed or assaulted write 'me too' as a reply to this tweet" [tweet]. Twitter. https://twitter.com/alyssa_milano/status/919659438700670976?lang=en.

Mitchell, C.L., & Glamb, L. (2012). "Sexual Assault, Drug Facilitated." In *Encyclopedia of Trauma: An Interdisciplinary Guide*. Thousand Oaks, CA: SAGE.

Munro, E. (2013). "Feminism: A Fourth Wave?" *Political Insight* 4(2), 22–25. https://doi.org/10.1111/2041-9066.12021.

Ohlleiser, A. (2017, October 19). "The Woman Behind 'Me Too' Knew the Power of the Phrase When She Created It—10 Years Ago." *The Washington Post*. Retrieved from https://www.washingtonpost.com/news/the-intersect/wp/2017/10/19/the-woman-behind-me-too-knew-the-power-of-the-phrase-when-she-created-it-10-years-ago/.

"Online Harassment 2017" (2017, July 11). Pew Research Center, Washington, D.C. https://www.pewresearch.org/internet/2017/07/11/online-harassment-2017/.

Ostby, I., Mic Staff (Interviewer), & Burke, T. (2018). "'Mic Dispatch' Episode 25: #MeToo Founder Tarana Burke on Brett Kavanaugh" [interview transcript]. Retrieved from:

https://www.mic.com/articles/191787/mic-dispatch-episode-25-metoo-founder-tarana-burke-on-brett-kavanaugh-transcript#.l4FKaJXRN.

Pennington, R., & Birthisel, J. (2016). "When New Media Make News: Framing Technology and Sexual Assault in the Steubenville Rape Case." *New Media & Society 18*(11), 2435–2451. https://doi.org/10.1177/1461444815612407.

Petsch, M. (2017, November 8). "Riverdale Season 2 Sexual Assault PSA Madelaine Petsch." Retrieved from https://www.youtube.com/watch?v=dbqifGbWMug.

Petsch, M. [madelainepetsch] (2018, October 9). "I'm a little late on this... #MeToo" [tweet]. Twitter. https://twitter.com/madelainepetsch/status/921031470315180033?lang=en.

Reinhart, L. (2017, November 10). "In light of the Harvey Weinstein allegations..." [Tumblr post]. Retrieved from https://lilireinhart.tumblr.com/post/166301255628/in-light-of-the-harvey-weinstein-allegations.

Rivers, N. (2017). *Postfeminism(s) and the Arrival of the Fourth Wave.* Cham, Switzerland: Palgrave Macmillan. doi:10.1007/978-3-319-59812-3.

Romero, A. (2017, November 9). "Riverdale's Date Rape Episode Is Its Most Important Yet." *Refinery29.* Retrieved from https://www.refinery29.com/en-us/2017/11/180400/riverdale-cheryl-nick-rape-sexual-assault-episode.

Silva, C. (2017, December 1). "The Worst #MeToo Apologies from Famous Men Accused of Sexual Misconduct." *Newsweek.* https://www.newsweek.com/worst-apologies-metoo-men-sexual-misconduct-726631.

Solomon, D. (Interviewer), & Valenti, J. (2009). "Fourth-Wave Feminism" [Interview transcript]. Retrieved from https://www.nytimes.com/2009/11/15/magazine/15fob-q4t.html?mtrref=www.google.com&gwh=C6B175803C7477CAEA6CECCE9EF5E841&gwt=pay&assetType=REGIWALL.

Sweeney, B. (2017). "Slut Shaming." In K. Nadal (Ed.), *The SAGE Encyclopedia of Psychology and Gender* (pp. 1579–1580). Thousand Oaks, CA: SAGE Publications. doi:10.4135/9781483384269.n530.

Teng, B. (2018, February 15). "How to Find Shelter in the Storm of #MeToo." *Slate.* https://slate.com/technology/2018/02/how-to-cope-with-trauma-in-the-tumultuous-era-of-metoo.html.

Usborne, D. (2018, August 5). "The Peacock Patriarchy." *Esquire.* https://www.esquire.com/news-politics/a22627827/matt-lauer-nbc-me-too/.

van Dijck, J. (2013). *The Culture of Connectivity: A Critical History of Social Media.* Oxford: Oxford University Press.

Watching Them, Watch Them
The Coded Movement of Betty's Pole Dance and Our Passive Audience Gaze

Hannah Meghan Celinski

I sat in stunned silence through "Chapter 21: House of the Devil" on *Riverdale*. Veronica and Archie were performing *Mad World* at the Whyte Wyrm bar for FP's retirement party. They abruptly left the stage and Betty appeared to complete the song by executing what had earlier been identified as the "Serpent Dance." When she finished the routine, FP offered her his coat, and she left the stage. I paused the television. I contemplated the age of the character in relation to the age of the on-screen observers, the sexualized nature of the movement, and my own participation as an at-home audience member. I sat in shock. I was not alone.

The episode debuted on December 6, 2017. An estimated 1.478 million viewers sat at screens watching a group of adults watch a teenage girl remove her clothes and dance around a pole in her underwear (tvseries-finale.com). It is not the only time a character on this show removes their clothing, as *Riverdale* has featured several intimate scenes between the couples. These scenes are troublesome—not because teenagers are engaging in sexual dynamics or intimate relationships, but because they do so with a confidence and a finesse that is incongruent with the reality of early exploration of the sexual self. They remove their clothes with ease and grace, slide shirts off easily, and exchange confident smiles. Nobody bangs noses, gets stuck in their pants, or otherwise falters during intimate scenes, and as a result, viewers consume adult relationships and engagement through these teenage characters. But when Betty begins to remove her clothes in public to perform the Serpent Dance, the discussion around the character's age, behavior, and confidence must shift to a discussion about the ethics of what is seen, by whom, and how.

There are several entry points for the discussion. The choreography, or dance steps that Betty executes, includes movements that communicate subtle messages about gender and sexuality. These movements, like many physical gestures, impart messages to observers and act as codes. For example, a person waving hello is a coded, physicalized greeting that communicates friendship and welcoming. Coded movement has both a sender or inviting performer (the person waving), and a receiver or consumptive audience (the person being waved at). The twist in "Chapter 21: House of the Devil" is that there is an additional layer or gaze: the audience watching the show at home. To clarify further examination of the episode, the inviting performer is Betty, the consumptive audience is the televised crowd at the Whyte Wyrm, and the passive viewers are the at-home audience. Each perspective is subject to its own distinctive view, and all parties look out at one another with their own gaze. The result is a multi-layered viewership that proves to be problematic because the character, Betty, is 16.

This essay will argue that *Riverdale* relies on coded movement (messages the movement sends to audiences about gender and sexuality) to further the show's intersected model of gender performativity (the performance of what society considers typical female and male behavior or attributes) and filter the audience gaze during problematic sequences through the manipulation of the gaze. Three specific gazes that were previously mentioned, which I have based on Alexandra G. Murphy's (2003) theory of dialectical gaze, will be applied: the inviting performer, the consumptive audience, and the passive viewer. The examination will also explore choreography and performance as coded movement, and how problematic messages are transferred or retained through observation and tradition. Close examination of *Riverdale*'s movement sequences lends itself to a broader conversation around gender and sexuality, including an examination of how the relationship between performer and audience is altered by age, and the role of mentorship and support in the coming-of-age process.

Riverdale is not the first production to circumvent the problematic tension between the movement of the characters and the passive viewer's gaze by managing the audience's view. It follows protocols established by previous productions that enact similar tension. Clare Parfitt (2005) explains the workaround in her article "The Spectator's Dancing Gaze in *Moulin Rouge!*" The film *Moulin Rouge* contains sexualized movement and interactions that are provocative, sometimes joyful, and in other cases, violent. Parfitt's article considers the director's approach to the intimacy explored in the film's racy sequences. She explains that

> this intimacy does not engender a sense of identification with the dancer. Rather, the voyeurism of the camera turns its subjects into objects of sexual and exotic titillation. While the movement of the camera provides the spectator with the sensation of being part of the action ... the camera sees the

spectators as well as the performers ... the film spectator ... watches the audience watching the dancers [p. 101].

Riverdale uses in-scene spectators at moments that require audience distancing to ease the audience gaze during sequences that include physical engagement. I use the term physical engagement here because it is not limited to dance sequences. Consider the following: we watch the Vixens watching Veronica and Cheryl during a dance-off ("Chapter 10: The Lost Weekend"); we watch the crowd reacting to Hiram Lodge and Archie wrestling ("Chapter 24: The Wrestler"); we watch the Serpents watching Betty pole dance ("Chapter 21: House of the Devil"); and we watch the crowd throughout Archie's underground fight-club battles during his third season arc in juvenile detention. Whenever there is a moment of sexual or exotic titillation, the audience's gaze is distanced to ease the gaze from consumptive viewer to passive viewer of the consumptive viewer. In other words, the at-home audience is watching the *Riverdale* characters watch each other. The removed position of the passive viewer is how the show navigates potentially inappropriate coding of movement sequences and physical engagement.

One such coded sequence is the Jailhouse Rock routine in "Chapter 37: Fortune and Men's Eyes." Veronica and the Vixens visit Archie and his friends while they are incarcerated in a detention center. Heather Laura Grey (choreographer seasons 3 and 4) took over as choreographer in Season 3, and leans heavily on athletic execution, including gymnastics and structured patterns that the director captures using overhead camera angles and wide shots to showcase the choreographic formations. In the Jailhouse Rock sequence, the Vixens interrupt a game of football at the detention center to sing and dance on the grass in their cheerleader uniforms. Archie and other male inmates show their appreciation by catcalling and climbing the fence, finally returning to their football game with renewed excitement and fortitude.

The opening of the routine reflects wartime performances in which female entertainers were sent overseas to lift the spirits of the troops. Kara Dixon Vuic (2019) writes of Marilyn Monroe performing in 1953 for "100,000 soldiers, sailors, airmen, and marines who clambered over each other, climbed telephone poles, and peered through telescopes to catch a better glimpse" (pp. 163–164). Women, and none more than Marilyn Monroe, were coded as desirable through their appearance, movement, and vocal tones to fortify the self-perception of male troops as masculine, strong, and brave, but objectification of the women resulted in the men clamoring for viewership by literally climbing over one another to get a better view of the female performers. To depict a group of teenage boys in the era of #MeToo as clambering over each other to whistle and cheer at young women in short skirts re-inscribes heteronormativity by continuing to draw from historically identified choreography and tropes that further patriarchal themes.[1] The Vixens present themselves to the inmates, through the fence, as positivity in visually attractive packages to satisfy the male gaze just as the troops were provided with visual stimulation in the form of performers like Marilyn Monroe. In this moment, the Vixens are relegated to the role of attractive support system cheering from the sidelines, instead of accessing the collective intellect of the group as a unified force to battle a corrupt system ("Chapter 37: Fortune and Men's Eyes"). The reaction of the guards and warden is used to offset the codes of performed gender within the sequence, by drawing the viewer to their presence. They are a form of authority that is present to ensure that inappropriate behavior is not tolerated. They do not interrupt the Vixens' performance or stop the inmates from climbing the fence, so the exchange is deemed as acceptable and therefore appropriate. The wardens are male adults who are responsible for the rehabilitation of a group of boys who have been detained due to concerns about their behavior. The lack of adult objection to the stereotypical feminization of the Vixens or masculinization of the boys signals to the viewer that behavior contributing to patriarchal narratives is acceptable and not worthy of addressing through either mentorship or education. It is appropriate for the girls to flirt and bounce around, and it is also appropriate for the boys to catcall and climb the fence to signal their approval. This may have the effect not only of causing young female passive viewers to wonder how they can encourage their male counterparts in the future, but it may also cause male passive viewers to ponder what they can expect to receive by way of fortification. It reflects the crisis facing teens which involves social media and images of the self as currency, which includes the way Betty's body is used as currency in the Serpent Dance. The difference between the two routines is that the adults stand idly by and observe the exchange unfolding at the jail, but FP steps in to manage Betty's experience at the Whyte Wyrm.

Early in "Chapter 21: House of the Devil" (2017), Betty states that she intends to get closer to Jughead by "being part of his world," then overhears an adult Serpent named Byrdie laughing at her expression of interest. Byrdie quips: "Sorry, Sweet Valley High, you wanna join the club, you gotta do the dance. The Serpent Dance." Though Toni (a Serpent, fellow high school student, and bartender) clarifies that the Serpent Dance is an "outdated, sexist, Serpent tradition" that is in the process of being phased out, Betty sees an opportunity to move closer to Jughead through the sexualized pole dance. The Serpent Dance demonstrator in the scene sets out the expectations of the sequence. She undulates smoothly and sensually but without athletic elements or tricks while looking straight out into an implied audience. She is shot from the ground up, and no spectator reaction shots are included. The act of the dance itself is presented, but the purpose, dynamics, and audience interaction are not explored. It is a preview of what Betty is expected to do, but it also captures the first gaze to be explored in this essay: the inviting performer gaze that is associated with professional exotic dancers.

In the article "The Dialectical Gaze: Exploring the Subject-Object Tension in the Performances of Women Who Strip" Alexandra G. Murphy (2003) considers the relationship between a female dancer and male audience members as a complex interaction. Though she acknowledges that the dynamic alters depending on the participants, for the purposes of her paper, Murphy focuses on male audience members of a specific venue that features professional female exotic dancers. The article discusses the gaze of the male viewer, and the gaze of the female dancer. Murphy asserts that the male subjugates the dancer through his viewership but is also subject to her control through the limitations of his viewership. As Murphy states, "[i]n strip clubs ... it is not always so clear who is watching whom. As numerous researchers describe, the female dancers watch the customers as much as they are being watched" (p. 310). Much of this observation relates to the transactional nature of the relationship, with patrons scanning for who they may wish to observe in closer proximity, and dancers looking to make eye contact to *invite* gaze and promote opportunities for paid personal interactions with the wealthiest customers. The inviting performer gaze is but one of the transactional features of the dialectical gaze, but it highlights the complexity of the transactional nature of Betty's performance.

To move closer to the boy she cares about, Betty is informed that she should adhere to a previously established rite of passage ("Chapter 21: House of the Devil"). This rite of passage includes presenting herself to an observing audience to perform sexualized movement for their pleasure. The legacy of the activity dictates its validity, and encourages continued participation, though real-life society continues to interrogate, dismantle, and evolve beyond dated practices that reaffirm gender stereotypes. (Pageants are an excellent example of a legacy that reinforces gender stereotypes while purporting female empowerment.) In the Introduction to *Bodies That Matter: On the Discursive Limits of "Sex,"* Judith Butler explains: "Performativity is thus not a singular 'act,' for it is always a reiteration of a norm or set of norms, and to the extent that it acquires an act-like status in the present, it conceals or dissimulates the conventions of which it is a repetition" (2014, p. 12). Butler captures the cyclical nature of being female as repeating recognized behaviors that have been passed along through time. Butler explains that often these behaviors are problematized during single events, which masks how the behaviors have been, and continue to be, reaffirmed through repetition. This reflects the ability for Betty's pole-dance to shock the audience through the one-time execution, while the show capitalizes on the audience's willingness to look to the legacy of the act as rationale for its inclusion ("Chapter 21: House of the Devil"). In the case of the Serpent Dance, participation in the ritualized performance is not up to individual choice; rather, it is a prescribed transaction that grants the performer membership to the group. Betty's performance is further complicated, as the feminized coded movement enhances the complexity of a minor entertaining a room of adults in a sexualized manner. Susan Foster's (1998) article, "Choreographies of Gender," explains: "Choreography, the tradition of codes and conventions through which meaning is constructed in dance, offer[s] a social and historical analytic framework for the study of gender, whereas performance concentrates on the individual execution of such codes" (p. 5). Foster points to the difference between choreography and performance, and how patriarchal, capitalistic, and oppressive frameworks are communicated through movement as physically enacted codes, and the execution of the steps is the continued demonstration and proliferation of these frameworks as codes. The Serpent Dance furthers codes of patriarchal dominance, female subjugation, the sexualization of women and movement, and coerced participation in sexual activities. The transactional nature of the Serpent Dance propels female participants toward accepting the practice as currency to be exchanged for membership, but it also serves to place the new member in a sexualized, subjugated light, before even donning the jacket. The dancer uses the inviting performer gaze to bring attention to her actions to satisfy the agreed-upon terms, but what, if any, are the ramifications of the performed invitation? As I stated earlier, the codes embedded in the choreography further patriarchal and capitalistic narratives, but the inviting performer gaze could be said to be limited to the "individual execution of such codes," meaning a one-time invitation. The complication is that the one-time invitation furthers the embedded repressive codes to endlessly prolong the invitation. It is this unending loop that contributes to societal repression of women.

The Whyte Wyrm itself offers conflicting messages, as its bar is tended by a minor, but the adult patron who addresses Betty early in the episode is obviously intoxicated ("Chapter 21: House of the Devil"). The licensed venue is bizarrely full of high school students, adults, and alcohol. Betty has reserved the bar for the retirement party of Jughead's father, FP (Forsythe Pendleton) Jones (II). Betty's mother Alice marches up to the bar upon arrival, and asks for a "shot of tequila, hold the worm." She then turns to Betty and asks, "Honey, what do you want? Shirley Temple?" Then she turns back to the bartender and quips, "Just give me two." Alice's comments frame the contrast of the moment. Public and private space intersect as the viewer assesses the entirety of the situation. It is uncomfortable for the audience because the setting is adult, but the introduction of the Shirley Temple reminds the audience that Betty is underage. An atmosphere of discord is created, where socially acceptable behavior and legality are brought into question without lingering on either side: there are minors in a bar, beer bottles littering the tables, intimidating adult men and women lounging at pool tables, and contrastingly, karaoke. Alice asks what Betty would like to drink from the bar, but only offers an option available on a child's menu. It is never clear if she does both shots or offers one to underage Betty. Despite the ambiguity of the beginning of the scene, audiences were quick to react to Betty's performance.

Viewer response was immediate and focused on the misalignment of the mature movement and Betty's age. This is a sampling of Twitter responses to the episode:

> Betty singing "Mad World" while stripping and then doing a pole dance for Jughead at his dad's retirement party while her Mom watches is one of the weirdest fucking things I've ever seen on a TV show. #Riverdale [@jester1436]
>
> RIVERDALE FUCKING MADE BETTY COOPER, A 15-year-old HIGH SCHOOL STUDENT, STRIP AND POLE DANCE IN FRONT OF A CROWD OF GROWN ASS MEN AND WOMEN BITCH WHAT THE FLYING FUCK [@saltzpark, since removed]
>
> #Riverdale has me 50 shades of fucked up why is Jughead's father clapping after Betty's STRIP TEASE!? And homegirl's mom somehow manages to not drag her off that **pole** by the ponytail!? The fuck is going on in this podunk town [@DixPeyton]
>
> Betty just did a pole dance with her mom in the crowd and then her bf's dad tells her good job. I love this god forsaken show [@beccaLader]

Viewer reactions highlight the dynamic that is created between performer and audience when the performer is underage, and the audience consists of adults. Dance competitions are an example of this phenomenon, as children as young as three years old take their turn to perform for an audience that includes adults. It is disconcerting for an adult who is new to competitive dance to observe a young dancer performing what the observer perceives to be a sexually coded routine while simultaneously observing adult audience members whoop and cheer in support. Dance competitions are a mild example of the potential discord experienced by those observing the young performer/adult audience dynamic compared to the outrage experienced by *Riverdale* viewers as they struggled to calibrate Betty with her adult audience. Viewers were so shocked by the scene that they did not realize that Alice only appears at the end. And FP does encourage the crowd to give Betty another round of applause, but he does so without any implication of sexualized enjoyment of the performance, more as a supportive parent or adult friend would encourage a child after performing a sexually coded routine at a dance competition ("Chapter 21: House of the Devil"). FP actively accepts Betty's effort to participate in Serpent tradition without further sexualizing the routine or encouraging responses like whistling or cheering through this moment of intentional support. He does not admonish Betty for her sexuality; instead, he offers a subtle indication that the performance is out of place considering the adults in attendance by offering Betty his jacket. There is an argument to be made that the jacket signals regulation of the female body or body shaming, but I argue that FP's reaction functions to navigate the space between child and adult. The gesture models that it is important to choose when and where you offer a sexualized portrait of yourself. After all, such performances are absolutely legal between consenting adults. But Betty is not yet an adult, so he ushers her along the journey by managing the moment for both the consumptive audience at The Whyte Wyrm and the passive viewer at home. It is one moment in the show where an adult extends themselves in a supportive manner to assist a teenager in navigating the complexities of realizing one's sexuality, without subjugation or admonishment. Through FP's actions, Betty's sexuality becomes part of a process that is supported through mentorship instead of a perpetuation of patriarchal conventions.

The audience at the Whyte Wyrm responds in kind to FP's example, and claps supportively. They are the performer's mirrored audience: the consumptive audience gaze. A group becomes a unified audience when they gather to observe, but each individual person will consume the material differently. A study conducted in 2011 by Corinne Jola, Shantel Ehrenberg, and Dee Reynolds examined the cognitive effects of audience experience by linking viewership to potential embodied physical empathy; essentially, how a person's body interprets another's movement. The article explains:

> A theatre dance performance is a multifunctional socio-cultural event constituted of many diverse strands, including the dancers, the music that accompanies the movements, the costumes, the lighting, the set, the other audience members, and so on, that work together to impact on the spectator in the moment of watching [p. 19].

Though Betty's pole dance is short, the lighting, music, and elevated platform she appears on contribute to the sense of theater ("Chapter 21: House of the Devil"). The audience consists of her peers, her boyfriend, the perception of her mother (though Alice arrives at the end), and an assortment of adults who merge to form her audience. Viewers struggled with their reactions and focused on the presence of Betty and Jughead's parents as problematic, though the "diverse strands" of Betty's performance also include the music, and a karaoke rendition of the song "Mad World" which was originally released by Tears for Fears in 1982 but was re-released featuring Gary Jules for the *Donnie Darko* film soundtrack (2001). In Betty's version, she partially sings and partially dances ("Chapter 21: House of the Devil"). As Betty steps up to the microphone and begins to sing, she unbuttons her top and removes her skirt, revealing a black lace bustier and bottoms with lace panels. The song continues with her voice as a back-track echo while she dances. Eventually, the lyrics repeat until Betty steps back to the microphone and sings the final line live. The song includes lyrics that evoke images of celebration and acting like a good girl, but she internalizes the lyrics that include darker content such as death through sexually coded movement with her voice continuing as a phantom track while she dances.

The entire scene is rife with the conflicts at the heart of the show itself. Betty is intelligent, driven, and community-minded, but she readily participates in a dated tradition meant to sexualize and subjugate women. She undresses to reveal lingerie that includes lace but also maximizes coverage. The top is a bustier, but the breast panels are made of fully opaque material and the top line is higher than a bathing suit. The bottoms sit high in the waist with a full waistband that visually allays any fear of slippage, and low on the thighs with extra lace panels for further coverage. There are no shots that encompass the entire ensemble for any period of time. The camera lingers on Betty's face. There is an overt effort to suggest a skimpy outfit, matched with an overt effort to suggest maximum coverage.

The movement of the dance is equally problematic, but I want to take a moment to separate the discussion around the dance itself from the execution. As stated earlier, Foster's article points to a separation between the codes of choreography and the performance (1998, p. 5). Each should be considered in their own right. I will start with the performance to properly frame the examination of the choreography.

Betty's movement during the pole dance lacks athleticism but is not hesitant ("Chapter 21: House of the Devil"). When she backs away from the microphone, she runs her hand over the top of her head and through her hair but does not actually touch the side of her face, as though she is unfamiliar with her own skin, or unwilling to commit to the sensuality of the movement. She then walks to the pole, moves to the other side of it by beginning a "pole walk around" (Savard, 2014, 61) where one hand is elevated and the feet remain tight to the pole, allowing the body to lean away, but she barely begins this technical aspect before she cuts it off to face the pole ("Chapter 21: House of the Devil"). She moves her body tightly against it and executes a lay out: the torso reaching out the top of the head to lead the upper body backwards like a waterfall, but her hands remain calm on the pole, and she does not extend her body to her full flexibility. She does roll through the body to return to an erect position, demonstrating technical proficiency that is not realized elsewhere. She then continues a brief pole walk around, before putting her back to the pole with her hands above her head and sliding slowly down the pole. She does not overtly move her hips or drop beyond a slight bent knee position. The steps are barely realized, but her delivery is internally fortified through a focused demeanor. She stares intently at Jughead for the entire routine and does not look anywhere else.

This is another contrasting point; her movement has no intention, but her focus and eye-line do. The inviting performer gaze is present, but limited to Jughead, which circumvents the cycle of sexualization. The sexualization of Betty is complicated by her focus on Jughead's attention and assessing his acceptance of her effort to join his social environment. She does not place herself on the stage with the purpose of seducing an audience; she steps on the stage and alters the parameters of the coded transaction between audience and performer to connect deeply with Jughead, and this crux is a dramatization of teenagehood. The formative years of a teenager include a desire to be mature and act with autonomy, but a lack of experience leaves young people open to finding themselves in situations that are out of their depth. Usually there are no life-altering consequences, and the teenager instead learns lessons that serve their decision-making later in life, but that is not always the case. Betty enters The Serpent Dance with the best of intentions: she wants to be close to a boy she cares about. But Jughead, the bar audience, and the passive viewer are all subject to the conflicting messages conveyed by the choreography, the legacy of the Serpent Dance, and the adult-oriented environment. These elements bump against one another. The scene works to capture a 16-year-old teenager's attempt to be mature, but the inviting performer (Betty) is meant to be a teenager. The age of the actress (21 years) is not enough to allow the passive viewer to suspend their concerns about the age of the character. Passive viewers have no agency in the scene, they are simply observers who are left with two options: watch the 21-year-old actress playing a teenager, or watch a teenager playing an adult. Neither is compelling.

The sexualization of Betty is also embedded in the coding of the choreography, which in turn sexualizes the audience gaze. The slow removal of her clothing realizes the stereotype of a pole dancer as a stripper, and a stripper as a product to be consumed by the male gaze. The pole walk around leans her out to the audience, bringing her body into closer proximity for easier consumption. When she presses into the pole and executes the layout, it alludes to an orgasm, and gently swaying hips act as an indicator of fertility. Even something as small as running her hands along the pole or microphone becomes a sexually coded movement representing gendered female encouragement of male arousal. In a *Glamour* magazine interview, Lili Reinhart, who plays Betty, expressed that the scene was supposed to make viewers uncomfortable, but she went on to say: "you're watching this girl do something completely out of her comfort zone for the man she loves. You're watching her make a personal sacrifice, and that is the most important takeaway" (Rosa, 2017). Reinhart also states that she choreographed the sequence herself, and though she was offered the opportunity to take pole lessons, she declined.

Pole dancing can include a wide variety of athletic and exciting steps and tricks, even at the most basic level. In a move referred to as a "forward chair," for instance, the dancer holds the pole with both hands and rotates around the pole, holding their body tight, as if they are sitting in a chair (Savard, 2014, p. 61). It would have been easy to include a step such as "forward chair" in Betty's routine, but Reinhart chose not to. It proved a wise choice. Should Betty have gone to the stage and presented as a proficient pole dancer, the message would have been entirely different, as the performativity would have been altered and the coding in the choreography would have included an aspect of preparedness and athleticism that was out of sync with the moment. Further to this, if she performed sexually aggressive movements, overly articulated thrusts and spins, the movement would have been coded as overtly sexual, and this would complicate the eventual return to her role as the good girl from the suburbs. Athletic execution of even a small step like "forward chair" casts Betty as a dancer, not as a conflicted potential Serpent. The movement does not allow for the intimate engagement and eye contact with Jughead, as it requires spotting (staring at one spot to keep the dancer from getting dizzy) and enough physical space to fully execute the steps. But despite the layers of contrast and confusion, the age of both the character and the audience remains deeply problematic, and Reinhart's choices result in different coding: a young woman steps out of the social constraints of the suburbs to engage with members of a different social class, the success of which relies on contrasts to laws and regulations of real-life that become acceptable within the *Riverdale* universe, such as minors serving alcohol to adults. The pole dance maintains the confused placement of the viewer, so Betty can visit the Serpent Dance with no intention of living there. This reinforces a different kind of coding, which allows Betty to participate from a position of privilege. The Serpent Dance has previously been used to secure women a place in the Serpent community, through the exchange of sexualized movement for consumption. But what opportunities are available to young women once they are secured within the Serpent community? Alice left. She evolved into a new version of herself by moving to the other side of the tracks to become a professional reporter and start a family. In this way, she and Betty both present as attending from a position of privilege. Once the evening is over, neither is limited by the position reserved for those who perform the Serpent Dance. Both return to their other life.

The privilege of returning to their other life is a powerful option that is not available to all women. This allows Betty security in her decision to participate in the Serpent Dance but does nothing to mitigate how the exchange is complicated by the ethics, appropriateness, and legality of adults observing a minor in a sexualized situation. The fact that the scene was broadcast because of the age of the actors, and despite the age of the character, raises the question of where we locate girls and women as they move from being a child, through their teenage years, to eventually becoming an adult. Megan Garber's 2019 article in *The Atlantic* titled "The Myth of the Underage Woman" tackles the nuances of how society and the media view teenage girls, considering reports about Jeffrey Epstein's sex-trafficking ring:

> [m]any media outlets referred to Epstein's victims ... as "underage women." *The New York Times* used the term. So did *New York* magazine.... The phrase is wrong in every sense: There is no such thing as an "underage woman." Underage women are girls [Garber 2019].

Becoming an adult is a journey. In Canada, the legal line between child and adult is drawn at 18 or 19 years of age, depending on the province or territory, and 18 years of age in the United States. Young people experiment with who they are and who they will become as they age, and through this experimentation, they begin to evolve into adults. This brings the discussion back to Butler, and the performativity of gender (2014, p.1). By casting Epstein's victims as "underage women," the diction capitalizes on the arrival at adulthood, bypassing the logistics of the journey through childhood. Children emulate pre-established norms, and this includes sexuality, which is why it is important for them to have mentors and trusted advisors to guide them as they grow (Garber 2019). Children need assistance in framing experiences with maturity to protect them from predators such as Epstein. In *Riverdale*, when Betty finishes her pole routine and FP manages the crowd, he is protecting and guiding her through the experience to safety. But Betty is an adult, playing a child, who is placed in jeopardy by writers and producers. The audience is expected to go along with her behavior because of the actress's age, not the character's. Epstein's victims are children, cast as "underage women," and the public is expected to go along with this label because of their behavior, not because of their age. This problematized narrative that intertwines the

Epstein case with Betty's pole dance brings into focus Butler's earlier statement about performed gender as a "reiteration of a norm or set of norms" (2014, p. 12). Popular media should not normalize the sexualization of children as it contributes to the notion of the "underage woman." In the pole dance episode, *Riverdale* uses the removed position of the passive viewer to attempt to navigate such a notion.

The minute Betty takes the stage and reaches for the first button on her shirt, the passive viewer interprets coded movement that signifies a woman's body being used as currency ("Chapter 21: House of the Devil"). Betty trades sexualized movement, in a public adult environment, for a spot with the Serpents and in Jughead's life. Reinhart explains that Betty does not do this for herself. It is not a moment of self-realization or empowerment, so it can be interpreted as a signal to viewers that in order to earn your place socially, and with a person you care about, you can make a sexualized display of yourself as a token of your affection. As Jughead sits taller in his seat and looks expectantly and attentively to the stage, we are also aware of Sweet Pea standing at the back, offering an approving nod. That nod is coded with the expectation of the male gaze, but not leering. He acknowledges Betty's decision to engage with the tradition. Toni moves her eyes to Jughead, and in the following shot, more of the crowd turns their focus in his direction. This focuses the passive viewer on Jughead's reaction and lifts some of the passive gaze off Betty's actions. If we interpret this choice as lining up with the approach taken in *Moulin Rouge*, shifting the passive viewer's gaze to Jughead is meant to temper the passive viewer's reaction to Betty's performance. This is where gazes collide. The passive audience at home is watching the consumptive audience watch Betty turn the inviting gaze on Jughead. This creates a buffer between the passive viewer at home and a child-character who is undressing in front of a room of adults. Betty uses the inviting gaze to become an object directed at Jughead, so we as the passive viewer are meant to observe the crowd bearing witness to Betty's Serpent Dance which is solely for Jughead's consumption. This, in turn, makes the entire scene more acceptable: the passive viewer watches adults watching minors engage in a sexualized performance of gender. This tactic is meant to circumvent the inappropriateness of the venue and the audience.

Though problematic, FP's actions following Betty's pole dance point to potential for the show to guide young people through the difficult landscape of maturing, exploring their own sexuality, and avoiding exploitation. Sexual expression is personal and does not warrant policing even by well-meaning critics. Women should not be shamed for expressing their sexuality, and men should not support structures that encourage sexism. However, as we see from the Epstein case, real-life exploitation, sex-trafficking, and the perils of social media all contort and complicate the process. *Riverdale* places Betty in a position to choose her own way forward through the Serpent Dance, but as Butler demonstrates, concerns raised by the one-time event of managing the experience in her own right conceals how repetition results in gendered subjugation. I for one, was too busy watching. Watching the crowd watch Betty. Watching Jughead watch Betty. Watching them watch them busies us as viewers until we are unable to grapple with the truth the moment reveals: The Serpent Dance contains too many established conventions for Betty to succeed in overcoming the sexually coded movement. Despite that, the pole dance does bring attention to how codes of movement re-inscribe patriarchal structures that subjugate and sexualize women, though it is masked by the passive viewer's placement behind the consumptive viewer. How society will untangle the damage done by continued repetition of gendered conventions remains to be seen, but by supporting Betty's choice to dance by examining the contrasting messages, codes, and viewer gazes through avenues such as this essay, perhaps society can begin to examine itself and consider a way forward. I hope FP has enough coats to go around.

Note

1. This moment—as well as other, similar scenes, including those involving characters engaged in wrestling and boxing, for example—would benefit from further unpacking to examine the heteronormative positioning of the scene through a binary gender lens that simultaneously leaves exploration of the queer gaze available for deep examination. As Molly Moss defines it, "[i]n theory, a queer gaze would deconstruct such gender-based power dynamics, changing not only the object but also the intent of the male and female gaze" (2019). J Halberstam's work on a transgender gaze in cinema in *In a Queer Time and Place* (2005) offers a potential model for thinking through the power dynamics, as well as the moral and ideological implications, of looking in *Riverdale*. Although compelling, such questions reach beyond the scope of this essay.

References

@beccaLader. Tweet. (2018, June 16, 10:32 a.m.). https://twitter.com/beccaLader/status/1008039692649095169.
Butler, J. (2014). *Bodies That Matter: On the Discursive Limits of "Sex."* New York: Routledge.
@DixPeyton. Tweet. (2017, December 6, 7:17 p.m.). https://twitter.com/DixPeyton/status/938970680414101505.
Foster, S.L. (1998). "Choreographies of gender. *Signs, 24*(1), 1–34.
Garber, M. (2019). "The Myth of the Underage Woman." *The Atlantic*. Retrieved January 10, 2020. https://www.theatlantic.com/entertainment/archive/2019/08/jeffrey-epstein-and-the-myth-of-the-underage-woman/596140/.
Grassi, M. (Writer), & J. Woolnough (Director) (2018, October 17). Chapter Thirty-Seven:

Fortune and Men's Eyes (Season 3, Episode 2) [TV series episode]. Roberto Aguirre-Sacasa (Developer/Executive Producer), *Riverdale*. Berlanti Productions; Archie Comics Publications; CBS Television Studios; Warner Bros. Television; Canada Film Capital.

@jester1436. Tweet. (2017, December 6, 7:03 p.m.). https://twitter.com/jester1436/status/938604879085481984.

Jola, C., S. Ehrenberg, & D. Reynolds (2011). "The Experience of Watching Dance: Phenomenological-Neuroscience Duets." *Phenomonology and Cognitive Sciences 11*, 17–37. DOI: 10.1007/s11097-010-9191-x.

Lawrence, Y. (Writer), J. DeWille (Executive Story Editor), & K.R. Sullivan (Director) (2017, December 6). Chapter Twenty-One: House of the Devil (Season 2, Episode 8) [TV series episode]. Roberto Aguirre-Sacasa (Developer/Executive Producer), *Riverdale*. Berlanti Productions; Archie Comics Publications; CBS Television Studios; Warner Bros. Television; Canada Film Capital.

Lundin, B. (Writer), B.E. Paterson (Writer), & D. Wilkinson (Director) (2017, April 13). Chapter Ten: The Lost Weekend (Season 1, Episode 10) [TV series episode]. Roberto Aguirre-Sacasa (Developer/Executive Producer), *Riverdale*. Berlanti Productions; Archie Comics Publications; CBS Television Studios; Warner Bros. Television; Canada Film Capital.

Murphy, A.G. (2003). "The Dialectical Gaze: Exploring the Subject-Object Tension in the Performances of Women Who Strip." *Journal of Contemporary Ethnography 32*(3), 305–335. DOI: 10.1177/0891241603252119.

Murray, G. (Writer), D. Turner (Writer), & G. Araki (Director) (2018, January 24). Chapter Twenty-Four: The Wrestler (Season 2, Episode 11) [TV series episode]. Roberto Aguirre-Sacasa (Developer/Executive Producer), *Riverdale*. Berlanti Productions; Archie Comics Publications; CBS Television Studios; Warner Bros. Television; Canada Film Capital.

N.A. (2018). "*Riverdale*: Season Two Ratings." *tvseriesfinale.com*. Accessed January 10, 2020. https://tvseriesfinale.com/tv-show/riverdale-season-two-ratings/.

Parfitt, C. (2005). "The Spectator's Dancing Gaze in *Moulin Rouge!*" *Research in Dance Education 6*(1–2), 97–110. DOI: 10.1080/14617890500373378.

Reinhart, L. (Singer), & R. Orzabal (Songwriter) (2017). "Mad World." Chapter Twenty-One: House of the Devil (Season 2, Episode 8) [TV series episode]. *Riverdale*.

Rosa, C. (2017). "Lili Reinhart Says Betty's 'Riverdale' Dance Was Supposed to Make You Uncomfortable." https://www.glamour.com/story/lili-reinhart-on-betty-riverdale-dance.

@saltzpark. Tweet. Since deleted.

Savard, A. (2014). *The Goddess Movement Method: Pole Fitness Instruction* (5th ed.). pp. 61.

Vuic, K.D. (2019). *The Girls Next Door: Bringing the Home Front to the Front Lines*. Cambridge: Harvard University Press.

Punk Rock Prom Queen to Covergirl
Teens and Consumption in *Riverdale* and *Josie and the Pussycats*

Kaarina Mikalson

When I taught the first episode of the Netflix/CW television series *Riverdale*, a live-action adaptation of the *Archie* comics, my undergraduate students were almost unanimous in their dislike. They found *Riverdale* to be too dark, too sexualized, too much like all the other teen dramas they had seen before. They felt the show had wandered too far from its sources: the cast of characters introduced first in MLJ Publications' *Pep Comics* in 1941, then adapted and re-adapted in endless comic, radio, and cartoon iterations. There is much to be unpacked in these critiques. Does *Riverdale* seem hyper dark and sexual compared to the original family of *Archie* comics series, which—at the height of the Comics Code Authority—marketed themselves as "clean and wholesome" (quoted in Robbins, 1999, p. 9)? Does the series' lack of originality, its similarity to other contemporary shows, imitate or diverge from the comic that took the subtitle "America's Typical Teenager" (Robbins, 1999, p. 11)?

Listening to my students' impassioned discussion, I thought about another *Archie* adaptation that seemed to wander—geographically, at least—from its origins in the small, timeless town of Riverdale: the 2001 film *Josie and the Pussycats* (*Josie*). *Josie* takes the eponymous Josie and her bandmates Valerie and Melody out of Riverdale and into the music industry of the new millennium. The plot certainly holds some darkness, including a military and corporate conspiracy and several attempted murders. But it is ultimately a comedic satire with a happy ending.

I explore the growing darkness in the Archie universe by analyzing these two adaptations' consumer politics, and how they situate teens—both their teenage characters and their teenage audience—in relation to power, capital, and culture. In this article, I close read the teenage girls in *Josie* and *Riverdale* in terms of their identities, their consumption and production of culture, and their style. I argue that *Josie*'s protagonists are primarily makers of culture and resistant to being influenced and positioned either as consumers or that which is consumed. In contrast, *Riverdale*'s protagonists are products of culture and capitalism, each carefully stylized and branded in keeping with their personalities and character arcs, but also in keeping with an increasingly individualistic and capitalist culture that ties identity to consumption. These different iterations of the Archie universe characters are products of their time: *Josie*'s protagonists grapple with the legacy of riot grrrl and the increasing capitalist pressure of girl power, while *Riverdale*'s protagonists are produced in an era of financial precarity, when becoming a social media influencer is a less risky path to success than accumulating student loan debt and precarious part-time jobs. Ultimately, these texts reveal how teenagers serve as barometers of economic and cultural flux, as they exist at the intersection of marketing, pressure, and risk.

The Archie universe offers excellent material for reflecting on girlhood and consumption. After all, girls have been consuming *Archie* comics for seven decades. Feminist comics historian Trina Robbins (1999) writes that

> the majority of *Archie* readers were girls, age six to thirteen. Demographics from within the past twenty-five years show that 60 percent of *Archie* readers are female and 40 percent male, and although there are no statistics from the early days, ads for feminine items like charm bracelets, handbags, belts, and even girdles ... that are in the *Archie* comic books of the 1940s and 1950s reflect the typical reader's gender [p. 12].

Robbins (1999) goes on to note that *Betty and Veronica*, the female-focused spin-off comic, has been "the best-selling title in the *Archie* comics line," further evidence of girls' consumption of the teen comics (p. 12).

As Robbins' attention to advertisements notes, *Archie* comics have devoted ample space and attention to fashion and style. Pinups and fashion spreads are common features in the comic books, appearing between stories and gags. Many of the stories include Veronica shopping, Betty sewing, and both girls and their friends experimenting with new styles. Even without accounting for the pages of advertisements that were typical of the early decades of *Archie* comics, the comics' attention to clothing and accessories has emphasized consumption as a central part of teenage life, and girlhood in particular. Teens be shopping, argues the *Archie* oeuvre; the 2001 film *Josie and the Pussycats* tackles this fact head on, with a plot line about the increasingly powerful consumer demographic of teenagers and their vulnerability under capitalism.

Many of the scenes in *Josie* play out in and around stores, including the Riverdale Mall and New York City's Times Square. The movie's side characters—the teens who eagerly consume the music of boy band Du Jour and the Pussycats—carry shopping bags from business to business, ready to buy into the next trend. But Josie, Melody and Valerie are introduced outside of this consumer context. A musical montage juxtaposes shots of them playing their instruments with shots from their daily lives: Josie juggling jobs in a music store, diner, and as a guitar teacher; Valerie working in a shoe store between volunteer gigs; and Melody holding handmade signs by the highway, eager to brighten commuters' days (Elfont & Kaplan, 2001). The montage presents the trio as busy getting by and giving back, rather than following trends. There are other hints at the band's low-cost, do-it-yourself (DIY) lifestyle: they share a pack of ramen, with Valerie observing, "I don't think people know how far one pack can go"; they try to be optimistic about a five-dollar profit on a gig, and they promote their band by playing on the street (Elfont & Kaplan, 2001). Unlike the teens of *Riverdale*, for whom money is rarely an issue, let alone a barrier, *Josie*'s protagonists work part-time jobs and live on a budget.

Their DIY lifestyle also translates into their aesthetic, especially in the case of Josie. When she is given designer gowns by the record label, she unabashedly takes scissors to them, cutting off sleeves and altering necklines to make them fit her own personal style. Unlike the teens who rush to stores to replace their red shoes with pink shoes, then orange shoes, at the behest of corporations, Josie does not want to be *told* what is stylish. She makes her own style—something that keeps the animal print, cat-ear trademark of the band but still sets her apart.

In both texts, Josie, Valerie, and Melody are stylistically united by shared accessories: their cat ears and leopard print clothing. But the other girls of *Riverdale* have distinct styles that are deeply tied to their personalities. Through the thirteen episodes of *Riverdale*'s first season, central characters Betty, Veronica and Cheryl rarely deviate from their signature color palettes, patterns, and accessories. Betty wears pastel pinks and blues, white, light grey, and the occasional floral pattern in similar pastel hues. She wears clothing best described as preppy and conservative: oxford shirts, cable-knit sweaters, cardigans, intact jeans, flats, simple stud earrings. She is introduced half-dressed in "Chapter 1: The River's Edge," but even then, she is modest: a pink lacy bra fully covers her breasts. Her styling in the comics has long been tied to her personality. Bart Beaty (2015) notes the significance of her trademark high ponytail: "The constant understanding among the *Archie* creators is that the ponytail is integral to any claim about Betty's innocence as the girl next door" (p. 57). When she goes bold, she stays within feminine shades, attending a dance in a candy pink dress. Even her food matches her palette: vanilla and strawberry milkshakes. Her consumption is as modest, as feminine, and as innocent as she is.

Veronica has long been Betty's foil, and this is made clear in the girls' contrasting styles. Where Betty is clean but casual, Veronica is sophisticated: pencil skirts, fitted dresses, capes, and brooches. Veronica wears dark, deep shades: burgundy, dark blue, black, purple, and dark grey. Veronica's long, dark hair is worn down, the opposite of Betty's blonde high ponytail. Veronica occasionally accessorizes with a headband—a visual nod to another teen protagonist, Blair Waldorf of the television series *Gossip Girl* (Schwartz & Savage, 2007). And, in many ways, Blair is Veronica-before-Riverdale, a New York City princess used to a lavish lifestyle and social standing upheld through her cruelty. But while the headband was Blair's signature accessory, Veronica's signature is pearls, a marker of wealth. Veronica does not dress like a high school student; pearls and brooches speak to a maturity and social standing inappropriate for Riverdale High. All in all, her sophistication seems to draw attention to Betty's youth. There is a sexual element here as well: Veronica is worldly, cosmopolitan, and experienced, while Betty is innocent, naive, and timid. Mere days into their friendship, Veronica pushes Betty to make a move on her long-time crush, a scene which is indicative of their contrasting approach to sex and relationships ("Chapter 1: The River's Edge"). Their dissimilar personalities and unlikely friendship are always emphasized by their visual styling, and any deviations from personality and social standing are registered on a stylistic level, as well.

It is through Betty's shifts in style that *Riverdale* begins to equate style not just with identity but moral allegiance. In "Chapter 3: Body Double," Betty plays out a revenge plot after her male classmates slut shame her friends. It is here that we first see Dark Betty, a figure whose full narrative arc is too much to take up in this essay. But Dark Betty is just that—Betty trading pastels for dark clothing, a black wig, and dark lipstick. When Betty first puts on the lipstick, a vibrant red borrowed from her sister Polly, it leads to an argument with her mother, Alice:

> ALICE: "Seduce Scarlet doesn't suit you, dear."
> BETTY: "It's Polly's. I'm borrowing it."
> ALICE: "Polly grew up too fast. I don't want you to make the same mistake."
> BETTY: "Well, I like it. It makes me feel powerful."….
> ALICE: "I don't want you associating with a girl like [Veronica]"
> BETTY: "A bad girl, you mean?...."
> ALICE: "Here. Pink Perfection. It's more you" ["Chapter 3: Body Double"].

During this tense exchange, the red lipstick takes on several meanings: the name of the shade, Seduce Scarlet, speaks to red lipstick's sexual connotations; it is associated with Betty's sister, Polly, a pregnant teen who has been institutionalized; and it is associated with "bad girl" Veronica, who Alice insults as she roughly wipes the lipstick off Betty's lips ("Chapter 3: Body Double"). The color red, and red lipstick especially, carries social and moral value: it is the accessory of "bad girls" and pregnant teens who "[grow] up too fast" and make mistakes ("Chapter 3: Body Double"). For Alice, the lipstick is serious business. It communicates to the world that Betty is a certain kind of girl, and it denotes actions and behaviors that have severe consequences. Lipstick and style here are not just a matter of play. Rather, they speak to the social and moral choices we make and to which we are accountable. Alice reminds Betty of Betty's signature shade, Pink Perfection, a name stripped of sexuality and moral risk.

That Betty sees power in the red lipstick is certainly meaningful and can be interpreted in a myriad of ways: the power that comes from acknowledging one's lack of perfection, the power of asserting independence in her life, the power that sexual women hold over men.

Most significantly for my purposes, this scene emphasizes the brand of the lipstick Betty is using. As Alice reaches to Betty's vanity for the Pink Perfection, the camera lingers on a lipstick tube, focusing on the brand name Covergirl. I will come back to the issue of product placement later, but for now I want to emphasize that teen audiences are being offered a certain narrative about make-up—that it is associated with power, independence, and sexual maturity—and then being reminded that they, too, can acquire this lipstick and the social and moral qualities associated with it. The identity of your choice is within reach, you just need to buy the right products.

Riverdale raises the possibility of buying your way into new identities, and of presenting yourself to the world in deliberate ways to clarify whether you are naive or sophisticated, perfect or seductive. *Riverdale*'s Josie is hyperaware of this potential, and from the moment she is introduced she uses the language of branding to describe her band and their social, cultural, and economic choices. When Archie asks to jam with them, Josie answers harshly and clearly:

> You're staring at our pussycat ears, which is rude, but let me break it, and them, down for you. The Pussycats are building a brand, creating a signature look, okay? We're telling a story. Last year, we won Rockland County's Battle of the Bands [....] This year, we'd like to build on that success, continue telling our story with songs we write [....] Read my glossed lips, Justin Gingerlake. Not. Gonna. Happen ["Chapter 1: The River's Edge"].

Throughout season one of *Riverdale,* Josie, Valerie and Melody are often pictured wearing matching outfits—cat ears, black chokers, and leopard print clothing—that lend them a unified look. Given Josie's monologue to Archie, this is less of a playful uniform and more of a curated image, managed for marketability as Josie attempts to usher herself and her band into fame and success.

Like Betty, Josie's success in building her brand depends on her accessories. And like Betty, she reaches for Covergirl in a critical moment. While she is applying her make-up before an important performance, the camera focuses in on the bottle: Covergirl blast pro mascara. *Riverdale* not so subtly reminds the viewers that Josie's personal journey is a commodity they can purchase ("Chapter 6: Faster, Pussycats! Kill! Kill!").

The blatant product placement in *Riverdale* is particularly striking given that in 2001, *Josie and the Pussycats* performed a feature film-length critique of product placement and consumer manipulation and pushed a narrative of media and consumer literacy. Product placement is a running joke in *Josie and the Pussycats*. The world that Josie, Valerie, and Melody inhabit is littered with branded products. At points, this branding becomes absurd: the plane that boy band Du Jour flies in is decorated with Target logos, and cleaning products like Bounce, Ivory soap, and Cheer are arranged around the plane and even pinned to the walls. Similarly, the Pussycats are flown out of Riverdale in a Motorola-branded plane, with cellphones on the plane's walls. The band's accommodations in New York City are similarly branded. The more successful the band becomes, the more these brand names accumulate, as the band becomes more deeply embedded in the mechanizations of capitalism.

Product placement as a phenomenon has a long and fascinating history, dating back to Jules Verne's 1873 novel *Around the World in Eighty Days*; reportedly, "a shipping company persuaded [Verne] to have the book's hero, Phileas Fogg, travel on one of their ships" (Shears, 2014, p. 60). Lynne Eagle and Stephan Dahl (2018) define product placement as "the insertion of a recognizable branded product into the content or background of a range of media formats" (p. 605). They differentiate between passive product placement, "the product is part of the setting but is not actually used by actors," and active product placement, "the product is used by an actor, with or without verbal acknowledgement, as part of the script" (Eagle & Dahl, 2018, p. 606). *Riverdale* notably uses active product placement, as watching the characters apply the Covergirl make-up builds the product's allure. In *Josie and the Pussycats*, active product placement uses dramatic irony, with characters engaging with brands in ways the viewers recognize as a result of subliminal marketing, such as vegetarian Melody announcing her desire for a Big Mac, or with product placements acting as visual metaphors, as when Valerie clutches a Target pillow to her chest as she deals with the emotional fallout of being the literal target of a capitalist and ultimately murderous conspiracy. While these scenes are heavily laden with branded products, these products contribute to the meaning of the film.

While *Josie*, as a major motion picture, is part of a mainstream industry, it is not necessarily as complicit in perpetuating consumption. The products that litter the sets of *Josie* do not fully qualify as product placement. Peter Shears (2014) distinguishes between product placement, that is, "the inclusion of, or a reference to, a product or service within a program in return for payment of some kind to the program maker or broadcaster," and prop placement, "the inclusion of, or reference to, products or services acquired at no, or less than full, cost where the inclusion can be justified editorially" (p. 68). Reportedly, the dozens of companies whose products appear in *Josie* did not *pay* for this inclusion; according to the film's directors, when the filmmakers approached the companies to propose sponsorship, the companies refused to pay for the inclusion of the products, which were left in anyway (Mogilevich, 2002, p. 44). This makes the products prop placement rather than product placement. It also makes the inclusion editorial rather than transactional. The makers of *Josie* were critiquing and mimicking product placement without profiting from it.

Significantly, given that *Josie*'s plot revolves around subliminal messaging, Eagle and Dahl (2018) differentiate between product placement and subliminal messages, which "are those below the threshold of consciousness; product placements do not meet these criteria" (p. 612). There is an ongoing debate on the vulnerability of youth and children to product placement; Eagle and Dahl (2018) report increased regulation around product placement in media aimed at children, as well as "international moves to deliver media literacy training to children" (p. 607). As a teen viewer of *Josie* back in the years after it was released, I was the target of a great deal of media literacy programming. Concerned Children's Advertisers released the famous House Hippo commercials to Canadian television in 1999 and adapted them for television in the United Kingdom in 2002, suggesting that they were regularly airing in the years around *Josie*'s release. The commercials were public service announcements that began by mimicking nature shows, with a narrator describing the tiny hippos who lived in North American houses. But a new narrative voice interjects, "That looked really ... real. But you knew it couldn't be true, didn't you? That's why it's good to think about what you see on TV, and ask questions, kind of like you just did" (Dempsey & Hamilton, 1999). The commercial's secondary narrator talks up to their audience of children and teenagers, implying that these viewers are already skeptical and smart, and encouraging them to *continue* approaching television critically. The House Hippo commercials acknowledge the vulnerability of young audience members to manipulation via media, but also emphasize these viewers as savvy and able to further develop their existing media literacy.

Concerned Children's Advertisers was not the only organization encouraging media literacy; from 1989 to 2006, the Canadian Broadcasting Corporation (CBC) ran a youth-oriented newsmagazine show called *Street Cents*, "a show about consumer awareness for the people who needed it most" (Jones, 2015). There are two things about the show I want to emphasize. Firstly, like the House Hippos campaign, it was on the air when *Josie* was released, suggesting that *Josie* was created in a culture of consumer awareness. Secondly, *Street Cents*' very existence acknowledged that "[t]eenagers are the demographic most susceptible to misleading advertising," and it often ran segments on shopping effectively in which "shitty consumer products were ... thrown into a fiery manhole" (Jones, 2015). In this sense, *Street Cents* seemed to be working on the same cultural wavelength as *Josie*: both shows were products in and of themselves that served a teen audience who is at once deeply vulnerable and cynically savvy, which has, as Mariana Mogilevich (2002) writes in her review of *Josie*, "the effect ... of a strange and simultaneous clarity and surreality" (p. 42). This surreality points to the tension in media that encourages consumer awareness while itself functioning as consumable media: Concerned Children's Advertisers imagined a magically adorable creature only to shatter the fantasy by acknowledging its own invention; *Street Cents* reminded viewers to be critical of consumer manipulation, while employing a Vietnamese potbelly pig as an attraction; *Josie* takes the form of a typical teen movie, complete with tie-in merchandise in the form of the soundtrack, while critiquing the industry that shakes teenagers down for cash. The absurdity or irony of all these texts points to an overarching question: how do you get youth to buy in—with their cash, with their time, with their attention—to texts that teach them to be more careful in their consumption? How do pedagogical texts of media literacy and consumer awareness draw in an audience?

Ultimately, *Josie* does not seem sure if it is a pedagogical tool or a product, and neither do its reviewers. Mogilevich (2002), while praising *Josie*, seems to think the film is undone by its own irony: "*Josie* is a film mocking the worldwide business of selling products, and the use of entertainment to 'subtly' compel people to consume.... *Josie and the Pussycats* is at the same time a product for entertainment (a film) whose sole real mission is to (not so subtly) compel teenagers to engage in unbridled consumption of consumer goods" (p. 42). Diane Negra (2013) refers to *Josie*'s "toothless critique of the calculation of corporate culture (as if the film itself were not fully complicit in such calculation)," and deems the film's discourse "superficial" (p. 86, 84). I see the film as more a product of its time. Building on the cultural chronology laid out by Marisa Meltzer (2010) in *Girl Power: The Nineties Revolution in Music*, I propose that *Josie* was situated at the moment when riot grrrl was co-opted into the more marketable girl power, and as such the protagonists struggle with how creative success becomes salability. *Josie* represents the struggle between empowering teenagers as creators and exploiting them as consumers.

In the early chapters of her book, Meltzer (2010) offers a kind of oral history of the riot grrrl movement, describing the music scene but also the zine culture, the fashion, and the sense of solidarity and resistance against male-dominated counterculture and mainstream visions of femininity: "Riot grrrl was girl power at its most brash and unfiltered. It created the most uncompromising (and defiant and audacious) female persona in music in recent history" (p. 19). The movement was girl-run, playful, and creative. This grassroots tone is imitated in the first act of *Josie*, when Josie, Valerie, and Melody take pleasure in their camaraderie, their fashion, and their music, regardless of how it is received by those around them. But, as Meltzer (2010) warns, "if one thing is a given, it's that counterculture movements become commodified and the underground becomes mainstream" (p. viii). She explains how the mainstream media came for riot grrrl, and how this disparate movement responded: "The core message of riot grrrl was about finding one's own voice, and to then see the media trying to interpret that for you could be deeply disconcerting" (p. 31). This is the exact scenario experienced by Josie, Valerie and Melody. During their first official recording session, they are surprised and delighted to hear the Megasound 8000 play back their music (Elfont & Kaplan, 2001). But the music becomes increasingly less recognizable to them, until they arrive at an industry party to hear a cover of one of their hit songs.

The band's discomfort with this commodification of their music speaks to a tension around concepts of empowerment and success, especially for girls and young women in the 1990s and early 2000s. Meltzer unpacks the fuzzy, pseudo-feminist message of girl power, which seems to offer agency to girls, but mostly only insofar as they are recognized as consumers. She writes that the Spice Girl phenomenon in particular "proved that a young, female demographic was ready and willing to become consumers, and that a feminist-lite message like girl power was an effective method of marketing to them" (Meltzer, 2010, p. 93). In *Josie*, the band is offered fame and success at the price of being re-packaged in increasingly violent ways. In the 2000s, girls were being offered power, but not to speak or change culture, simply to buy it. At the turn of the millennium, Meltzer (2010) identifies a boom in "pop culture creations geared toward teenagers.... Teen girl audiences emerged as one of the most powerful demographics of the era, making movies like *Clueless*, *Scream*, and *Titanic* massive hits" (p. 78). *Josie* is one of these hits, but it is also a reflection on them, and on the creation and exploitation of this new teen demographic.

However, Meltzer's narrative of co-optation is overwhelmingly white, and it seems to erase major Black musicians like Destiny's Child and T.L.C. entirely. This erasure of Blackness from a cultural narrative of adolescence and consumption is significant, particularly as the *Archie* comics universe diversifies. After decades of comics and cartoons in which Josie and Melody were white,[1] *Riverdale* cast Ashleigh Murray as Josie and Asha Bromfield as Melody alongside Hayley Law's Valerie Brown, resulting in an all-Black trio. This is an example of blackwashing or staining, which John G. Russell (2018) describes as "the casting of actors of color in traditionally white roles" (p. 267). Russell (2018) notes that blackwashing has many different ends, including exemplifying Hollywood's commitment to diversity (p. 269). But it can also be a destabilizing moment for white audiences who expect whiteness on screen: "by decentering whiteness and casting actors of color in traditionally white roles, staining potentially forces white audiences to become reflexively and retroactively aware of the implicit 'whiteness' of both the original displaced white character and other surrounding white characters" (Russell, 2018, p. 270). In the case of *Riverdale*, the blackwashing may serve as a belated diversification of an overwhelmingly white community. As Beaty (2015) writes, *Archie* often made a claim to all-Americanness that was belied by its lack of racial diversity: "The myth is that Riverdale was a typical American community. The fact is that the almost total absence of nonwhite characters makes Riverdale one of the least typical locales in the United States" (p. 52). *Riverdale*, which also casts Latinx performers in canonically white roles (the Lodge family) and queers other core characters (Cheryl Blossom), seems interested in a diversity that is more representative of its audience.

Russell (2018) also argues that blackwashing can be for profit, as it may "attract a heretofore neglected demographic—nonwhite audiences" (p. 269). This raises questions about the consumability of girls and teenagers, and how their appeal or profitability hinges on their normativity. *Josie* satirizes a culture in which girls and young women are produced to be more consumable and to encourage consumption by a younger demographic. When Josie challenges MegaRecords CEO Fiona's violence toward the band, insisting that MegaRecords needs her to perform the concert, Fiona bites back: "Need you? Doll, I created you, and believe me, I can destroy you" (Elfont & Kaplan, 2001). Fiona's response highlights two things about teen celebrities: their malleability—like a doll, they can be dressed and presented in whichever way pleases the creator or entices the consumer—and their disposability. Let me unpack both malleability and disposability in both these texts and its consequences for teen culture more generally.

When 2001's Josie, Melody and Valerie sign on with MegaRecords, they are transformed in a makeover montage. A team of stylists and make-up artists descends on the frightened-looking musicians, but the montage becomes more playful as it goes on: the bandmates dance and sing along, strike goofy poses, and even interfere with the process, as when Josie rips the sleeve off a designer dress to the horror of a nearby stylist. The musicians are being produced and presented by the record company, dressed up and styled like dolls, but they still maintain their sense of fun. The final looks are not a major departure from their original style, if a little more polished and high-end. Notably, this is one of the only scenes of the movie that is not saturated with brand names. In the white, minimalist studio, there are occasional glimpses of the faded brand names for Streetwear, a clothing company, and John Frieda, a hair studio. But the cosmetic products themselves, which we see close up as they are applied to the characters, are not branded. Though the movie represents the process of someone being produced and transformed for consumption, they do not provide a string of brand name clues as to how to imitate the process.

In contrast, the girls of *Riverdale* conspicuously consume Covergirl make-up: Betty's lipstick brand is visible in "Chapter 3," the camera lingers on Josie's mascara in "Chapter 6," and in "Chapter 11: To Riverdale and Back Again," Cheryl and Polly apply make-up in a room littered with Covergirl products. This conspicuous consumption is part of a long-term branding partnership between *Riverdale* and Covergirl. As the final episodes of season one aired, the Riverdale YouTube channel released advertisements titled "RIVERDALE: Becoming Josie McCoy" and "RIVERDALE: Becoming Veronica, Betty et Cheryl." The videos include sped-up footage of each actress in the make-up chair as they are styled for a day of shooting. Voice overs from the actresses describe their characters, highlighting certain personality traits and drawing attention to the make-up that best communicates these traits. The video slows down to focus on these key moments of styling: the application of foundation, eye shadow, and lipstick. These narrations relate identity and appearance to power and social standing: Camila Mendes describes how her character Veronica's "mystery and allure ... are reflected in her eyes" and Cheryl actress Madelaine Petsch argues that "a bold strong lip" is "part of [Cheryl's] ability to control and to persuade" (Riverdale, 2017a). And finally, echoing the dialogue of the show, Josie-actress Ashleigh Murray links Josie's success in music to her personal presentation:

> Josie is all about ambition. She's going places. Josie knows that in order to succeed, she's got to get noticed. That means, her look has got to pop, it's got to turn heads. And that's why she always plays with colors. Her eyes, her cheeks, her lips. Her whole look says "See me. Hear me. Now watch me turn up the volume" [Riverdale, 2017b].

The campaign is very explicit in arguing that make-up, and style in general, is a way to make one's self. If you want to be a risk-taker like Veronica, or as ambitious as Josie, or as controlling as Cheryl, here is a line of products to make that possible.

Of course, Covergirl's *Riverdale*-themed campaign is not particularly shocking or innovative. Make-up and fashion companies have long constructed narratives of power, allure, and potential. And make-up does carry the power to shape how we present ourselves in the world and how the world receives us, for good and for bad. But it is a step further into consumer culture than the makeover scene in *Josie*. While 2001's Josie was a fleshed-out character who could be polished by stylists but maintain her own identity and agency, *Riverdale*'s Josie is produced in the make-up chair. By her own admission, she is concerned with "branding" ("Chapter 1: The River's Edge"). *Riverdale* exists in a social media era, when, as Axel Bruns (2008) argues with his concept of the "produser," consumers are expected to create much of the very content they consume (p. 2). Sarah Banet-Weiser (2011) studies YouTube as one site of produsage and personal branding; building on YouTube's former slogan "Broadcast yourself," she argues,

> "Broadcasting yourself" is also a way to brand oneself, a practice deployed by individuals to communicate personal values, ideas, and beliefs using strategies and logic from commercial brand culture, and one that is increasingly normative in the contemporary neoliberal economic environment [p. 278].

"Online self-branding," Banet-Weiser (2011) notes, "utilizes the labor of consumers in re-imagining a 'product' *as* the self" (p. 286). *Riverdale*'s Josie is fully aware of herself as product and tries to make herself as consumable as possible in the hopes of achieving success.

But as ever, the neoliberal dynamics of personal branding are driven by normative concepts of celebrity and beauty. Noting the rise in YouTube stars and wannabe-stars, and the increase in articles and guides on how to achieve this type of success, Banet-Weiser (2011) writes:

> the notion that there are clear—and accessible—steps one can simply follow in order "to be a star" renders invisible how bounded those steps are in terms of age, race, and class. Individuals who are culturally marginalized (through law, policy, media representation, etc.) because of race or class, for instance, do not have the same access to the practice of self-branding as white, middle-class girls and women [p. 288].

Riverdale's Josie is certainly aware of her disadvantage, as she pushes back against the desire of (white, male) Archie to be a part of her success: "do you know why we're called the Pussycats? Because we have to claw our way into the same rooms that you can waltz into" ("Chapter 3: Body

Double"). A few episodes later, Josie's mother Sierra asks Josie to find a new bandmate, "Someone skinny and beautiful. But not more skinny and beautiful than you. And a woman of color, please. Josie, don't forget our branding" ("Chapter 6: Faster, Pussycats! Kill! Kill!"). Sierra's emphasis on the Pussycats brand as beautiful, thin, women of color speaks to the band's navigation of an industry that prioritizes certain bodies over others.

Ultimately, Covergirl's partnership with *Riverdale* echoes Banet-Weiser's concerns over the disproportionate success of white girls and women. In October 2019, Lili Reinhart, who portrays Betty on *Riverdale*, signed on as the new face of Covergirl cosmetics (@covergirl, 2019). Though there are certainly many factors in Reinhart's success, I want to cite the 2017 advertisement, in which Reinhart tells us that "Betty's looks match her personality: simple and clean. It all starts with her skin. It's clear, it's pure, it's bright" (Riverdale, 2017a). While she narrates, the camera focuses on foundation, which is applied to her skin to both produce and emphasize its pureness. This video fits in a long tradition of women emphasizing their whiteness through cosmetics, which Kimberly Poitevin (2011) dates back to Early Modern England, when "English women … us[ed] make-up to accentuate differences between themselves and their foreign, darker-skinned counterparts, and making whiteness a visible English trait" (p. 62). After two years working closely with *Riverdale*, Covergirl embraces its whitest, blondest actress as their new model. Their announcement on Instagram describes Reinhart as "authentic," a term which seems to highlight the contradictory nature of describing Betty's personality and white skin as "simple and clean" when the skin, at least, is carefully painted with product (@covergirl, 2019; Riverdale, 2017a).

The economic investment in whiteness and white-centered culture ties into the disposability of teen celebrities but particularly of non-white bodies. In *Josie*, MegaRecords begins centering Josie and actively excluding Valerie. They rename the band "Josie and the Pussycats," plaster Josie's name and image on products and marketing materials and leave Valerie out of cars and parties. Melody, the other white band member, is not actively targeted like Valerie is, suggesting that Valerie's Blackness is a part of why she is excluded. In fact, Valerie finds herself alone watching a *Behind the Music* episode about another Black musician pushed out of a band. The fictional "Chief" is pictured mopping floors, performing menial labor after he contributed to, but did not benefit from, the successful musical group "The Captain and Tennille." The television episode builds on Valerie's sense of rejection and enforces the racial dynamics at play, in which white musicians are valued over their Black collaborators.

Disposability as experienced by Valerie, and by the musicians in general, relates back to an increasing precarity in late-stage capitalism.

Kimberly Ann Hall (2015) defines precarity as "a lived condition of dependence on economic and social systems over which we exercise minimal amounts of control" (p. 129). Creative professionals, including the Pussycats in both texts, are precarious as they seek to build careers in an unpredictable industry. Though *Josie* takes the volatility of the music industry to the extreme by representing record labels that kill off bands who are deemed unmanageable, *Riverdale*'s Josie's invocation of "clawing" her way into opportunities speaks to this instability as well.

Riverdale's Valerie is also considered disposable, this time because she is not willing to take direction or prioritize the brand over her own desires. In "Chapter 6: Faster, Pussycats! Kill! Kill!" Josie complains about Valerie's disloyalty to the band to her mother, Sierra McCoy, who is calmly ruthless in her response: "Replace her [....] Find yourself a new cat" ("Chapter 6: Faster, Pussycats! Kill! Kill!"). Valerie's decision to sing with Archie temporarily puts the Pussycats at risk, but ultimately reinforces the branding effort behind the band. Josie and her mother know that the brand—women of color, conventionally attractive, stylized—does not rely on the individuals within the band. Personal branding, the production of the self into product, something consumable, this is a fairly ruthless process, and one that often prioritizes success over community or creativity. The Pussycats of 2001 follow the motto "Friends first, band second," but *Riverdale*'s Pussycats seem to have no such motto (Elfont & Kaplan, 2001).

Perhaps, then, *Riverdale*'s darkness is a reflection of a growing precarity and a capitalist emphasis on individual branding. Covergirl's advertisements outline how to take control of one's image, offering a way to buy into Veronica's sophistication, Cheryl's power, Josie's talent, or Betty's innocence. This emphasis on self-branding, on carefully controlling how you present yourself to the world, is a neoliberal argument that you can work your way through precarity and into success. This neoliberal argument for self-branding seems to efface inequalities in privilege, or at least suggest that it is the responsibility of the marginalized individual to "claw [their] way into" opportunities and success ("Chapter 3: Body Double"). The implied violence of this metaphor is lateral: it speaks to the disposability of Valerie in favor of another thin, pretty woman of color. It is also a heavily gendered metaphor, hinting at cat fights and direct competition between women and girls for the few slots allotted to them at the top. When read alongside the Covergirl advertisements and the Covergirl branded scenes in *Riverdale*, there is a social, aesthetic, and economic pressure put on girls and women: highlight your best features, choose your personal and moral qualities, shape the way the world sees you, be conscious—always—that you will be judged on your appearance. The playful rebellion of riot grrrl is fully in the past. In fact, *Riverdale* is far beyond even the vaguely empowering materialism of girl power. Rather, I see the potential for future analysis on *Riverdale* as a post-feminist text. Alyxandra Vesey (2015) uses the term "post-feminist entrepreneurialism" to analyze pop stars' endorsement of fragrances, arguing that this term "describes the contradiction between empowerment and the erasure of agency" (p. 995). The girls of *Riverdale*, with their signature products and color palettes, are living in a post-feminist era, where they are encouraged to embody certain moral qualities—seduction, innocence, manipulation, ambition—under the guise of controlling their narrative, when truly they are being asked to limit themselves to a consistent, consumable brand.

Note

1. Valerie was canonically Black, and was, in fact, "the first African-American cartoon character to star as a TV series regular" when she was voiced in the 1970s by Patrice Holloway (Tunzi 2006).

References

Aguirre-Sacasa, R. (Writer), & Krieger, L.T. (Director) (2017). Chapter 1: The River's Edge [television series episode]. *Riverdale*. United States: Berlanti Productions and Archie Comics Publications.
Aguirre-Sacasa, R. (Writer), & Sullivan, K.R. (Director) (2017). Chapter 11: To Riverdale and Back Again [television series episode]. *Riverdale*. United States: Berlanti Productions and Archie Comics Publications.
Banet-Weiser, S. (2011). "Branding the Post-Feminist Self: Girls' Video Production and YouTube." M.C. Kearney (Ed.), *Mediated Girlhoods: New Explorations of Girls' Media Culture* (277–294). New York: Peter Lang.
Beaty, B. (2015). *Twelve-Cent Archie*. New Brunswick: Rutgers University Press.
Bruns, A. (2008). *Blogs, Wikipedia, Second Life, and Beyond*. New York: Peter Lang.
[@covergirl] (2019, October 30). SURPRISE! The secret is out: @lilireinhart is our newest #Covergirl!... [Instagram photograph]. Retrieved from https://www.instagram.com/p/B4PXScBngqq/.
Dempsey, S. (Writer), & Hamilton, T. (Director) (1999). The Hidden World of the House Hippo [television commercial]. Canada: The Concerned Children's Advertisers.
Eagle, L., & Dahl, S. (2018). "Product Placement in Old and New Media: Examining the Evidence for Concern." *Journal of Business Ethics 147*, 605–618.
Elfont, H., & Kaplan, D. (Directors) (2001). *Josie and the Pussycats* [motion picture]. United States: Universal Pictures.
Hall, K.A. (2015). "The Authenticity of Social-Media Performance: lonelygirl15 and the Amateur Brand of Young-Girlhood." *Women & Performance 25*(2), 128–142.
Jones, A. (2015). "An Oral History of Street Cents: The Best Kids' Show Ever on Canadian TV." *Vice*. Retrieved from https://www.vice.com/en_ca/article/znwpgj/an-oral-history-of-the-best-kids-show-ever-on-canadian-tv-852.
Lawrence, Y. (Writer), & Krieger, L.T. (Director) (2017). Chapter 3: Body Double [television series episode]. *Riverdale*. United States: Berlanti Productions and Archie Comics Publications.

Meltzer, M. (2010). *Girl Power: The Nineties Revolution in Music*. New York: Faber & Faber.
Mogilevich, M. (2002). "Charlie's Pussycats." *Film Quarterly* 55(3), 38–44.
Murphy, J. (Director), & Sarwer-Foner, H. (Director) (1989). *Street Cents* [television series]. Halifax, NS: Canadian Broadcasting Company.
Negra, D. (2013). "'Queen of the Indies' Parker Posey's Niche Stardom and the Taste Cultures of Independent Film." In G. King, C. Molloy & Y. Tzioumakis (Eds.), *American Independent Cinema: Indie, Indiewood and Beyond* (pp. 71–88). London: Routledge.
Riverdale. (2017, April 20). "RIVERDALE Becoming Veronica, Betty et Cheryl" [video file]. Retrieved from https://www.youtube.com/watch?v=8Pl7cmAfsqw.
Riverdale. (2017, May 1). "RIVERDALE Becoming Josie McCoy [video file]. Retrieved from https://www.youtube.com/watch?v=0b9gT9vMLyA.
Robbins, T. (1999). *From Girls to Grrrlz: A History of Girl Comics from Teens to Zines*. San Francisco: Chronicle Books.
Russell, J.G. (2018). "Trading Races: Albescence, Staining, Xenoface, and Other Race-Switching Practices in American Popular Culture." *The Journal of American Cultures* 41(3), 267–278.
Sauer, A. (2011). "Announcing the Brandcameo Product Placement Awards." *Brandchannel*. Retrieved from https://www.brandchannel.com/2011/02/22/announcing-the-brandcameo-product-placement-award-winners/#single.
Schwartz, J. (Producer), & Savage, S. (Producer) (2007). *Gossip Girl* [television series]. New York: Warner Bros. Television.
Shears, P. (2014). "Product Placement: The UK and the New Rules." *Journal of Promotion Management* 20(1), 59–81.
Tunzi, K. (2006). "Mileposts." *Billboard*, 104.
Vesey, A. (2015). "Putting Her on the Shelf: Pop Star Fragrances and Post-Feminist Entrepreneurialism." *Feminist Media Studies* 15(6), 992–1008.
Williams, T. (Writer), & Adelson, S.A. (Director) (2017). Chapter 6: Faster, Pussycats! Kill! Kill! [television series episode]. *Riverdale*. United States: Berlanti Productions and Archie Comics Publications.
Zeisler, A. (2016). *We Were Feminists Once: From Riot Grrrl to Covergirl, the Buying and Selling of a Political Movement*. New York: Public Affairs.

Archie Got Hot

How Embracing the Queer Art of Failure Allows the Chilling Adventures of Sabrina to Shift Queer Readings Away from Identity

Mat Wenzel

In a "first look" preview for *Riverdale,* aired by the CW, the camera quickly takes the viewer from a street corner of suburbia into the bedroom of Betty Cooper. It takes about 5 seconds to get a close-up of her lips, 12 for a view of her in her bra. But in 44 seconds, for gay male viewers, there's a bigger reveal. Kevin, Betty's confidant, looks out the window and exclaims, "Oh my God," as the camera follows his gaze. KJ Apa, Archie, stands in front of the window shirtless.

"Archie got hot," Kevin exclaims.

And in less than a minute, the CW has revealed a gay character and a ridiculously good looking red head. A lot of gay fans were instantly hooked. But as the series continued, the show might not have lived up to the expectations of LGBTQ+ viewers; though, with so much eye candy, and a long history of queer viewers using their imagination to identify with straight characters, many kept watching.

In contrast, the teasers and trailers put out by Netflix for *Chilling Adventures of Sabrina* (*CAOS*) fail to titillate queer viewers or firmly establish queer characters like promotions for *Riverdale* did. From these previews and one-minute spots, viewers don't get even hints that *Sabrina* actually has a spectrum of queer characters including Ambrose, Sabrina's pansexual cousin, and Theo, her transgender friend.

CAOS, though, has been widely praised for its representations of queerness (Bowen, 2019; Souza, 2019; Platt, 2018; Prance, 2018; Yandoli, 2018)—not just for having queer characters and queer characters of color, but for avoiding tropes like using coming out as a plot twist or plot arc, or isolating a character's sexuality as their only or major characteristic. While representation isn't necessarily the focus of my work here, it is still an important issue. A brief look at how queer identities are represented in the Archie universes can inform how queer readings can work with and on top of queer representation.

Riverdale has taken more criticism for its representations of queerness, or lack thereof. Before the show even started, some *Archie* fans were hoping to see the character of Jughead represented as asexual. Many argued that Jughead was always asexual, even in the earlier comics before the prevalence of that term, preferring food over romantic relationships (Brinkley, 2017). In 2016, a year before Riverdale aired, the writers of *Jughead* (an *Archie* comic) explicitly labeled Jughead as asexual, and people like *Vulture* writer Abraham Riesman were predicting that *Riverdale* might honor this "canonical" characteristic in the show (Riesman, 2016). The hashtag #AroAceJugheadOrBust sprang up as queer fans called for queer representation in *Riverdale*. Annemarie Navar-Gill and Mel Stanfill discuss this hashtag campaign and others in their analysis of queer fan hashtag campaigns and their potential queering effect on heteronormative plot and characters in television (Navar-Gill and Stanfill, 2018). Even the actor who portrays Jughead, Cole Sprouse, seemed to support this queer portrayal as well. In an interview with *Teen Vogue*, he said, "I hope that huge corporations like the CW recognize that this kind of representation is rare and severely important to people who resonate with it," even going so far as to say that these underrepresented identities "demand representation" (Elizabeth, 2017). But *Riverdale* has yet to pursue any plotlines that explore Jughead's asexuality, a move condemned by many fans (Alexander, 2017).

The show, too, has been accused of gaybaiting (Prance, 2018; Reilly, 2018; Idika, 2017; McGrath 2017). Veronica and Betty share a performative kiss in the very first episode but no queer relationship between them or with others is pursued throughout the first season, making this queer act of affection appear as just a plot device, a way to get the attention of the cheerleading captain, and some might argue to titillate viewers. In a later season, a preview was released showing gay character Joaquin kissing Archie, suggesting to some queer viewers that Archie might be involved in a gay relationship or sexual encounter, not entirely impossible in the *Riverdale* world. But this kiss was just a Judas kiss in the episode, as immediately after kissing Archie, Joaquin stabs him (Reilly, 2018). Again, a queer act of affection is turned into a titillating plot device. To be fair, not all the reviews of *Riverdale*'s queer representation are negative. Sam Prance praises the show for its "Bizzarodale" episode in the third season that tries to focus on characters that are usually backgrounded by the main characters and their heteronormative relationships (Prance, 2019).

Sabrina isn't free from criticism concerning queer representation either. In an early episode Sabrina shuts down transphobic male football players by casting a spell that causes them to engage in sexual activity with each other and then she takes pictures, threatening to release them if the transphobic bullying continues—a problematic instance of fighting-queer-phobia-with-queer-phobia (Sobel, 2018). Some criticism about the marginalization of Theo, the transgender character, has circulated as well. Iman Hariri-Kia brings up criticism about the scene of Theo "coming out" to his father not being developed enough and Lachlan Watson, the actor who plays him, doesn't necessarily disagree: they say, "The fact that I was given anything at all, that Theo even exists ... for now, that's enough" (Hariri-Kia, 2019). Kaila Hale Stern's *The Mary Sue* article "*The Chilling Adventures of Sabrina*'s Non-Binary Character Deserves Better" goes in depth about how the show might make Theo a stronger character instead of a side-character who is the victim of trauma/bullying (Hale-Stern, 2018).

In these types of representations of queerness on the screen, we see that there is much work to be done on the part of both shows, and, of course, in television and cinema overall. But *CAOS* does provide a unique way to view queer representation. It's easy to make analogies between Sabrina's witchyness and queerness, to see the historically marginalized world of witchcraft as a metaphor for that of queerness. Both worlds are seen as minorities, aberrations, and silenced through taboo and acts of violence both unadjudicated and encoded by law. Under this metaphor a sort of binary starts to appear: witch/mortal, gay/straight. But Sabrina Spellman becomes a representation of the complexities that exist in, among, and between these worlds, as she is—at least initially—half-witch, half-mortal. Sabrina's constant failure to even maintain that solid identity models queerness and opens up opportunities for queerer possibilities. In this essay, I argue that Sabrina's quest to fail at moving fully toward either pole on the witch/mortal binary (further queered by the fact that she actually has three essences, as she is simultaneously divinely/satanically empowered as neither human nor witch), makes her a queer character whom queer viewers can see themselves in. Using Jack Halberstam's *Queer Art of Failure*, I argue that this embrace of failure is essentially queer, that the writers' failure to solidly define the sexuality of the show's characters and metaphors is essentially queer, and that this celebration of the failure to adhere to heteronormative standards is how writers, artists, and scholars can move toward queerer work.

Jack Halberstam writes,

> Rather than just arguing for a reevaluation of these standards of passing and failing, *The Queer Art of Failure* dismantles the logics of success and failure with which we currently live. Under certain circumstances failing, losing,

forgetting, unmaking, undoing, unbecoming, not knowing may in fact offer more creative, more cooperative, more surprising ways of being in the world. Failing is something queers do and have always done exceptionally well [2011].

It's important to note that I am trying to employ the term "queer" here not as a term strictly related to sexuality. I'll sometimes distinguish between the traditional identitarian markers of LGBT (Lesbian, Gay, Bisexual, Transgender) and queerness, while remaining hyper-aware of the danger of creating another false binary between these markers and queerness. Identitarian markers can be essential to survival, power, relationships, and functionality in everyday life. An individual may choose to move between identitarian markers at certain points (or consistently) or not at all. That letters are being added to the identity acronym and that they persist is representative of the fact that they are useful but incomplete. The "alphabet soup" of LGBGTQIA+ may be limited, but using queer to lump them all together is equally problematic. The statement "Everyone's a little queer" has its own set of issues. Siobahn Somerville explains,

> "Queer" causes confusion, perhaps because two of its current meanings seem to be at odds. In both popular and academic usage in the United States, "queer" is sometimes used interchangeably with the terms "gay" and "lesbian" and occasionally "transgender" and "bisexual." In this sense of the word, "queer" is understood as an umbrella term that refers to a range of sexual identities that are "not straight." In other political and academic contexts, "queer" is used in a very different way: as a term that calls into question the stability of any such categories of identity based on sexual orientation. In this second sense, "queer" is a *critique* of the tendency to organize political or theoretical questions around sexual orientation per se. To "queer" becomes a way to denaturalize categories such as "lesbian" and "gay" (not to mention "straight" and "heterosexual"), revealing them as socially and historically constructed identities that have often worked to establish and police the line between the "normal" and the "abnormal" [Burgett, 2014].

Here I model my definition of queerness after Halberstam, Muñoz, and E. Patrick Johnson: Halberstam's use of "queer" to refer to "nonnormative logics and organizations of communities" as well as sexual identity; Muñoz's call for queerness to be "more than an identitarian marker," a term that "articulate[s] a forward-dawning future," and also about "a desire for another way of being both in the world and time [and] a desire that resists mandates to accept that which is not enough"; and Johnson's assertion that "queer studies, like black studies, disrupts dominant and hegemonic discourses by consistently destabilizing fixed notions of identity by deconstructing binaries such as heterosexual/homosexual, gay/lesbian, and masculine/feminine as well as the concept of heteronormativity in general" (Halberstam, 2005; Muñoz, 2007; Johnson, 2005). It's with these ideas in mind that I approach failure in *CAOS*.

Sabrina's failure in *CAOS* is a major element of the show, especially her failure to sign her name in the Dark Lord's book at her dark baptism. On her 16th birthday, Halloween, a full moon and eclipse, this act represents Sabrina's allegiance to the witch world, and her witch identity. The first two episodes build up to this formative event, and all the signs point to her accomplishing this normal part of being a witch. Every witch in the *CAOS* world has signed their name in the book—it is one of the ways in which a witch is defined as a witch. Ambrose, perhaps Sabrina's most honest guide in witchdom, after confirming that Sabrina takes pleasure in casting spells, tells her "your gifts, that euphoria, fade to nothing if you aren't baptized" ("Chapter 1: October Country"). According to the logic, as of yet in the traditional rules of the witch world, if Sabrina doesn't perform this act, she really won't be a witch at all, or at least won't have the power and pleasure that comes with being a witch. But even without watching the previews that "spoil" this plot element, viewers get the sense that she will not sign the book, and that this long-held belief that it is essential, will end up not being true. This decision is supposed to be a defining moment in choosing "between the witch world of her family, and the human world of her friends" as Sabrina puts it in the narration at the very beginning of the series. In explicit narration a solid line is drawn between these two worlds, and it seems as if Sabrina must deny one half of herself in order to embrace the true side of herself. The in-between doesn't seem to exist. And Sabrina's words themselves consistently reinforce this throughout the first two seasons. While she has doubts and hesitations, she sees the line as a real one. In many ways, the viewer, being instructed on how to read the fictional world of *CAOS* and its rules, sees it this way too.

Though not entirely. The initial scenes of the series set viewers up for a kind of queerness. Sabrina's narration tells us plainly that she is "half-witch, half-mortal," but the scenes being played out seem to undermine binary. One of the first things we learn about Sabrina is that she doesn't abide by typical social boundaries. In the movie theater with her boyfriend she smiles and eats popcorn while everyone else reacts to a jump scene in the horror film, instead of inhabiting the well-known identity of the girlfriend grabbing the boyfriend in such a scene. Later she'll tell Harvey as he pretends to be a zombie that the only one he'll be scaring is himself. This could just be a role reversal within a traditional binary of gender expectations. But in a few beats, Sabrina is swept away by Harvey's gift of devotion and affection—a locket. Sabrina moves into a more traditional gender role here as she is enthralled by this gift of jewelry. Though, as she leaves Harvey with a kiss and enters her house she flips on the radio with her magic and celebrates in dance that reads, to more than one viewer, as an homage to Winona Ryder's final scene in *Beetlejuice,* and it is difficult not to read this moment as an act of feminist celebration (Goldstein, 2018).

As the friends leave the theater in the very first scene, Sabrina runs into her teacher, Ms. Wardwell (still in her human/unpossessed form) and invites her to hang out and discuss the film with her friends. Sabrina's friends seem confused that she is choosing to break the sacred boundary between teacher and pupil, but Sabrina seems unfazed. Later, as the scene cuts to Dr. Cerberus's bookstore where the four friends are discussing the film, we hear Theo through the shop window say, "The whole thing functions as a metaphor." Harvey responds that it's just a monster movie. Sabrina says, "Devil's advocate, can't it be both?" to which Roz and Theo enthusiastically agree. Of course, as we the viewers are also watching a "monster movie" of sorts, we are instructed to read it as both entertainment and a metaphor. This is much of the pleasure of watching the show, as there are moments of entertainment, the nostalgic feeling of teenagerdom and the pleasure of being frightened by visual effects and jump scenes, but often confronted with more than just a faint feeling that maybe it is trying to represent something more. For many, this metaphor reads as a distinction between fundamentalist religion and agnosticism—the witch world has definite oppressive fundamentalist values rooted in misogyny and exclusionary and predatory practices. But the witch world could also represent an LGBT community, as referred to earlier. Or, to play Sabrina's advocate, "can't it be both?" In any case, Sabrina's deliberate act of failure to sign her name, a potential giving up of pleasure, power, and protection, opens up a spectrum of possibilities (Bowen, 2019). Sabrina's choice not to outwardly commit to the witch world (whether that encodes organized religion or gayness) opens the viewer to a queerer experience—one in which it isn't possible to make clear distinctions about exactly what these two worlds and the characters within them represent.

That the metaphor falls apart quickly, and that the rules of the mortal world and witch world seem unclear and arbitrary could be seen as itself a type of failure. *CAOS* Vulture recapper Jessica Goldstein voices frustration with the lack of concrete rules in the fictional world. An example from her recap of "Chapter 16: Blackwood":

> I am still very confused about what makes Sabrina so special, beyond the accident of her birth. The fact that she's a half-mortal/half-witch is all very cool material for her own soul-searching journey, but that alone does not explain why everyone is so obsessed with her. Why does the Dark Lord even want a half-witch by his side to reign over hell?
>
> Also still totally unclear: how magic works here. We don't even know what

Sabrina is learning at the Academy; it feels mostly like summer camp for witches and warlocks, not real school with classes and exams and homework and such. Which, whatever, I don't need to see her study, but can you at least tell me what she does and doesn't know? Is she good at magic? In this world, is that even a thing? Or is it binary—you sign the Book of the Beast and boom, you're a full-blown witch with the same powers as anybody else? [Goldstein, 2019].

Goldstein's questions don't really get answered, though some progress is made in the final episodes of the season. Additionally, some of her questioning is the type one might expect from a fan in the middle of a series. But later Goldstein does make a more pointed critique of the show's writers/runners:

> I'm not asking for, and would not even enjoy, a magical world that held up to scientific scrutiny. But the absence of all this crucial context and information is extremely distracting. It pulls me out of the show. Does it do the same to you?

Viewers have come to expect a high standard of "world building" and *CAOS* may not always meet that standard. The witch world of Greendale and beyond is vague at times, and the rules and roles are changing. Fans also wonder what connection Greendale has to *Riverdale*, as they are both based on the *Archie* comics series. Prior to *Riverdale* season 6, episode 4 ("The Witching Hour[s]"), when Sabrina returns from the dead to help Cheryl with a troublesome spell (she even fails at dying!), crossover between the shows consisted of small "Easter eggs" like the fact that Sabrina carries an Archie lunchbox and thermos (Truong, 2019), though a much talked about "crossover" is when a character from *Riverdale*, Ben Button, appears in *CAOS* as a pizza delivery boy—whom Wardwell devours (@KinkleWhore, 2018; Aguilera, 2018; Fuster, 2018). *ET* reporter Leanne Aguilera interviews Roberto Aguirre-Sacasa, showrunner of *Riverdale* and director/writer/producer of *CAOS*, about the appearance of a *Riverdale* character on *CAOS*. He says, "It suggests a very deep, deep mythology where time and space bends. I love that kid. I'm sad that he keeps turning up and horrible things keep happening to him. [...] It seemed like it was pretty final, but yet there he is in Greendale. But in Greendale, everyone pops up—the dead don't stay dead long in Greendale." It is just a "suggestion" of a deeper mythology, a mythology which fans may want more of than just a suggestion. Lincoln Michel, in an essay called "Against Worldbuilding," argues that "world conjuring" over worldbuilding may offer readers/viewers a new way of seeing realities, and, I argue, queerer ones. Michel asserts, too, "it isn't a coincidence that the celebrated SFF 'worldbuilders' are Western writers, typically white, while imaginative writers from so many other cultures get lazily lumped together as 'magical realism.' Worldbuilding insists on a certain concept of supposedly logical 'realism' that pretends it is the only way to see the world." (Michel, 2017). Again, I might argue that the failure to create a "logical" (read: heteronormative) world in *CAOS* is an act of queering. Whether this ambiguity is deliberate on the part of Aguirre-Sacasa or not, I assert that it still falls under the category of queer failure, though I have strong doubts about the deliberateness of it, an issue I'll return to later. For now, back to Sabrina.

In many ways Sabrina seems set to sign the Book of the Beast and fully embrace her witch identity in the first two episodes, though, as I've stated before, the previews spoil that she won't be signing it. It seems that she will sign it under her own terms; she's a witch, but not a regular one. She tells Aunt Zelda she is going to let a familiar choose her instead of choosing from a catalog. She calls the traditional practice of choosing from a book "dehumanizing." Aunt Zelda retorts that familiars aren't human at all: "They're goblins taking the shape of animals" ("Chapter 1: October Country"). Sabrina persists, though, and goes into the woods to invite a familiar. In this early scene, Sabrina is progressing in the "path of night" but failing to adopt its oppressive traditions—questioning its authority to decide who gets equal treatment and who does not.

Later, Sabrina voices her "doubt" to her cousin Ambrose when he questions whether she has told her friends she will be leaving them. For many queer viewers, the pressure of the "grenade of truth" is palpable in this scene. Sabrina does not want to hurt her friends with the truth of her witch identity, or even a version of it (one in which she just tells them she is going to a private school). But Ambrose promises Sabrina, "You will belong in every sense of the word" ("Chapter 1: October Country"). It's hard not to read this as the promise of an LGBT community that will fully accept you after a long-enough period of not fitting in, or outright hostility/violence, free even, perhaps, of racism and ableism. Though that promise dissolves quickly, as the very next scene is one in which The Weird Sisters threaten and put a hex on Sabrina, making it clear that she won't be fully accepted. Now once-doubtful Sabrina seems even more sure of her decision to sign the book as she stands up to the sisters and insists she won't be bullied, "not in the woods, and not at the academy" ("Chapter 1: October Country"). Sabrina rushes off to the safety of her school (not her witch home) to hit the showers in the girls' locker room and wash off the hex. It's there that a link between Sabrina and Theo is made that never really goes away in the series, but also suffers from being a marginalized side-plot. Theo is a guest character; Lachlan Watson doesn't appear in the opening credits for the first two seasons of the show. But the link seems crystal clear in this first episode. Sabrina, free to be naked in the shower at school, and now in a towel, finds Theo crying in the girls' locker room.

Theo, crying, tells her, "They pulled up my shirt," and when he looks at the camera, he has a bloodied lip. Immediately Sabrina marches to the principal's office seeking justice, though Theo is now nowhere to be found. Sabrina tells the principal, "They pulled up her [sic] shirt because they wanted to see if she [sic] had breasts, to see if she [sic] was really a boy or a girl under there" ("Chapter 2: The Dark Baptism"). Sabrina spells it out for viewers and the principal: this isn't just bullying, it is transphobic violence. To connect Sabrina's struggle with her own identity in proximity in plot and scene to conflict with trans identity almost demands a queer reading of Sabrina's failure to fully identify as witch or mortal—though a problematic one in which Sabrina here doesn't just use her privilege to "help" Theo, but Theo is completely side-lined and unable to save himself. Sabrina serves as a straight-white-savior; Theo is represented as lacking the power to save himself. I'll speak more on this later, but it should be noted that at a later point in the series Sabrina's "helping" her mortal friends is portrayed as highly problematic, and her privilege of being able to move freely between her worlds, just temporarily dropping out of Baxter High, is directly addressed by the characters that are her closest friends.

Sabrina's "coming out" to Harvey, a few scenes later, is a major failure. First of all, Sabrina has put off telling her friends that she is a witch and/or that she is abandoning them until a week before her dark baptism. She provides no space for her friends to absorb this information, no room for discussion. Not that she needs to, but if it's some sort of acceptance she is looking for, she's setting herself up for failure. She decides to tell her boyfriend, Harvey, in the woods. She tells him that she's a witch, half-witch (this distinction is clarified by both Sabrina and Harvey in this conversation). Harvey begins to react poorly, starts to walk away, and immediately Sabrina turns him around and casts a forgetting spell on him, sealed with a kiss. Later she tells Ambrose that the whole thing was "wrenching." She also tells Ambrose that she told Harvey she was a witch, now dropping the "half" modifier. She calls the situation "impossible," but she does not regret the telling or the failure to tell. This type of failure is repeated throughout the series, a failure as Halberstam defines it, which "dismantles the logics of success and failure" (2011). There's not a way to see this event as success or failure when the logics of the witch world and the mortal world, or the gay and straight ones, are at play.

In the fifth episode of the first season, the Spellmans encounter a sleep demon that confronts them with their deepest fears. It's Sabrina who unwittingly released this demon by solving a complex puzzle that her dad created. After a spell has been cast to keep the demon from leaving the house to inflict pain on others and trapping the demon in an urn, the family celebrates around the kitchen table. Sabrina reveals that the code for cracking the puzzle was her mortal mother's name. Aunt Hilda is pleased when she says that it took a "half-witch, half-mortal" to solve the puzzle. But Aunt Zelda does not, saying, "Sabrina's duality almost got us killed!" The aunts often represent poles of commitment to the Church of Night. Zelda ascends to high-priestess while Hilda is excommunicated, though both of them often betray their own allegiances.

It turns out that the demon isn't actually trapped in the urn, only the house. She puts the family to sleep and walks their nightmares. In Sabrina's nightmare, dream-Zelda warns: "Hear this: Your attempts to conciliate your duality will only bring you pain and suffering" ("Chapter 5: Dreams in a Witch House"). This dark prophecy comes to pass in the dream, and later in real life. In the dream Sabrina comes out to Harvey on her wedding day, telling him, "I'm a witch." He responds positively this time, though his sense of déjà vu cues Sabrina to say that she wiped his memory the first time she told him. This time Harvey accepts her fully, promising to make her the "happiest woman and witch of all time." "He knows what I am and he loves me," Sabrina beams. But then, as Harvey's family bursts in to stop the wedding, Harvey starts choking Sabrina, saying, "It would have been fine if you just hadn't told me." Then he literally shoves her back into the closet, or here, an iron maiden, quoting the Old Testament: "Thou shalt not suffer a witch to live" (Exodus 22:18). This commandment, perhaps not coincidentally, echoes a later one in Leviticus which reads, "If a man lies with a male as with a woman [...] they shall surely be put to death" (Leviticus 20:13). The sleep demon appears and promises to release Sabrina if Sabrina will give her the spell to unlock the house. Sabrina chooses to stay in the dream, and in the iron maiden.

In "Chapter 9: The Returned Man," Sabrina is forced to reveal to Harvey that she is a witch. It's a long and complicated story involving necromancy, but when she tells Harvey, "I'm a witch," he again has a sense that this happened before. She again admits to wiping his memory. She does not really apologize for this memory wipe. In fact, it seems as if she believes Harvey will accept her. Harvey rejects her. That a form of the truth is out there seems somewhat successful, but the overall sense of this event is that of failure. It won't be the last time Sabrina fails at these reveals.

In the final episode of the first season, Roz and Theo confront her in the girls' bathroom. "Are you a witch?" Theo blurts out. "I wanted to tell you so many times," Sabrina "confesses" ("Chapter 10: The Witching Hour"). She's actually more outed than coming out here. In many ways, it's a recipe for disaster as Sabrina hasn't answered calls for weeks, just broke up with her boyfriend who was nearly killed in a mining accident, and when her friends ask her in this vulnerable moment if she is a witch or not, they don't even check the stalls for interlopers. But the confrontation seems gentle and kind, and her friends embrace her unconditionally. Of note, Sabrina also says that she is sorry for lying at this point. Sabrina doesn't really apologize much for her failures. She'll hide more from her friends in the future, and she'll keep messing things up even though characters in the privy along with viewers know that she's about to make a big mistake—maybe most obviously how she keeps using magic to help Harvey even though he has clearly said he doesn't want to be involved in magic at all. More on Sabrina's other failures in just a minute. But there is one more failure to come out in the second season.

There's a kind of coming-out narrative that circulates heavily in the LGBT community: first you come out to your close friends, or maybe your family because also maybe your family already knows, and then you gradually enlarge that circle as you feel comfortable or safe. Social media has added a new element to this progression, as changing your Twitter bio can also be part of a "public" coming out. And while this narrative helps queer the binary between "out" and "not out," it's not a complete picture. Many LGBT individuals find themselves coming out over and over again, each time they get a new job, are in a new social interaction, or just waiting for the bus listening to homophobic slights. In the second season, Sabrina starts to fully embrace her "duality" as half-witch, and half-mortal. She even becomes a kind of prophet, preaching "intermingling" between mortal and witch, perhaps to bring on a new kind of magical being of which she may be one of the first because she has developed powers that no witch or mortal known has demonstrated—the ability to heal, raise the dead, change the weather. But Sabrina doesn't change her Twitter bio to tell Greendale about her newfound pride in her identity. In fact, there's only one cell-phone scene in the whole series: the timeframe is fuzzy at worst, in a queer time and place at best. She throws a party at her house filled with mortals (many of them church-kids that Roz invited) and witches from the academy. Just as she is about to make a glorious step out of the closet by flying off the roof on a broomstick, Harvey bursts on the scene asking her not to do it and to come down and check out some witchy things he and Theo found in the mines. Sabrina walks back down from the roof, failing to reveal her identity to the crowd.

I'd like to return now to the link between Sabrina's failure to identify and the sub-plot of Theo's journey. I'm not the only one to make this link. In the first episode of the second season ("Chapter 12: The Epiphany"), the two characters' stories are linked again—Sabrina has to choose to go to The School of Dark Arts or Baxter High (or both) and Theo is choosing to try out for the boys' basketball team. Goldstein notices this "parallel" and writes:

> I guess we need this extremely no-duh parallel to make us see that sexism is oppressive and everywhere? I think it would actually be a lot more interesting if Sabrina's witch-world were the place with all the patriarchal bullshit and her mortal world were more progressive and modern. Because then there'd be real tension: Is she coming into her power by embracing her identity as a witch, or giving it up to abandon a place where the gains of feminism are more well-established and no anachronistic laws will prevent her from running for class president or whatever? But no one asked me, so here we are [Goldstein, 2019].

It's in this episode that Theo "comes out" and tells Roz and Harvey that he goes by Theo now, instead of his dead name. Roz and Harvey accept this joyfully, though later Roz has to have a little talk with Harvey about pronouns. It's a very positive and "successful" coming out, though inflected by a problematic "straight savior" plot line. It's only by Sabrina's spellwork that Theo is able to perform so spectacularly at the tryouts that he makes the team. It's in the confidence boost that Theo feels free to "come out" to his friends. Importantly, though, this coming out, and a later scene with Theo and his dad aren't functioning along the lines of the expected logic of coming out. Theo never uses the word "transgender," he simply informs his friends and dad what he would like to be called. And neither of the events are overblown "bomb-dropping," plot twist events. Theo's identity and relationships are largely the same as before and after these events. It helps, too, that Theo was called a young man before this event by Roz's grandmother and others. As viewers, we aren't surprised at all by some sort of false "big reveal."

"The closet" is a problematic paradigm, and one that the show could have adopted fully, as the showmakers did in *Riverdale* to a certain extent. The paradigm of coming out has served its purposes. Harvey Milk famously called the LGBTQ community to come out in his fight for equality. Though he may already have been aware of the problems with the metaphor, saying that if a bullet entered his brain it would be the bullet that destroyed "every closet door." This pressure to come out cost many people dearly, and it cost some much more than others, especially people of color. Eve Sedgewick's *Epistemology of the Closet* (1990) worked to place this paradigm in a dominant position in academia as well. Marlon B. Ross addresses the problems with this universalizing metaphor in "Beyond the Closet as Raceless Paradigm" (Johnson, 2005) arguing that the paradigm largely works for metropolitan gay men, but fails for just about everyone else.

Lachlan Watson, the actor who plays Theo, is outspoken about their role on the show, and encouraged the showmakers to avoid the pitfalls of the closet and show the fluidity and freedom between identities. "I talk so much about myself and my identity as a non-binary person and I think they listened, and if anything it helped them understand that labels aren't everything. [Theo] is on an ongoing queer journey, just like myself," they said in an interview, adding, "You don't have to label yourself so quickly, you don't have to just be one thing or another. Just like Sabrina choosing her own path of light and dark, you are allowed to forge your own path and you can do it brilliantly and independently" (Carlin, 2019). Watson, in their own life, has identified as transgender, now non-binary. They've been open about their top surgery but choice not to take hormones. "I had almost every queer or straight person in my life go, 'Wait, wait, wait, you didn't want to do testosterone, why are you doing top surgery? That's not how this works. You're doing this wrong'" (Carlin, 2019). This wrongness is a type of queer failure—failure to meet even "queer" expectations of what it means to be transgender or gender non-binary. And Theo's "not knowing" can be seen as a type of failure too, or at least being ok with not knowing, as the expected result is that he'll figure it out. But as Watson points out, "It's not as linear as the world sort of believes it is. It's not just jumping to Point A to Point B and then stopping. There really is no Point B, you just leap off Point A headfirst and just dive through the weird world of gender until you stop" (Carlin, 2019). In fact, in the show, Theo doesn't really officially identify as transgender, though Watson seems to interpret it that way. Theo just tells people he's Theo now, without label or explanation. Watson says, "We're telling a queer storyline, but we're telling it right—because they're listening to me" (Netflix, 2018). In a way, the writers are queer failing, too. It seems at first they wrote Theo as a trans character, but they put that aside and allowed for a kind of not-knowing. Perhaps the show's leaning toward world-conjuring instead of world-building is a kind of queer failure as well. In the *CAOS* world perhaps there isn't a clear movement from Point A to Point B, and the rules of the magical world may be unclear, or changing—fluid. And Sabrina, of course, is a vital part of that change and fluidity as she demonstrates that some of the expectations and traditions within the strange world of witchcraft are just not true, for her and others.

Sabrina's failure to come out or clearly identify certainly demonstrates queer failure. But what of her other failures? From the beginning Sabrina can be very successful at spells and magic, but also a spectacular failure, often doing "the one thing you aren't supposed to do." In the first episode Ambrose tells her to find a fortune-telling apple but to make sure it doesn't have a worm in it—she eats the one with the worm. She tries necromancy even though everyone says it's the one thing witches shouldn't mess with—she ends up turning her boyfriend's brother into a zombie. She's late for her dark baptism and fails at signing the Book of the Beast, with no real exit plan. She even wears white to a dark baptism—a wedding dress, which she also wears to a Halloween party, like *Mean Girls*' Cady Heron. She fires the only lawyer that can help her win her court case against Satan, though she "wins" the court case because she was baptized in the Roman Catholic Church—a witch "failure" unto itself. Hilda's participation in it gets her excommunicated from the Church of Night—she still plays into the devil's hand with the deal the court strikes that she'll attend the Academy of Dark Arts. She fails to recognize that mousy Ms. Wardwell, her favorite teacher, is possessed by the sexy Queen of Demons. She fails at Nick Scratch's offer to have a sexy witch boyfriend *and* a cute mortal one. At her witch school, she can't stand up to the hazing so she calls in her Aunts for help. She fails at getting a demon's real name so she can exorcise him—she thinks Maerceci, Ice-cream backwards, is his real name. She views that whole exorcism as a failure on her part, announcing, "How am I ever going to outwit the Dark Lord?" which Goldstein sharply points out is a failure to keep her secret plan a secret. She fails at resurrecting Harvey's brother, saving him from limbo, and then fails at returning his zombie body to the grave (Harvey ends up shooting his own brother). She fails at her first séance (mostly). She ends up signing her name in the Book of the Beast after all, which is a failure to not sign as she had planned. She volunteers as tribute for the Feast of Feasts and ends up serving her nemesis who is actually chosen as tribute. She does this to end the practice of cannibalism in the Church of Night, but the whole thing ends in a "long pig" food orgy. Speaking of orgies, she turns down the chance to participate with the sexiest group of witches on God's green earth, no judgment. But later, she sets a plan to lose her virginity at a witch bacchanalia and just ends up killing her (new) boyfriend's wolfmother. She fails to get her father's church reformations read by the dark pope. She also must be failing all her classes at mortal school and witch school because she never seems to attend class at either place and gets a free pass to show up only when she wants to. And then, toward the end of the second season, she tries to save her witch friends from witch-hunters (who apparently are Mormons but also angels) and ends up getting shot up like St. Sebastian. The holy arrows kill her, but she resurrects as Dark Phoenix Sabrina, where she does enjoy some success: raises the dead, gives sight to the blind, calms a storm. But then she gives all that power up by making a mandrake double of herself. At first we think she fails at creating the double, but it's actually a success. When she kills the double, and her powers, it fulfills the prophecy she was trying to avoid, bringing the return of sexy Satan himself, and Armageddon. Her elaborate plan to trap the devil in the puzzle her dad made fails too, and Nick ends up possessing the Dark Lord or the other way around (either way it's homoerotic AF). It also turns out (I think) that Sabrina isn't really half-witch, half-mortal at all, because her father is actually Satan, not a witch. And, luckily, Sabrina also fails at becoming her father's "consort," whatever that means.

Through all of these failures, though, Sabrina seems to come out as a kind of hero, and she seems completely unfazed by her failures, even welcoming them. In "Chapter 3: The Trial of Sabrina Spellman" she tells her family, "there are a lot of people facing their fears right now, fighting battles they know they're not gonna win. So if this is mine, well, then let's get it over with." Her failure demonstrates the type of queerness that Muñoz and others imagine, one in which a person finds themselves in a world but also to reject "mandates to accept that which is not enough" (Munoz, 2007), one that "disrupts dominant and hegemonic discourses" (Johnson, 2005).

Under Halberstam's definition, "failing, losing, forgetting, unmaking, undoing, unbecoming, not knowing may in fact offer more creative, more cooperative, more surprising ways of being in the world" (Halberstam, 2011). While more creativity and surprise is clearly ahead for the show, it seems that a more cooperative future could be possible as well. Throughout the first two seasons, Sabrina calls on a friend sometimes to help her, but largely does things on her own, often against the advice of her friends. Her failures, too, have consequences for them—the worst one probably being that Harvey had to kill his brother's zombie. But the failures also open up the possibility of collaborative world-changing. The mine accident lets Theo use his ability to communicate with his dead ancestor and go down into the mine to try to save the trapped miners. When the Greendale 13 are released because Sabrina won't sign her name in the Book of the Beast, Theo also keeps death at bay for himself and Roz. Roz is able to help in the mine accident as well, as she discovers "the cunning," an ability to see past, present, and future visions. Harvey's artistic skills end up sealing the gates of hell. A community comes together, too, to help cast the spell that will trap the Dark Lord in the puzzle. I wouldn't label these interactions as particularly "cooperative," but the final scene of the second season seems to promise a more cooperative future, the kind of disruption that only the banding together of all intersections of oppression can create. Sabrina, Roz, Theo, and Harvey are at Dr. Cerberus's bookshop. Sabrina sums things up, saying that she has realized she's not half-witch, half-mortal but "something else." And then she says, "You three saved the world this weekend" ("Chapter 20: The Mephisto Waltz"). The four take vows of friendship to work together even if the mission is "impossible" and might get them killed. The fight for the impossible is a fight in failure, but one worth pursuing. In this way, queer failure is also a call to fight together for social and political change, for conflict resolution, and the dissolution of structures and logics once believed to be indissoluble. Perhaps, too, shows and show makers that are willing to listen to queer voices on their teams, even handing over the reins to new voices and risking failure, are opening more creative, cooperative, and surprising ways of being in this world.

References

Aguilera, L. (2018, October 27). "'Chilling Adventures of Sabrina" Boss Explains 'Riverdale' Cameo!" *Entertainment Tonight.* https://www.etonline.com/chilling-adventures-of-sabrina-boss-explains-that-shocking-confusing-riverdale-cameo-exclusive.

Alexander, J. (n.d.). "Riverdale's Jughead Is No Longer Asexual, and That's a Problem for Fans." *Polygon.* https://www.polygon.com/tv/2017/1/26/14403700/jughead-riverdale-asexual.

Anderson, J. (2019, June 11). "Chilling Adventures of Sabrina Promotes Two Cast Members to Series Regulars." *Comicbook.com.* https://comicbook.com/horror/2019/06/11/chillingadventures-of-sabrina-season-3-cast-gavin-leatherwood-lachlan-watson/.

Betancourt, M. (2019, April 25). "How 'Riverdale' Turns Masculinity into a Queer Thirst Trap." *Electric Literature.* https://electricliterature.com/how-riverdale-turns-masculinity-into-a-queer-thirst-trap/.

Bowen, S. (2019, April 8). "Why Queer People Love 'Chilling Adventures of Sabrina.'" *Nylon.* https://nylon.com/chilling-adventures-sabrina-queer-people.

Brinkley, N. (2017, March 1). "#AroAceJugheadOrBuse: An Ace/Aro Jughead in Riverdale." *Book Riot.* https://bookriot.com/2017/03/01/aroacejugheadorbust/.

Burgett, B., & Hendler, G. (Eds.). (2014). *Keywords for American Cultural Studies* (Second edition). New York University Press.

Carlin, S. (2018, October 29). "Susie's Journey on 'The Chilling Adventures of Sabrina' Is an Honest Look at Being Non-Binary & That's Exactly What Lachlan Watson Wanted." *Bustle.* https://www.bustle.com/p/susies-journey-on-the-chilling-adventures-of-sabrina-is-honest-look-at-being-non-binary-thats-exactly-what-lachlan-watson-wanted-12965144.

Combs, C. (2018, October 20). "Pansexuality & Genderqueer Roles in 'The Chilling Adventures of Sabrina.'" *Black Girl Nerds.* https://blackgirlnerds.com/gender-sexuality-on-the-chilling-adventures-of-sabrina/.

Corcione, A. (2018, October 29). "Susie Doesn't Need a Label in 'CAOS'—Lachlan Watson Explains Why That's So Important." *Teen Vogue.* https://www.teenvogue.com/story/lachlan-watson-susie-putnam-chilling-adventures-of-sabrina.

Elizabeth, D. (2017a, January 25). "Cole Sprouse on "Riverdale's" Jughead and Asexual Representation." *Teen Vogue.* https://www.teenvogue.com/story/cole-sprouse-interview-riverdale-jughead-asexual-representation.

Elizabeth, D. (2017b, July 25). "Fans Accuse 'Riverdale' of Queer-Baiting Viewers." *Teen Vogue.* https://www.teenvogue.com/story/fans-accuse-riverdale-queer-baiting-viewers.

Fuster, J. (2018, October 28). " Sabrina' Surprise: Yes, THAT Dead 'Riverdale' Character Showed Up in Greendale." *TheWrap.* https://www.thewrap.com/sabrina-riverdale-greendale-ben-button/.

Goldstein, J. (2018, October 26). "Chilling Adventures of Sabrina Premiere Recap: Not a Girl, Not Yet a Witch." *Vulture.* https://www.vulture.com/2018/10/chilling-adventures-of-sabrina-season-1-episode-1.html.

Goldstein, J. (2019a, April 5). "Chilling Adventures of Sabrina Recap: You Wanna Be on Top?" *Vulture.* https://www.vulture.com/2019/04/chilling-adventures-of-sabrina-recap-part-2-episode-1.html.

Goldstein, J. (2019b, April 6). "Chilling Adventures of Sabrina Recap: 'Til Death Do Us

Part." *Vulture*. https://www.vulture.com/2019/04/chilling-adventures-of-sabrina-recap-season-2-episode-5-blackwood.html.
Halberstam, J. (2011). *The Queer Art of Failure*. Duke University Press.
Halberstam, J. (2005). *In a Queer Time and Place: Transgender Bodies, Subcultural Lives*. New York University Press.
Hale-Stern, K. (2018, November 5). "'Sabrina' Doesn't Know What to Do with Its Non-Binary Character." *The Mary Sue*. https://www.themarysue.com/sabrina-non-binary-character-susie-putnam/.
Hariri-Kia, I. (2019, June 3). "Lachlan Watson on Fighting for Queer Representation—On 'Sabrina' & in Everyday Life—EXCLUSIVE." *Elite Daily*. https://www.elitedaily.com/p/lachlan-watsons-gender-identity-breaks-the-binary-but-theyre-busy-breaking-the-internet-exclusive-17868495.
Idika, N. (2017, May 4). "Riverdale Let Down Fans with Its Lackluster LGBTQ+ Representation." *PopBuzz*. https://www.popbuzz.com/tv-film/features/riverdale-lgbt-representation/.
Johnson, E.P. (2005). "'Quare' Studies, or (Almost) Everything I Know About Queer Studies I Learned from My Grandmother." In E.P. Johnson & M.G. Henderson (Eds.), *Black Queer Studies: A Critical Anthology* (pp. 124–157). Duke University Press.
@KinkleWhore. (2018, October 26). **Raquan** on Twitter: "Ben button from riverdale appeared on sabrina #SabrinaOnNetflix #riverdale https://t.co/NTrUg3yb7Z. Twitter. https://twitter.com/kinklewhore/status/1056031116132532224?ref_url=https%3a%2f%2fwww.thewrap.com%2fsabrina-riverdale-greendale-ben-button%2f.
Lutkin, A. (2017, April 19). "Shannon Purser Comes Out as Bisexual After Getting in a Twitter Fight with Riverdale Fans." *Jezebel*. https://jezebel.com/shannon-purser-comes-out-as-bisexual-after-getting-in-a-1794449713.
McGrath, M.K. (2017, April 20). "Queer-Baiting, Explained, in Light of the Convo Surrounding 'Riverdale.'" *Bustle*. https://www.bustle.com/p/riverdale-queer-baiting-how-one-tweet-exposed-the-fan-conversation-we-need-to-pay-attention-to-52319.
Michel, L. (2017, April 6). "Against Worldbuilding." *Electric Literature*. https://electricliterature.com/against-worldbuilding/.
Muñoz, J.E. (2007). "Cruising the Toilet: LeRoi Jones/Amiri Baraka, Radical Black Traditions, and Queer Futurity." *GLQ 13*(2–3), 353.
Navar-Gill, A., & Stanfill, M. (2018). "'We Shouldn't Have to Trend to Make You Listen': Queer Fan Hashtag Campaigns as Production Interventions." *Journal of Film and Video 70*(3–4), 85–100.
Netflix (2018, October 26). "Chilling Adventures of Sabrina | Lachlan Watson's Casting Story." https://www.youtube.com/watch?time_continue=33&v=N6eY6EnRpKE&feature=emb_title.
Ouellette, L., & Gray, J. (Eds.) (2017). *Keywords for Media Studies*. New York University Press.
Platt, J. (2018, November 7). "Chilling Adventures of Sabrina Is a Big Queer Moment." http://www.mtv.co.uk/chilling-adventures-of-sabrina/news/chilling-adventures-of-sabrina-is-big-queer-moment-positive-lgbtq-representation.
Prance, S. (2018a, November 7). "Why 'Chilling Adventures of Sabrina' Is Groundbreaking for LGBTQ+ Representation." *PopBuzz*. https://www.popbuzz.com/tv-film/chilling-adventures-of-sabrina/ambrose-susie-gay-trans-non-binary-queer/.
Prance, S. (2018b, November 15). "'Riverdale' Needs to Stop Queerbaiting Its LGBTQ+ Audience." *PopBuzz*. https://www.popbuzz.com/tv-film/riverdale/queerbaiting-archie-joaquin-kiss-lgbt/.
Prance, S. (2019, February 7). "'Riverdale' Finally Centred Its LGBTQ+ characters but It Can Still Do Better." *PopBuzz*. https://www.popbuzz.com/tv-film/riverdale/recap-gay-lesbian-characters-bizzarodale/.
Reilly, K. (2018, November 14). "'Riverdale' Accused of Queerbaiting Over That Joaquin/Archie Kiss." *Refinery29*. https://www.refinery29.com/en-us/2018/11/216897/riverdale-queerbaiting-joaquin-archie-kiss.

Riesman, A. (2016, February 8). "Archie Comic Reveals Jughead Is Asexual." *Vulture*. https://www.vulture.com/2016/02/archie-jughead-asexual.html.

Sasso, S. (n.d.). "Lachlan Watson Reveals the Beauty of Top-Surgery Scars & Self-Care." *Refinery 29*. Retrieved January 14, 2020, from https://www.refinery29.com/en-us/2019/05/232331/lachlan-watson-top-surgery-scar-interview.

Sedgwick, E.K. (2005). *Epistemology of the Closet*. University of California Press.

Sobel, A. (2018, October 30). "The 'Chilling Adventures of Sabrina' Features Ice Cold Homophobia." https://www.advocate.com/commentary/2018/10/30/chilling-adventures-sabrina-features-ice-cold-homophobia.

Souza, G. (2019, April 11). "The 'Chilling Adventures of Sabrina' Representing the LGBT+ in the Mainstream." GCN. https://gcn.ie/chilling-adventures-sabrina-representation-lgbt-mainstream/.

Streeby, S. (2018). "Heroism and Comics Form: Feminist and Queer Speculations." *American Literature 90*(2), 449–459. https://doi.org/10.1215/00029831-4564382.

Truong, P., & Lundgren, A. (2019, April 8). "Did You Notice All These 'Riverdale' Easter Eggs in 'Chilling Adventures of Sabrina?'" *Cosmopolitan*. https://www.cosmopolitan.com/entertainment/tv/a24480796/riverdale-sabrina-easter-eggs/.

Yandoli, K.L. (2018, October 31). "Meet the Actor Who Plays Susie, the LGBT Character on 'Chilling Adventures of Sabrina.'" *BuzzFeed News*. https://www.buzzfeednews.com/article/krystieyandoli/chilling-adventures-sabrina-susie-lachlan-watson-lgbt.

Disability in *Chilling Adventures of Sabrina*

WHITNEY TIFFANY RENVILLE

I would like to acknowledge Dr. Mary McCall and Olivia Vogt, who generously took the time to read this essay and give their feedback. As always, I am thankful to my husband and my son for their patience and support.

This essay is dedicated to the memory of Elaine M. Firecloud.

John Milton, upon losing his sight, wrote, "To be blind is not miserable; not to be able to bear blindness, that is miserable" (2016, p. 680). Milton's observation provides a framework, three centuries old, for the way in which the contemporary social theory of disability creates a distinction between the physical impairment itself and the disabling conditions imposed on a body by society. In the first and second seasons of *Chilling Adventures of Sabrina* (*CAOS*), the viewer is introduced to a rhetorically familiar disability storyline in Roz's blindness, as well as two depictions of the perceived psychiatric disabilities of Tommy Kinkle and Jesse Putnam. In contrast to these commonly seen tropes, Sabrina's narrative provides a very different story of someone using her body to challenge societal norms and expectations—if Sabrina is also seen as a disabled person—diseased by her humanity, the way the witches see her, and incomplete. Judith Butler argues that "not only are we culturally constructed, but in some sense we construct ourselves," and it is this journey of blending her witch and human selves on which we follow Sabrina (Butler and Salih, 2004, p. 23).

There is a wealth of feminist literature that discusses the misstep of describing the female experience through the gaze of a male character. In the case of Roz, *CAOS* makes the misstep of treating Roz's blindness as something which makes Sabrina miserable. She and the other characters perceive Roz as broken. Roz, it can be argued, was on a journey which may have landed her in a philosophical space like her grandmother—who has accepted her cunning ability as a trade for her sight. Before this can happen, however, Sabrina steps in and Roz is able to have both her sight and her cunning. In contrast, it is Sabrina who we see going on the journey toward acceptance that we wish we saw Roz get to go on. As Sabrina goes further down this road, we see her body physically change—her hair becomes white after one encounter with a demon, and her clothing and make-up take on a more gothic appearance. She is physically scarred by the claws and arrows of her adversaries. Her outward appearance becomes more wanton and less like that of her human friends. She begins, instead, to represent what Bart Beaty calls the "token unattractive female" in the original *Archie* comics—in other words, a nonnormative body, one whose individuality has come at the cost of her traditional femininity (1992, p. 29). This is not to say that Sabrina ceases to be attractive to viewers, but rather that the changes in her appearance represent a change in *what* she is and what she is capable of. Jose Alaniz, in *Death, Disability, and the Superhero*, describes the double-bind of the "supercrip" character: a "wondrous figure" who "pays a heavy price—namely its humanity—for all the prominence and acceptance" (2014, p. 33), which is exactly what Sabrina does when she chooses to sign the Dark Book.

Sabrina outwardly carries the marks of her attempts to be a full witch, but her true victories are almost always the result of her craftiness as a human. She, like women in literature often labeled invalids, learns to use her body and "her illness as negotiation of agency" (Davidson, 2013, p. 6). She comes to possess a body of knowledge—because of her body—that is unique to her. Ultimately, she cannot be complete without accepting both sides of her nature, and the next hurdle for her is demanding that the other characters accept it as well.

This essay will ask the questions: what is the definition of disability in the Greendale universe, what social codes and norms are exposed by the disability experience in Greendale, and what is the take-away about what it means to have a disability for the viewing audience? Finally, I believe that *CAOS* can be read reparatively, as described by Eve Sedgwick. She writes, "wide-spread critical habits ... may have made it less rather than more possible to unpack the local, contingent relations between any piece of knowledge and its narrative/ epistemological entailments for the seeker, the knower, or teller" (2006, p. 124). I want, as Sedgwick does, to "try to hypothetically disentangle the question of truth value from the question of performative effect" (p. 129). The question becomes does *CAOS* show the viewer how "to connect knowing to knowing what to do," a necessity of reparative reading according to Sian Melville Hawthorne (2018, p. 160). In other words, is it possible to look at the *CAOS* characters from a social disability theoretical standpoint, and judge them by their potential performative effect? I will argue that while Roz especially represents the misguided "truth value" of traditional disability storylines, it is possible to extract some value on creating agency through disability from Sabrina's story.

What Is CAOS About?

CAOS debuted on Netflix on October 26, 2018. The character of Sabrina, a half-mortal half-witch teenage resident of the fictional town of Greendale, has been a part of the Archie universe since 1962. The early comic version of Sabrina appears with teased hair and tight sweaters: she represents a normative body in the way that Betty and Veronica do—she is attractive, able, and, upon first inspection, available. She first appears lounging in front of her television (Archie and Betty are on screen) surrounded by the accouterments of '60s teendom: records, snacks, and comic books, and declaring to the reader, "Everywhere I go the boys are simply wild over me! But you'll never catch me falling in love … that would mean I would lose my powers and become human … and that would be bad!" (*Archie's Madhouse*, #22, Oct. 1962). She is a cheerleader at Greendale High School, however, she does not interact with the Riverdale characters in her early appearances. While Sabrina bears all the physical attributes of a "normal" *Archie* girl, it is her abilities as a witch that could potentially render her more powerful than any of the mortal male characters, and that set her apart from the human girls. This early Sabrina storyline sets up the possibilities for seeing Sabrina as a nonnormative body. She is outwardly a glamorous specimen of normed beauty, but she is neither a complete witch or a complete mortal. Her powers as a witch embody what Jay Dolmage describes as an "intersection of sex, sexuality, and disability" (2014, p. 71). As a witch, Sabrina has great power and strength compared to the mortal males around her, and so her powers are portrayed as a dangerous rather than positive thing. Therefore, she must remain untouchable and alone. The difference between this Sabrina and the *CAOS* Sabrina is that 1962 Sabrina appears to be satisfied to have traded the possibility of love in exchange for keeping her powers.

In 1996, *Sabrina the Teenage Witch* premiered on NBC, and ran for seven seasons. Here, a live-action Sabrina is told she is half-witch by her guardian aunts on her sixteenth birthday. The fates of her warlock father and mortal mother are introduced, as is Salem the Cat, who speaks and often is a source of comic relief in the show. The idea of Sabrina maintaining a balance between her mortal and witch lives is the focus of the plot. She is not made to choose one path or the other. As a young witch, her spells often misfire with disastrous consequences. Sabrina begins the show with a crush on Harvey Kinkle, and eventually enters into a relationship with him. The two are revealed to be soulmates in the final season, and—quite literally—ride off into the sunset together. This version of Sabrina allows the character to have it all without having to choose between being powerful and being desirable to mortal males.

In 2014, Robert Aguirre-Saracasa and Francesco Francavilla revived Sabrina's character for *Afterlife with Archie*. Set in an alternate Riverdale following a zombie apocalypse, Aguirre-Sacasa and Francavilla's Sabrina is decidedly darker than previous incarnations, and is the first comic in the series to be aimed at an older audience with its Teen + rating (Arlington, 2013). Sabrina's primary role in *Afterlife* is minimal. She brings Jughead's beloved pet Hot Dog back from the dead, inciting the zombie apocalypse that dominates the storyline, but Sabrina herself disappears.

Aguirre-Sarcasa and Francavilla then introduced the graphic novel *Chilling Adventures of Sabrina*. In this version, Sabrina, the child of a warlock and a human woman, again must choose between life as a witch and life as a mortal. The storyline from the original comic is revived where Sabrina has to choose between being powerful and being wanted by human males. Becoming a witch means giving up her human boyfriend, Harvey. Sabrina's body is not considered to be "whole" by those around her, and in order to become whole, she must deny a part of herself. In this sense, she will always be broken and imperfect. Sabrina's aunts, Hilda and Zelda, reappear in the comic, and her cousin Ambrose is introduced. Salem the cat has a role as Sabrina's familiar. Sabrina's father, Edward, is ultimately revealed to be a treacherous character who had her mortal mother committed to an asylum. The Spellman family are followers of the Church of Night, which worships Satan as its higher power. Veronica and Betty appear as witches from a coven in Riverdale.

The television adaptation of *Chilling Adventures of Sabrina* introduces the characters of Theo Putnam and his family, and creates a different personality for Roz. In the print comic, Roz appears only briefly and as a rival with Sabrina for Harvey's affections. In the series, Roz is Sabrina's best friend, and only begins to date Harvey after he breaks up with Sabrina when she reveals she is a witch. The television version of Greendale is home to a more diverse population than previous incarnations. In particular, the writers have developed several pansexual and transgender characters, and there are actors of color in supporting roles. The show has, however, been criticized in online forums for its lack of commentary on race and misuse of Indigenous African and Diaspora magic and Indigenous American imagery. The casual, repeated use of the term "half-breed" is problematic. The same can be said about the show's inclusion of disabled bodies.

Who Has a Disability?

Contemporary disability study has been dominated by variations of two conflicting models: medical and social. In the medical model, disability is determined by diagnosis and is generally viewed as something that needs to be diagnosed and treated or fixed, which implies that the person with the disability is somehow broken. The idea that something requires fixing is directly tied, according to Snyder and Mitchell, to the question of whether or not the recipient is morally deserving, and has "precipitated the rise of ... empirical evaluations of the incapacitated body" (2006, p. 61). In this model, as Michel Foucault describes it in relation to the development of asylums, disability "would always be only in the order of organization and classification. It would not be a dialogue" (1965, p. 250).

In contrast, the social model is about the ways in which the idea of disability is constructed by society. Disability is not a physical state of being (that is an impairment), but rather the ways in which a body is restricted by societal norms. The social model draws attention to and offers criticism of the ways in which the physical act of seeing (in the case of Roz's storyline) is privileged in a culture. In the Greendale universe, sighted bodies move freely, whereas blind bodies are confined. Not only are they physically confined, but their experiences are further restricted by only having access to the information that the abled characters bring to them. Community and freedom of movement are the hallmarks of ableist privilege in Greendale.

Also vital to the analysis of disability in Greendale is Snyder and Mitchell's concept of narrative prosthesis, which asks the question does disability appear in the narrative "as a stock feature of characterization" or as "an opportunistic narrative device" (2001, p. 205)? Both of these forms of narrative prosthesis plague the *CAOS* storyline. That the use of disability as a situational plot device that can be fixed and then forgotten when a plot point is resolved, is plain in the storylines involving Roz's blindness and Uncle Jesse and Tommy's psychological differences. Using disability as a way of establishing a character trait—particularly a trait that is seen as weak or treacherous—is implied by Jesse when he accuses Roz of going blind because she has no faith in God. Ultimately, this is not true, but Roz believes it and this belief guides her actions for several episodes.

The portrayal of human disability is unique to the television version of *Chilling Adventures of Sabrina*. In *Twelve Cent Archie*, Beaty describes the town of Riverdale as a "1960s wish-dream of white privilege, and normative sexualities, where all difference could be banished and opportunities were eternally endless" (2017, p. 31). This is, in many ways, echoed in Roberto Aguierre-Sacasa's graphic novel version of Greendale, Sabrina's home. In *The Occult Edition*, the author places *CAOS* in the mid–1960s. The television series, however, is set in the present day. The comic being set before the passage of the Americans with Disabilities Act of 1990 or ADA would explain, then, the lack of building accommodations in the print Greendale, as well as perhaps the lack of visibility of disabled characters.[1] The characters who are disabled in the television show, however, are either non-disabled or completely absent in the print version. Most notably, Rosalind Walker—Sabrina's best friend in the show is, instead, her red-haired rival for Harvey Kinkle's affections in the comic. Graphic novel Roz makes only brief appearances, is sighted, and we never meet her family. In print, Greendale maintains many of the "normative wish-dream" attributes of a traditional *Archie* comic (Beaty, 2017, p. 31). The television show, instead, makes substantive efforts to include an entire population of "othered" bodies, including characters with disabilities. This is illustrated by the abundance of what Foucault calls "heterotopias," or places that challenge our notion of utopia and throw it back at us in mirror image, in the new *Sabrina*.

If 1960s Greendale is a utopia, a place that presents "society itself in perfected form" (1984, p. 3), then *CAOS* Greendale is rife with heterotopias, places that exist outside or operate within the utopia. There are "crisis utopias," like Greendale High and the Academy of Unseen Arts, where traditional teenage rites of passage take place. The word crisis is not a negative thing, rather it refers to places where people who are "in relation to society and to the human environment in which they live, in a state of crisis" can go to have that crisis (p. 4). Teenagers fit that description, and the Greendale stories have always primarily centered around teens. There can, however, also be heterotopias of deviation: places "in which individuals whose behavior is deviant in relation to the required mean or norm are placed" (p. 5), and the new Greendale gives life to these as well. Foucault specifically mentions rest homes and psychiatric hospitals as examples of utopias of deviation, and both are visited or alluded to in *CAOS*. Nana Ruth appears to be living apart from her family in some kind of assisted living facility. There is discussion of sending Uncle Jesse to an asylum. These kinds of heterotopias align with Snyder and Mitchell's concept of "cultural locations of disability," which they describe as places that "exist largely at odds with the collective and individual well-being of disabled peoples" (2006, p. 4). In this way, even the traditional crisis heterotopias in Greendale can become uncomfortable and even dangerous to characters who live outside of the heteronormative utopian Greendale, as the high school becomes to Theo when he comes out as transgender or to Roz when she becomes blind. The Academy of Unseen Arts is often not a safe place for Sabrina.

In order to discuss how disability is portrayed in the *CAOS* universe, we must first define what disability is in Greendale. Doing this can move the discussion back and forth across the length of the theoretical spectrum. With the first, we can define disability by more conventional medical standards—those things which have rendered a human body non-normative and relegated to the place of "other." Hawkes and Kanake lay out how this storyline commonly works in American and British fiction: "When a character with a disability arrives ... the narrative must halt in order to inspect them, generally to diagnose the disability, then to discuss the difficulties that have arisen from their inclusion, and finally to overcome their presence within the fictional world" (2019, p. 1468). The Walker women's blindness is the primary example of this.

Rosalind Walker (Roz) is first threatened with the possibility of blindness when she is visited by Jesse Putnam, who has been possessed by a demon ("Chapter 6: An Exorcism in Greendale"). Jesse tells Roz, "There is no faith in you, girl, so as punishment you shall be made blind," enacting the common trope of "disability as a sign from above" (Dolmage, 2014, p. 36). Roz's supposed lack of faith (in fact just a different kind of faith from her father's) is going to manifest itself upon her physical body in a way that the characters deem to be tragic. This prompts Roz to visit her grandmother Ruth in "Chapter 8: The Burial." Nana Ruth, who has been blind since she was around Roz's age, introduces Roz to the gift of the "cunning," which originated as a curse on the Walker family women by another Greendale woman they accused of being a witch. Grandma Ruth tells Roz, "I don't know if being cursed gave us the cunning or if it brought out what was already there." The Walker women's cunning abilities skirt several of Dolmage's disability tropes, including that of "disability as an object of pity or charity," and namely "disability as isolating and individualized" (2014, p. 42). She explains that, as one begins to develop the cunning, she will also lose her eyesight. Nana Ruth does not seem bothered by this, but Roz is willing to go to great lengths to prevent herself from going blind because she is already aware that the impairment brought on by blindness in Greendale is isolation. Nana Ruth lives alone and has "spent the better part of 30 years" sitting in her chair ("Chapter 10: The Witching Hour"). When she becomes blind herself, Roz stops attending classes and sequesters herself in the school library. Going to a separate school for the blind is mentioned several times. "In cultural narratives," Alec Cattell explains, "disability is frequently understood as something that is isolating and individual" (2018, p. 3). In Roz's case, she is following the example she has seen with her Nana Ruth.

The second category of disability in Greendale is instances of witchcraft which the human population perceives to be disability. Theo's uncle

Jesse Putnam is included in this category because he is perceived as being mentally ill and violent. His disability is only discussed in terms of what he might do to other people, for his actions are what make the disability visible to them. According to Theo, Jesse became sick while working in the mines owned by Harvey's father. "One day he just went crazy," Theo explains to Roz ("Chapter 15: Doctor Cerberus's House of Horror"). Jesse is kept medically sedated, and the Putnams explore the possibility of committing him to an asylum. For the time being, he is confined—literally—to his room, kept tied to his bed. He appears to be breaking out in sores and feverish. His mental illness has manifested itself on his body. In social disability terms, he loses the privilege of movement reserved for abled people. In fact, Jesse (or the demon possessing him) is clever enough to outwit Sabrina and Miss Wardwell on several occasions, but this is not acknowledged. By both mortal and witch standards, Jesse needs to be "fixed" so that he can be changed back into a form that is socially acceptable to them and does not require so much of their energy.

Harvey's brother Tommy also inhabits this area of acquired disability by medical standards because the mortals believe his condition to be the result of trauma and not of supernatural origin. When Tommy is killed in a mine collapse, Sabrina goes to purgatory to bring him back, unwittingly leaving his soul behind. At first, Harvey, who is oblivious to the interference of witchcraft in his brother's return, tells Sabrina that a doctor told him that "the collapse was a trauma ... he should be back to his old self—eating and talking—in no time" ("Chapter 9: The Returned Man"). This does not happen, and when Tommy attacks Mr. Kinkle in an attempt to defend Harvey, Mr. Kinkle declares that Tommy is "an animal. He's not my son" ("Chapter 9"). Aside from this single violent outburst, Tommy's trauma manifests itself through him not talking or eating, reacting but not attempting to initiate communication, and scratching at his reflection in the mirror. In the cases of Tommy and Jesse, violence is the perceived characteristic of mental illness most noted by the other characters, and it is their potential for violence that makes their disability visible to the other characters and allows the other characters to justify their being confined and isolated.

There is the possibility of a third category of disability in Greendale—those perceived to be weakened by virtue of their mortal attributes. The Weird Sisters, particularly Prudence, repeatedly call Sabrina a "half-breed," and tell her that her humanity makes her weak in comparison to the full-blood witches. Sabrina, instead, could be considered to be a disabled character by Dolmage and Hawhee's definition of *metis* or "adaptive intelligence" (Dolmage, 2014, p. 5). *Metis*—sometimes described as cunning, adaptability, or even street smarts—challenges the tradition in classical texts to privilege abled bodies over disabled ones or to erase disabled bodies altogether. The ways in which Sabrina uses her body, like Hephestus, "are evidence of a particular form of intelligence that Hephestus was said to symbolize ... his disability was his ability" (p. 366). She is rejected by the witch community, and often has to rely on her cleverness rather than her skills with witchcraft to resolve situations. Sabrina learns—in the sense of Seiber's concept of complex embodiment—to navigate the world through her disability. She gains a knowledge base that the other characters—witch and mortal—do not possess, and becomes identifiable as a person with a disability "by [her] possession and use of the knowledge gathered" as an inhabitant of her own othered society (2013, p. 8). As she gains understanding of herself as a whole person rather than two conflicting halves, Sabrina's body physically changes: her "very physicality and movement employs rhetorical tactics beyond language" (Johnson et al., 2015, p. 40).

This kind of transformation is also referenced by Seibers: "Sooner or later, whatever we think an object is, we come to esteem it not for what we think it is but for what it really is—if we are lucky" (2001, p. 750). Sabrina, perceived as vulnerable by her family and classmates at the Academy, begins to use her lack of witch blood as a way of establishing power among the other witches. In doing this, however, she must assume the role of what Glasberg calls an "undesirable female" in the Archie universe. In the early *Archie* comics, "all males appear to possess an individuality inasmuch as they are the choosers rather than the chosen. Only undesirable females have individuality and that comes from the fault of being unattractive and not being the object of choice by males" (1992, p. 31). In Sabrina's case, while her body remains normative, what she does with it provokes fear and revulsion from Harvey. *Metis* can also be characterized by difference of movement, both in body and in thought. Dolmage explains, "*Metis* is characterized by sideways and backward movement." For Sabrina, her witch powers give her the ability to move up and over that the mortal characters do not have. Although Sabrina uses it like a super-power, the mortals are disturbed when they see her levitate or fly in spite of the fact that her having the power is often to their benefit. She is now able to *do* more than her mortal friends, Harvey in particular. In this sense, Sabrina is disabled not by any lack of ability, but by how mortal society looks at her when she uses the ability.

This does not come without consequences. Sabrina does not choose to give up her relationship with Harvey. It is Harvey who breaks up with Sabrina when she admits to using witchcraft. Ending the relationship is Harvey's choice, but it is through the loss of this relationship that Sabrina gains agency. This move has been used in past incarnations of the *Archie* comics, as with the character of Ethel whose "individuality has been purchased at the cost of her feminine desirability" (Glasberg, p. 29). Of course, this is television, and so Sabrina does not become undesirable, just different. Her new-found agency draws the attention of Nick Scratch, who becomes her boyfriend. It should be noted that, in contrast to this trope, Sabrina's outward appearance actually becomes more gothic as she becomes more insistent on identifying with both sides of her nature, but as Dolmage argues, for the female body, "any departure from the bodily norm is seen as potentially 'crippling'" or "monstrous" (p. 70).

Seibers, however, cautions us, "it is easy to mythologize disability as an advantage. Disabled bodies are so unusual and bend the rules of representation to such extremes that they must mean something extraordinary" (2001, p. 745). Viewing Sabrina as disabled treads dangerously on the edge of characterizing her as what has been termed the "supercrip" by Robert McRuer, who defines the term as disability being represented as "an adversity over one must triumph" (2018, p. 20). Dolmage describes the trouble with the supercrip in popular culture is its use as a way to mitigate audience fears that they, too, could become disabled. The audience is relieved of the work of having to "focus on the disability, or challenge the stigma that the disability entails, but instead focuses attention towards the 'gift'" (2014, p. 39). This most certainly happens with Roz, whose sight is returned through Sabrina's intervention, but is able to retain her "cunning" abilities. Following this turn of events, there has been little growth in Roz's character—she is chosen by Harvey after his break-up with Sabrina and loses her agency as an independent female (as Glasberg describes). The focus of her character is now her "cunning" exclusively. Whether or not Sabrina represents the "supercrip" stereotype is debatable, since her attempts at using witchcraft often have disastrous outcomes and are the result of being manipulated by The Dark Lord and Lilith.

What Social Codes and Norms Are Exposed by Disabled Characters?

In his 2001 article "Disability in Theory: From Social Constructionism to the New Realism of the Body," Tobin Siebers observes, "Disability exposes with great force the constraints imposed on bodies by social codes and norms" (p. 740). As previously mentioned, human disability in Greendale is punished with confinement and isolation. Roz, her Nana Ruth, Jesse Putnam, and Tommy Kinkle's bodies all become physically confined. The idea of death as being preferable to living with a disability—or the "kill-or-cure" trope as described by Dolmage, is promoted in the storylines of the latter three characters (p. 34). Following his uncle's passing, Theo says, "Honestly, maybe it's better. He would've rotted away in there. At least he's free now" ("Chapter 6: An Exorcism in Greendale"). If Jesse had lived, Theo and his father would have knowingly sent Jesse to an asylum where Theo admits he would've rotted away. His disability made him dangerous, and the solution—before his death—would have been to remove him from the community entirely.

In Roz's storyline, her individuality as a person with impairment is overshadowed by the reactions of her non-disabled peers, thus creating a world of disability all around her. Roz not only becomes blind, blindness becomes all that is Roz—and rather than allow her character to develop as a person without sight, her disability is depicted as so unbearable that Sabrina must intervene and "fix" her friend. "Members of a society may fear and even resent people with disabilities based on a fear of becoming disabled themselves," and in this case Sabrina is directed to "heal the blind" in order to strengthen her own powers (Reid-Cunningham, 2009, p. 106).

Previous research has addressed the pro-feminist and queer-positive elements in Sabrina, but less so the subject of disability. In the Greendale universe, it is acceptable to be a powerful woman (under certain circumstances), to be transgender (within Sabrina's circle of friends), and to worship Satan. These storylines serve to bring characters together. Yet, when Roz goes blind, she becomes isolated from her friends. While her exile in school appears to be self-imposed, it can be argued that she is moved to this decision by the accommodations—or lack thereof—around her. Greendale does not appear to have much in the way of assistive technology. Hawkes and Kanake discuss how, in fiction, a disabled character's storyline will become "about disability and not a story that includes a character who has a disability" (2019, p. 1464). This is what happens in the case of Roz. When Roz becomes blind, she can no longer navigate the high school, and no one seems moved to assist her in doing so. Everything else about her—the potential romance with Harvey, her book club—gets pushed aside to make room for her blindness, which then becomes the only thing about her that is important to the other characters. Likewise, her grandmother is never seen outside of her nursing home room. Nana Ruth's entire purpose in the story is to explain what is happening to Roz. When the explanation is complete, her character passes on and disappears from the narrative.

While Nana Ruth, Jesse, and Tommy all "escape" their disabled lives through death, Roz instead begs Sabrina to return her sight through a spell. Roz falls prey to the dominant view of disabled bodies as "'lacking,' and in need of repair if a 'good' life is to be made possible" (McLaughlin and Fountain, 2014, p. 76). Sabrina (fresh off of healing Ambrose's wounds, thus already fulfilling that piece of the Dark Bargain) obliges Roz through a spell, telling her "all you gotta do is wash your eyes out" with water that Sabrina has cast a spell on ("Chapter 18: The Miracles of Sabrina Spellman"), implying that Roz is not only disabled by her blindness but also made unclean by it. Roz echoes this belief when her sight returns and she tells Aunt Hilda, "Sabrina de-cursed me" ("Chapter 18"). Roz is imbued with "the cunning" at this point, which should make way for her to embody and enact *metis*. She, however, lacks the qualities of *metis* according to Hawhee in that she has no "mode of negotiating agonistic forces" without her sight (2004, p. 47).

In the witch world, where Sabrina arguably embodies non-normality, isolation is again a repercussion of disability. Sabrina is repeatedly told that she is the only one of her kind and that she is not meant to be at the Academy for the Unseen Arts. Aside from Sabrina, there are no other disabled bodies, although witches of many gender identities and races seem to belong there. Ultimately, Sabrina is labeled by the other witches not because her powers are deficient compared to theirs, but simply because her blood is different. As the series progresses, the Church of Night's patriarchal nature is further exposed, and—as Cheu asserts—both "disease and woman form threats to the dominant paradigm of masculinity" (2015, p. 79). Sabrina, as a diseased woman in the witch world, is doubly threatening. Sabrina embodies the social theory concept of disability vs impairment. In spite of her ability to outshine the witches and protect the mortals with her "diseased" blood, she is disabled by their attempts to isolate her and restrict her use of her body and abilities.

CAOS' *Chaotic Message*

Ria Cheyne writes, "The narratives circulating in popular culture play a significant role in shaping wider understandings of disability and impairment" (2012, p. 117). The depiction of disabilities in *CAOS* provides multiple perspectives from which the audience might explore the nature and meaning of what it means to have a disability. But what does the viewing audience learn about disability based on these representations? This depends on who the audience believes is disabled. The same societal constraints are placed on Sabrina as are on the other characters with disabilities: she is isolated from alternately the human or witch community, she is treated as though her mixed blood is a sickness. This difference causes the witch community to treat her as someone who is diseased, and therefore—as the Greendale universe requires—she needs to be either fixed and made like them or destroyed. If Sabrina has a disability, then the message is one of someone exploring her agency, and displaying *metis* in her ability to outwit the full-blood and more experienced witches who see her as less than.

Sabrina exemplifies "the disabled body's vacillating degree of incompatibility with its ever-shifting material surroundings" (Cleary, 2016). In *CAOS*, Sabrina's body moves back and forth between two school settings—Greendale High School and Blackwood Academy—and represents a non-normative state in both. She embodies a change in graphic heroines over the latter half of the 20th century and beginning of the 21st in which "transgressive representations of the female body re-code the female body in comics not to satisfy the male gaze, but rather to represent a less glamorous female body experience" (Diamond and Poharic, 2017, p. 408). Sabrina gets sweaty, she gets bloody, we see her flesh torn open. Season 2 ends decidedly with Sabrina in control, and on her way to save her boyfriend. In this case, her warlock boyfriend is comfortable with being saved by a female.

Nana Ruth, Uncle Jesse and Tommy are medical disability model examples of what it means to have a disability. The human residents of Greendale see Tommy and Uncle Jesse as disabled because they do not recognize the presence of witchcraft. The changes they exhibit are assumed by the mortals be medically based, and the mortals act accordingly by trying to "fix" their family members through medical interventions because "lodged in the medical model is not only the fantasy that disability can be easily eradicated through the joint miracle of a doctor's skillful use of a scalpel and a patient's positive thinking" (Cleary, 2016). Unfortunately, all three fall victim to the trope that they are better off dead than living with their disabilities. Only Roz survives because Sabrina is able to return her sight. This is ironic, of course, because Tommy already is dead. "By othering people with disabilities, the inevitability of one's own corporeal vulnerability can presumably be ignored" (Ahlvik-Harju, 2015, p. 225). Therefore, to "other" Tommy is to dismiss mortality.

Both Tommy and Jesse are completely without agency, and their bodies no longer belong in their homes or in the human world. Jesse has to be tied down to keep him from hurting himself or anyone else. He is, in effect, already institutionalized. Tommy no longer interacts with anyone around him, except when their father threatens Harvey. Then Tommy also reacts with violence. What the witches know is a loss of a soul, the humans believe is a loss of mental capacity. In both cases, the response is to first attempt to change him back and then to remove him altogether.

Equating disability with a lack of faith or soullessness is a common trope used in *CAOS*. This convention of "disability as internal flaw" describes the body by "accentuating its abnormality or exoticness (to) allow for insinuations of internal deviance" (Dolmage, 2014, p. 41). This is extremely problematic in the portrayal of Roz, since she is also one of a minority of Greendale residents who is a person of color. Although the storyline would have us believe that Roz was never marginalized before her blindness, she is exoticized in a number of ways, for example, with her "cunning" abilities, and that her family appears to be members of some extremely strict religion.

It is the portrayal of the Walker women that is given the most shallow treatment within the show, but that also has the most potential to show non-normative bodies in a recontextualized sense. Although the Walker women's storyline follows the familiar tropes of being better off dead (Nana Ruth) and needing—in fact, begging—to be "fixed" (Roz), previous plotlines where Sabrina has "fixed" something through magic have ended with something going terribly wrong, and this leaves open the possibility that Roz's experience with disability might not yet be resolved.

For the time being, however, with the break-up between Harvey and Sabrina opening the door for a romance between Harvey and Roz, the show has followed a less progressive convention of teen romance literature "in which her pursuit of a nondisabled and 'healthy' male love interest parallels and positively affects her process of 'getting well'" (Elman, 2012, p. 175). Elman calls this genre "teen sick lit." Although in-line with teen romance literature, sick-lit is in opposition to more contemporary comics where Elman continues that, in teen romance, "Characters with disabilities or diseases are often desexualized within dominant culture" (2014, p. 186). Roz becomes non-sexual. While her appearance becomes more sensual, Sabrina maintaining her virginity remains a plot point. It is Roz's relationship with Harvey that can potentially defy the conventions of sick lit, and "offer significant opportunities to challenge negative stereotypes around disability" (Cheyne, 2013, p. 37).

For the time being, however, the disabled characters serve a function as plot devices rather than having active roles in the plot, in accordance with Snyder and Mitchell's metaphor of narrative prosthesis. Roz, Jesse, and Tommy are all part of a storyline that has Sabrina manipulated into performing the rituals that will begin an apocalypse. She believes that they are examples of *her* witchcraft capabilities, but—in fact—the Dark Lord and Lilith have put her up to healing the blind, performing an exorcism, and raising the dead. Only Sabrina herself gains agency as she establishes herself among the witches. In order to regain their agency and again become "players," the mortal disabled characters have to lose their disabilities or be removed from the storyline.

The Trial of Sabrina Spellman

Disability, according to Diamond and Poharec in their examination of Harley Quinn in the Batman universe (2017), is often portrayed in comics in terms of freaks, outcasts, post-humans, and medicalized others:

> Which bodies are permitted depiction as heroic or innocent, as antagonist or distraction, as expendable or not, and how does their representational embodiment determine their casting? To use the character formula established by superhero comics, the question then becomes: who is the hero, the super villain, the bystander (which often includes the sidekick or love interest), the common criminal? [p. 407].

The bodies in *CAOS*, however, are complicated not only by the social constraints of disability, but also because they are teenagers and are in conflict with not only the adult world, but also with the crisis (as Foucault labeled adolescence in need of a heterotopia) of their own changing bodies. McLaughlin and Fountain describe the teenage body as that person's "body project" (2014, p. 84). This concept is echoed in Elman's description of teen "sick lit" in which the heroine's body has to change (grow up, get better) in order for her to get the guy. Sabrina and her friends are all involved in their own individual body projects. Problems with depictions of disability arise when one character (namely Sabrina) interferes with another's project. Then we are returned to Milton: disability is made unbearable by Sabrina's refusing to bear it.

CAOS does both a very good and very poor job of challenging the tendency to "presume that there is one normative body (white, male, hetrosexual, middle-class, abled) that is neither labeled 'cultural' or 'signifier'" (Johnson et al., 2015, p. 40). In part, the charm of the series is that the central characters are just kids, normal kids in the crisis of being teens with a variety of non-normative bodies, in their respective human and witch worlds. Ultimately, though, *CAOS* fails to challenge the audience through the stories of Nana Ruth, Tommy, and Jesse that end in the familiar "cure-or-death" trope. There is still an opening for Roz's character to re-develop as a blind woman, but it is questionable, had the series continued, whether the writers would have taken the opportunity given that her blindness was presented as a problem for Sabrina to fix, and—once fixed—the "problem" was deemed resolved. This returns us to Butler's question whether it is possible to derive sustenance or joy from a culture that doesn't acknowledge you. In looking for ways to find joy in *CAOS*, I see multiple opportunities to present Sabrina as someone whose body increasingly becomes the platform for her inner "practicality, success, or resourcefulness," as Hawhee defines *metis* (2004, p. 46), however, the show fails to use them as such, choosing instead to further isolate Sabrina from her family and peers (albeit as their supreme ruler). Supernatural powers are neat, but real sustenance will be found in a story about a girl whose body teaches her to be cunning, and whose cunning establishes her as part of something rather than an exile from it or a ruler over it.

NOTE

1. The Americans with Disabilities Act of 1990 mandates that public places, including public schools, be accessible to persons with disabilities.

REFERENCES

Aguirre-Sacasa, R. (Creator) (2017). *Chilling Adventures of Sabrina.* Warner Brothers Television. Retrieved from https://www.netflix.com/watch/80230071?trackId=200257859.
Aguirre-Sacasa, R., Hack, R., & Morelli, J. (2019). *Chilling Adventures of Sabrina: Occult Edition.* Archie Comic Publications, Inc.
Ahlvik-Harju, C. (2015). "Disturbing Bodies—Reimagining Comforting Narratives of Embodiment through Feminist Disability Studies." *Scandinavian Journal of Disability Research 18*(3), 222–233. doi: 10.1080/15017419.2015.1063545.
Alaniz, J. (2014). *Death, Disability, and the Superhero: The Silver Age and Beyond.* University Press of Mississippi.
Archie Superstars (2014). *The Complete Sabrina the Teenage Witch: 1962–1965.* Archie Comic Publications, Inc.
Arlington, J. (2013, October 18). "World War R: New Comic Pits Archie and Friends Against the Undead." Retrieved from https://www.npr.org/2013/10/18/236230146/world-war-r-new-comic-pits-archie-and-friends-against-the-undead.
Beaty, B. (2017). *Twelve-Cent Archie.* Rutgers University Press.
Butler, J., & Salih, S. (2010). *The Judith Butler Reader.* Blackwell.
Cattell, A. (2018). "'Hopefully I won't be misunderstood': Disability Rhetoric in Jürg Acklin's Vertrauen ist gut." *Humanities 7*(3), 71. doi: 10.3390/h7030071.
Cheu, J. (2015). "Blind Female Gaze." In *Problem Body: Projecting Disability on Film.* Ohio State University Press.
Cleary, K. (2016). "Misfitting and Hater Blocking: A Feminist Disability Analysis of the Extraordinary Body on Reality Television." *Disability Studies Quarterly 36*(4). Doi: 10.18061/dsq.v36i4.5442.
Davidson, M. (2013). "Introduction: Women Writing Disability." *Legacy 30*(1), 1. Doi: 10.5250/legacy.30.1.0001.
Diamond, A., & Poharec, L. (2017). "Introduction: Freaked and Othered Bodies in Comics." *Journal of Graphic Novels and Comics 8*(5), 402–416. Doi: 10.1080/21504857.2017.1355833.
Elman, J. (2012). "'Nothing feels as real': Teen Sick-Lit and the Condition of Adolescence." *Journal of Literary & Cultural Disability Studies 6*(2), 175–191. Doi: 10.3828/jlcds.2012.15.
Foucault, M. (1965). *Madness and Civilization.* Random House.
Foucault, M. (1984, October). "Of Other Spaces: Utopias and Heterotopias." *Architecture, Movement, Continuity,* 1–9.
Garland-Thomson, R. (2017). *Extraordinary Bodies: Figuring Physical Disability in American Culture and Literature.* New York: Columbia University Press.
Glasberg, R. (1992). "The Archie Code: A Study in Sexual Stereotyping as Reflective of a Basic Dilemma in American Society." *The Journal of Popular Culture 26*(2), 25–32. Doi: 10.1111/j.0022-3840.1992.260225.x.
Hawhee, D. (2004). *Bodily Arts: Rhetoric and Athletics in Ancient Greece.* University of Texas Press.
Hawkes, L., & Kanake, S. (2019). "Structural Boundaries That Affect the Representation of

Gender and Disability in Works of Fiction from the United States and United Kingdom." *Gender, Place & Culture* 26(10), 1459–1471. doi: 10.1080/0966369x.2018.1553855.
Hawthorne, S.M. (2014). "'Reparative reading' as Queer Pedagogy." *The Journal of Feminist Studies in Religion* 34(1), 155–160.
Johnson, M., Levy, D., Manthey, K., & Novotny, M. (2015). "Embodiment: Embodying Feminist Rhetorics." *Peitho Journal* 18(1), 39–44.
Mclaughlin, J., & Coleman-Fountain, E. (2014). "The Unfinished Body: The Medical and Social Reshaping of Disabled Young Bodies." *Social Science & Medicine*,120, 76–84. Doi: 10.1016/j.socscimed.2014.09.012.
McRuer, R. (2018) *Crip Times: Disability, Globalization, and Resistance.* New York University Press.
Milton, J., & Graham, J.J.G. (1972). *Autobiography of John Milton; or, Milton's Life in His Own Words.* Folcroft Library Editions.
Mitchell, David T., and Snyder, Sharon L. (2001). *Narrative Prosthesis: Disability and the Dependencies of Discourse.* University of Michigan Press.
Parker, Robert Dale (2020). *How to Interpret Literature: Critical Theory for Literacy and Cultural Studies.* Oxford University Press.
Reid-Cunningham, A.R. (2009). "Anthropological Theories of Disability." *Journal of Human Behavior in the Social Environment* 19(1), 99–111. Doi: 10.1080/10911350802631644
Sedgwick, E.K. (2006). *Touching Feeling: Affect, Pedagogy, Performativity.* Duke University Press.
Shakespeare, Tom. (2016). "Just What Is the Disability Perspective on Disability?" *Hastings Center Report* 46(3), 31–32.
Siebers, T. (2001). "Disability in Theory: From Social Constructionism to the New Realism of the Body." *American Literary History* 13(4), 737–754. Doi: 10.1093/alh/13.4.737.
Siebers, T. (2010). *Disability Aesthetics.* University of Michigan Press.
Snyder, S., and Mitchell, D. (2006) *Cultural Locations of Disability.* University of Chicago Press.
Stabile, C.A. (2009). "'Sweetheart, This Ain't Gender Studies': Sexism and Superheroes." *Communication and Critical/Cultural Studies* 6(1), 86–92. Doi: 10.1080/14791420802663686

"First as tragedy, then as farce"
The Chilling Adventures of Sabrina and Satanic Moral Panic

BRETT PARDY

The *Chilling Adventures of Sabrina* (*CAOS*), following *Riverdale* in Archie Comics' attempts to break away from the company's clean-cut image, embraced imagery and themes drawn from occult and Satanic themed horror. In "Chapter 1: October Country," Sabrina receives a vision after biting into an evil apple, the malum malus, of witches hanging from a tree being consumed by flames. Satan himself steps out from within the tree, seconds before Sabrina is snapped out of this vision by spitting out the apple. The horror tropes help to clearly differentiate the show from the popular sitcom *Sabrina the Teenage Witch*, which ran for seven seasons between 1996 and 2003. While *Sabrina the Teenage Witch* drew inspiration from the witches of *Bewitched* (1964–1972), who used magic to navigate various misadventures in suburbia, *CAOS* draws inspiration from *Rosemary's Baby* (1968), where witches conspire to serve Satan. The plot of the first two seasons focuses on Sabrina's initiation into the world of her local witch coven of Satanists, the Church of Night. The Church of Night serves as a malleable representation of various hierarchical institutions, allowing *CAOS* to use Satanism to critique contemporary religious institutions.

Since *Rosemary's Baby*, American popular culture's understanding of Satanism has gone through a macabre feedback loop, where popular culture depictions fueled imaginings that such terror could exist in reality. Subsequent pop culture must now grapple with not only remixing and commenting upon Satanic horror tropes, but also with how these tropes were mobilized and weaponized in the 1980s as a moral panic fueled by the nascent New Right. One of *CAOS*'s strongest features is how it engages with Satanism not to perpetuate moral panic, but rather to investigate, expose, and critique the underlying attempts to restore traditional authorities which initiated the 1980s Satanic moral panic.

Referring to the differences between the regimes of Napoleon I and Napoleon III, Karl Marx wrote that history occurs "the first time as tragedy, the second time as farce" (1852/2005, p. 7). This remark also describes *CAOS*'s relationship to Satanism, albeit in this case the farce is intentional rather than inadvertently trying to restore the past. From 1980 to the early 1990s, the United States experienced a moral panic around alleged secret Satanic cults abducting, abusing, and/or murdering children. Tragically, hundreds of people were charged, thousands of children experienced suggestive questioning which coerced them to admit false stories of abuse, and several people received lengthy prison sentences (Nathan & Snedeker, 1995; Rodriguez McRobbie, 2014). For example, in 1991, Frances and Dan Keller of Austin, Texas, were sentenced for sexually assaulting children to 48 years in prison and served 22 years before being released after the medical expert who testified in the case admitted making a mistake (Rodriguez McRobbie, 2014).

Typical Satanic ritual abuse accusations included animal and child sacrifice, cannibalism, and orgies, all of which are featured in the Satanic world of *CAOS*. However, unlike how *Riverdale* handled its depiction of the related 1980s moral panic over fantasy tabletop role-playing games, *CAOS* does not use these elements merely to shock. *Riverdale*'s Gryphons and Gargoyles plays off fears the fantasy role-playing tabletop game *Dungeons & Dragons* could lead to suicide and murder (Laycock, 2015). *CAOS* could have mined the lurid fears of the Satanic panic to create the Church of Night. Instead, *CAOS* offers a subversive vision of Satanism. Despite maintaining the visual elements, the rituals are remixed. The Satanists mostly do not prey upon the mortal world, but keep their violence to within the magic community. There are only hints of violence against the mortal world, such as when under a demon's spell, Sabrina's aunt Zelda dreams Satan is coming to dinner and prepares his favorite dish, "roast child" ("Chapter 5: Dreams in a Witch House"). Satan refuses to eat it because she used a child from the Church of Night and not a mortal. Witches do not aspire to install Satan as ruler over the mortal plane, but instead pursue a primarily isolationist policy, much to Sabrina's dismay. The Church of Night does not attempt to recruit, as the ability to use magic is genetic.

While versions of Satanism and other occult religions are practiced in the real world (none of which involve anything approaching ritual torture or murder), the world of *CAOS* does not borrow from these traditions, beyond a few symbolic elements like the pentagram and statue of the goat-headed demon Baphomet. Instead, many forms of Satanic worship in the world of *Sabrina* are carnivalesque inversions of Christian practices.

Characters replace "God" with "Satan" in common phrases like "Thank Satan" or "Satan Bless Us, Everyone." Sabrina participates in a "Dark Baptism" and knows the "13 Commandments." The head of the Churches of Darkness resides, like the Catholic Pope, in Vatican City and is addressed as the "anti-Pope." The theology of the Church of Night consists of simultaneously lurid Satanic tropes and versions of recognizable Christian practices. Yet despite Satan being a character who interacts with others in the show, the emphasis in religious practice is not on dogma passed down by sacred absolute authority. Instead, *CAOS* uses Satanism as a farce to pull back the curtain on how people in positions of power institute particular practices for particular reasons. Michel Foucault (1976/1990) emphasized that it is not enough to explore a specific discourse, but to investigate "the will that sustains ... and the strategic intent that supports" (p. 8) these discourses. To explore importance of the Church of Night is not just how it uses the mixture of Satanic tropes and Christian ritual, but to figure out how that combination expresses *CAOS*'s "strategic intent," a main theme of challenging tradition. Taking the discourse of Satanism from two locations, the 1980s American moral panic and *CAOS*, I demonstrate how the discourses are deployed in ways that create tragedy, and then farce.

Satanism as Tragedy: American Moral Panic

While the panic would not begin until the 1980s, the roots of the Satanic moral panic stretch back more than a decade earlier. Historian Philip Jenkins (2008) describes a "decade of nightmares" that killed the optimism and potential radicalism of the late 1960s youth counterculture and birthed a reactionary new form of conservativism. Jenkins' overall thesis is that the shift in American culture from the 1960s to the 1980s required a pessimistic view of human nature, in opposition to the 1960s counterculture's emphasis on love. Instead, Jenkins argues that Americans increasingly saw danger lurking both abroad and at home, and that discussion of the causes of these dangers flattened out nuance and lapsed back into simplistic explanations of human failings.

Stuart Hall et al.'s *Policing the Crisis* (1978) provides a framework for understanding why moral panics occur. Hall et al. locate the 1960s counterculture, shared by both Britain and the United States, as a crisis of hegemony. A new social emphasis on the pursuit of material pleasures strongly contradicted the 1950s consensus of conservative social values, internalized authority, and "respectability." In addition to the 1960s counterculture's political upheavals over the pursuit of pleasures, 1973–1975 saw a major economic crisis in both Britain and the United States, with simultaneous high unemployment and high inflation. Hall et al. (1978) argue that rather than the complexity of discussing structural issues, the simpler narrative put forward by conservative interests of a moral panic about a clear, external enemy, created by the decline in "values," won the public debate.

The 1980s lent itself to a climate ripe for moral panics (of which Satanic ritual abuse was just one among many) as it was a period of dramatic restructuring of the American way of life. President Ronald Reagan and his advisors introduced a new economic vision for the United States, where the economy should be left up to the "free market." Deregulation removed the rule which banned networks' entertainment divisions from running content which appeared as new, which allowed such a television program as *Devil Worship: Exposing Satan's Underground* to be aired (Hughes, 2017). Reagan's "new right" formed a coalition between believers in neoliberal economics and evangelical Christians. The two shared a disdain for liberal rights movements of the prior two decades: neoliberals because of fear of left-wing economic policies, and evangelicals because feminism, the civil rights movement, and the gay rights movement threated the white hetero-patriarchy that ordered their way of life. The New Right pushed the idea that America faced economic problems because it had lost its values. Neoliberal policies did upend the way Americans work—unions disappeared, many jobs were sent out of the country to places where labor could be cheapened, and wages stagnated while the cost of living dramatically increased (Desilver, 2018). Focusing on social change as the cause of economic ills was an effective narrative to sell as an explanation and allowed for the unlikely alliance between economists encouraging profit as the only social value and evangelical Christians.

But why was Satanism one of the scares that captured public imagination? Other moral panics around serial killers, drugs, and terrorism had roots in actual events. Yet no evidence of Satanists kidnapping and/or murdering people for dark rituals was ever produced. One driving factor was that Satanists were the ultimate inversion of the idealized American—Christian, rule following, respectable. And enough Satanic imagery was present in American popular culture to fuel panic. *Chilling Adventures* both builds on and departs from the usual depictions of Satanism in American media. These depictions also were key in producing the moral panic and require further discussion to set up how *Chilling Adventures* comments on the past.

Dyrendal, Lewis, and Petersen (2016) identify a "satanic milieu" developing in the late 1960s, which gained media attention beyond the fringes of the counterculture with Anton LaVey's Church of Satan. The Church of Satan did not believe in a theistic Satan, but as LaVey explained, "my religion is just Ayn Rand's philosophy [of acting always in one's own self-interest] with ceremony and ritual added" (Andrade, 2018, p. 39). The Church of Satan experienced a schism in 1975 over the question of whether Satan is an existing supernatural being or a symbol for someone who defies Christian traditions and instead pursues individualism and self-enlightenment (Dyrendal, Lewis, and Petersen, 2016).

In 1969, LaVey published *The Satanic Bible*, introducing what had previously been a circle limited to San Francisco's counterculture scene to a wide audience. Dyrendal, Lewis, and Petersen argue that "in societies used to viewing scripture as the hallmark of religion, it has acquired many of the usages of other scripture" (2016, p. 71). The book's title derives more from shock appeal rather than a conventional understanding of scripture as supernaturally inspired. *The Satanic Bible* does not present itself as being the literal word of Satan, unlike the Book of the Beast in *Chilling Adventures*. Yet the book did not function in public discussions as a text to be engaged with, but rather as an actual object of evil, one that was potentially too dangerous to even open (Dyrendal, Lewis, and Petersen, 2016).

Further attention toward The Church of Satan roughly corresponded with three blockbuster horror films: *Rosemary's Baby* (Roman Polanski, 1968), *The Exorcist* (William Friedkin, 1972), and *The Omen* (Richard Donner, 1976). *Rosemary's Baby* writer Ira Levin explained that his inspiration for the book was about the fear of what a fetus might be growing into over the course of nine months. He recalls that because his first choice, an alien, was already taken by *The Midwich Cuckoos* (John Wyndham, 1957), he "was stuck with Satan" (Levin, 2012). LaVey, a dedicated self-promoter, tied the Church of Satan to the success of *Rosemary's Baby*, falsely claiming to have been an advisor on the film and to have had a cameo as Satan himself (Dyrendal, Lewis, and Petersen, 2016).

Perhaps the main reason for the cycle of Satanic horror films was that the Motion Picture Production Code, in place since 1934, was replaced by the Motion Picture Association of America rating system in 1966. The Code had made the production of films about Satan difficult because films were not to depict "ridicule of the clergy" nor profane use of religious iconography and words (Lewis, 2000, p. 301), features subsequent Satanic films reveled in. With the box office struggling due to competition with television, Hollywood studios were willing to experiment with what had been previously off limits (Rubin, 1999). *Rosemary's Baby* was one of the first of the new horror films unrestricted by the code. In the film, Rosemary (Mia Farrow) is a newly married woman whose husband (John Cassavetes) conspires with the seemingly friendly elderly neighbors (Ruth Gordon and Sidney Blackmer) to have Rosemary give birth to Satan's son. Heather Greene (2018) outlines that while not the first Hollywood film to mention Satanism, it was the first to explore the topic in such thematic and visual clarity. Greene writes that Hollywood conflated "Christian-based Satanic themes, occult ritual practice, modern day Witchcraft, and other common witch tropes ... into a singular narrative identity" (p. 125), a narrative identity that informs *CAOS*. The Satanic witch became a horror sub-genre staple, one that Greene emphasizes "was then sensationalized further with displays of physical violence, nudity, and implied sexual perversions" (p. 125).

B-movies followed the leads of the big Satanic blockbusters, with films like *The Devil's Rain* (Robert Fuest, 1975), where LaVey did serve as advisor and have a cameo role, and *Satan's Cheerleaders* (Greydon Clark, 1977). Television mogul Aaron Spelling produced a made-for-TV movie *Satan's School for Girls* (David Lowell Rich, 1973). The eighth and final film of Hammer Horror's Dracula series was retitled *The Satanic Rites of Dracula* (Alan Gibson, 1973), despite the cultists in the film trying to summon Dracula and not Satan. Marvel Comics publisher Stan Lee wanted to cash in on the Satanism phenom, resulting in writer Roy Thomas and artist Gary Friedrich creating the new hero Daimon Hellstrom, the Son of Satan (Cronin, 2018).

Sean M. Quinlan (2014) argues Satanism hit a nerve with 1970s American culture because it represented the tension between traditional and counter-cultures which created a crisis of authority. Satanism was a metaphor for the collapse of belief in traditional authority. Beginning in the 1960s, many Christians left traditional Protestant denominations for rising evangelical Christian churches while at the same time, many Americans rejected traditional beliefs for exploration of New Age spirituality. The Church of Satan was just one of many new religious groups to form in the late 1960s. New religious movements, either Christian or New Age, led to an increase in what the media deemed "cults." In 1969, media reports on the Manson Family Murders began to refer to the group as both "hippies" and "Satan worshipers" (Hughes, 2017, p. 707), suggesting an interchangeability of terms which offered "proof" of darkness lurking in the nation's spiritual restructuring. In 1972, Christian evangelist Mike Warnke published his memoir *Satan Seller*, which detailed his ascent to a Satanic high priest in lurid detail, including that he had met both Anton LaVey and Charles Manson at a ritual, further establishing a link between Manson and Satanism.

Warnke became an expert on anti–Satanism, first within evangelical churches, but later appearing on *20/20*, *Larry King Live*, and *The Oprah Winfrey Show* (Trott and Hertenstein, 1992). Warnke's recollections of Satanism were highly malleable. While his book never mentions child sacrifice, when that became one of the key moral concerns a decade later, he backed up claims that Satanists sacrificed between fifty and sixty thousand children a year, which Dyrendal, Lewis, and Petersen (2016) emphasize would be more than double the number of homicides per year in the U.S. at the time. Warnke's claims were thoroughly debunked only twenty years later in evangelical magazine *Cornerstone* (Trott and Hertenstein, 1992). Other supposed ex-Satanic cult converts became associated with the growing evangelical right, including John Todd who inspired the content of many of Jack Chick's widely distributed comic tracts (Roman, 2016).

Outside of evangelical circles, in 1980 Canadian psychiatrist Lawrence Pazder collaborated with his patient Michelle Smith on *Michelle Remembers*, a memoir they claimed was produced by retrieving, under hypnosis, Smith's supposed repressed memories of suffering Satanic ritual abuse. Suddenly Satanism was everywhere because of course it was—it had been a popular pop culture motif in the 1970s and people were familiar with its imagery and could draw upon it as material to tell narratives. But in the same way zombie imagery today does not indicate that there are actual zombies, the presence of Satanic iconography did not indicate there were any Satanists. But people believed there were, because of the secrecy Satanism supposedly entailed.

Satanism flowed from fictional media to "news" media as part of the larger trend of news focusing increasingly on "entertainment" as by the 1980s, network news and entertainment were merging. In addition to *20/20*, which launched in 1978, the decade saw the launch of further tabloid news shows, like *Unsolved Mysteries* (1987), as well as daytime talk shows like *Sally Jesse Raphael* (1985), *The Oprah Winfrey Show* (1986), and *The Geraldo Rivera Show* (1987), most of which covered the Satanic Panic. Soon the national news on the big networks began doing features on the most sensational stories to increase ratings, in turn confirming the legitimacy of the tabloid and daytime talk shows (Hughes, 2017). By spreading allegations of Satanic abuse, Hughes argues television reinforced "the particular cultural sway of conservative evangelicals, who identified the perceived threats to the sacred suburban nuclear family norm as demonic" (2017, p. 707). What attracted viewers was also, bizarrely, what scared them.

The combination of news coverage alerting people to Satanists' supposed existence with information from recovering repressed memories and suggestive interviews, led to over a hundred investigations of Satanic ritual abuse, primarily in preschools and daycares, almost entirely in wealthy, predominantly white suburbs (Hughes, 2017), possibly because this demographic was most able to afford the rapidly expanding industry of daycare, yet leaving children with strangers rather than friends and relatives was a potential source of anxiety. It also coincided with the audiences of tabloid news on television (Hughes, 2017).

McMartin Preschool in Manhattan Beach, California, was the most prominent of the schools investigated, and was involved in one of the longest and costliest trials in U.S. history (Pendergrast, 2017). After a woman called the police suspecting her son had been abused at the preschool, police sent a form letter to the parents of over 200 children at the preschool to ask their child if they had seen or been victims of abuse. Concerned parents, even those who did not receive the letter, began taking their children to the Children's Institute International abuse therapy clinic. At the clinic, unorthodox interviewing which included leading questions resulted in children describing an increasingly wild and bizarre narrative of abuse that involved many of the preschool's staff members, the drinking of blood, animal sacrifice, hot air balloon trips, and secret tunnels under the school. News media reports of the story spread the idea that "children wouldn't lie about such things" (Pendergrast, 2017, p. 188). However, it turned out while they would not lie, children could be easily suggested into confirming accounts that were not true (Pendergrast, 2017). Therapists, police, social workers, and parents, spurred by the knowledge of repressed memories, believed that the truth could be obtained from the children if they just pressed hard enough and took children's initial denials as walls that needed to be broken down rather than the truth (Pendergrast, 207).

The McMartin case eventually ended in acquittal, despite Lawrence Pazder testifying as an expert witness (Nathan and Snedeker, 1995), because of lack of evidence. However, other charges of Satanic abuse did send innocent people to prison on lengthy sentences (Nathan and Snedeker, 1995; Romano, 2016). One of the last cases was that of The West Memphis Three in 1994, where teenager Damien Echols was sentenced to death and his two accomplices, Jessie Misskelley, Jr., and Jason Baldwin were sentenced to life in prison for the murders of three boys in West Memphis, Arkansas (Rich, 2013). The police assumed the murders were cult based and assigned an investigator to assemble of list of youth involved in cult activities. Echols, a working-class high school dropout previously hospitalized with depression and a fan of heavy metal music, which was often associated with Satanic imagery, was singled out as the likely ring leader (Rich, 2013). The three men were finally exonerated in 2010, largely from public pressure spurred by HBO's *Paradise Lost* documentary (Joe Berlinger and Bruce Sinofsky, 1996). While Berlinger and Sinofsky had come to West Memphis to make a documentary on Satanic murders, to continue feeding the media narrative, they soon realized in their investigations the better story was how moral panic had led to an unfair trial against teenagers who were likely innocent. The popularity of their documentaries was a contributing factor to the public understanding Satanism as a moral panic (Rich, 2013).

Berlinger and Sinofsky's skepticism was generally lacking from media that latched onto the Satanic panic after the release of *Michelle Remembers*. The media's love of the sensationalistic Satanic ritual abuse story climaxed in a 1988 NBC "documentary" *Devil Worship: Exposing Satan's Underground*. Produced and hosted by Geraldo Rivera, this program broke ratings records for televised documentary (Diamond, 1988). The feature offered "warning signs that might indicate a child's drift towards Satanism," which included "abrupt emotional changes," "rejection of parental values," and "preference for being alone"—in other words, normal teenage behaviors. At the time, NBC news anchor Tom Brokaw said the idea of "news" being purchased by the network's entertainment side "troubles me greatly" (Sharbutt, 1988).

While some news coverage of Satanic ritual abuse was well intentioned under the idea that the children could not possibly make up such accusations, much of the coverage was as motivated by the fact that it was attention grabbing. Gone was the idea that news was to be separate from the profitable areas of a network, but that the "news" itself could be a source of revenue. Despite the ease with which many of the figures in the Satanic ritual abuse cases were discredited, including Warnke and later Lawrence Pazder in 1995 (Nathan and Snedeker, 1995), news media did not go deeper into investigations because challenging power is hard and salacious stories of satanic abuse were easy. In contrast, *Chilling Adventures of Sabrina* uses this salaciousness *to* challenge power.

Chilling Adventures

CAOS is much braver, albeit with the luxury of hindsight. The America of 2018 shared several similarities with the Satanic Ritual Abuse panic of the early 1980s. Both eras feature reactionary conservative governments tying themselves to a mythic past when America was great as the answer to unsettled social consensuses about the nation's future direction. Both saw economic growth for the wealthy, but precarity for the majority. And both eras saw people look toward strong-man leaders for simple answers, a return to tradition, and enemies to scapegoat. However, instead of Satanism being used as a smokescreen away from some conservative ideals, *CAOS* takes on these ideals through the metaphor of Satanism.

In "Chapter 2: The Dark Baptism," Father Faustus Blackwood corrects Sabrina's accusation that Satan is the "embodiment of evil" by suggesting he is actually the "embodiment of free will," which echoes the Church of Satan's position. But Satanism in the show is the embodiment of a carnivalesque approach to Christian ritual. The internal coherence of the Churches of Darkness depicted in *CAOS* is best not thought about too deeply. Satan is a literal being who interacts with many of the show's characters, but much conflict also revolves around the doctrinal interpretation of Satan's will. The members of the Church of Night hardly pursue their own free will, but often acquiesce to tradition. Yet when Satan arrives back on earth at the end of season two, many members of the church actively fight back against him (unlike traditional depictions of Satanic cults, which work towards the goal of bringing about Satan's power on earth, like in *Rosemary's Baby*). The lack of coherence allows the writers flexibility to direct the farcical depiction of hierarchical institutions to suit their larger themes over necessities of world-building. Instead of trying to figure out a coherent ideological and theological stance in *CAOS*, I turn to "Chapter 7: Feast of Feasts" as the best and clearest example illustrating how the show utilizes Satanism to critique institutions that seek to rule through obedience.

Sabrina, who is new to the world of Satanism, works as an audience surrogate in discovering the unusual rituals in which her new religion participates. The Church of Night is led by Father Faustus Blackwood, a charismatic and ambitious man who emphasizes his knowledge of ancient texts. Father Blackwood is less Anton LaVey, and has more in common with the 1980s rise of the televangelist, where right wing evangelists like Jerry Falwell, Pat Robertson, and Oral Roberts reached over 13 million viewers and raised hundreds of millions of dollars preaching their message of returning to patriarchal values (Hughes, 2017). Like a televangelist, Blackwood emphasizes only by returning to tradition can the Church members reach contentment.

The Church of Night's members are members for a variety of reasons beyond blind adherence to the doctrine. For some, like aunt Zelda, it provides a necessary guidance on how magic is to be used. In contrast, for Sabrina's aunt Hilda, the Church's doctrine is not important. She helped Sabrina's parents give her a Christian baptism, in major violation of the Church of Night's laws, yet continued to participate in Church of Night activities for another 16 years. Hilda is surprised to find herself excommunicated when this information comes to light, but is more disappointed at the loss of community than the religious rebuke.

One of the traditions Blackwood emphasizes is the "Feast of Feasts," an annual ritual where one female member of the church's 14 families participates in a lottery ("Chapter 7: Feast of Feasts"). The "winner" is named Queen, who for three days is treated as royalty, and then sacrificed and her body consumed by the rest of the coven.[1] Ritual murder and cannibalism was a frequent trope of recovered Satanic abuse memories in the 1980s, including *Michelle Remembers* (Pazder & Smith, 1980).

Sabrina's rival Prudence is selected as Queen and Sabrina as her handmaiden, who must serve her for the three days before her sacrifice. During this time, Sabrina and Prudence debate what happens after Prudence's sacrifice. Prudence is unconcerned about death, confident her sacrifice will ensure she lives on with Satan. Sabrina is unconvinced and wonders if it is worth the risk that there is no afterlife. Sabrina's questioning causes Prudence to tell Sabrina she pities her lack of faith, much in the same way the evangelical Right emphasizes rewards in the afterlife over trying to improve living conditions in the present. By focusing on eternal rewards, Prudence is distracted from the question of who benefits in the present by such rituals.

While Sabrina's aunt Zelda assures Sabrina it is an honor to even be nominated for Queen because it is an important tradition, Sabrina refuses to take tradition as an answer and continues to question. She learns from fellow student Nick that Sabrina's now deceased father, Edward, had banned the Feast for being barbaric. Only when Father Blackwood replaced him was the event brought back as tradition. Blackwood links the Feast to honoring a witch who sacrificed herself to save her coven from starvation centuries ago. The Feast of Feasts is what historian Eric Hobsbawm called an invented tradition, one that "seek[s] to inculcate certain values and norms of behaviour by repetition, which automatically implies continuity" (1983, p. 1). The tradition of the feast returns not because it is a timeless repetition whose purpose has been forgotten or is no longer relevant, but because it serves particular contemporary goals. Sabrina further determines that Lady Constance Blackwood rigged the lottery so that Prudence, who is Father Blackwood's illegitimate daughter, is killed. The new tradition of the Feast of Feasts serves several purposes for Father Blackwood's rule of the church, beyond allowing for the potentiality of killing particular members. More broadly, it focuses the members, and particularly the women, of the Church on both the past and the future, but not the present. By emphasizing the timeless nature of an event that has been stopped and started, it depicts progress as interfering with a world view that provides direction and certainty. By emphasizing the better afterlife than this life, it redirects attention from making progress on Earth because the afterlife is already perfected.

Thomas Frank (2004) traces how the New Right successfully shifted political discussion to a "culture war" between values rather than a discussion about policies. Jenkins (2008) summarizes "at home and abroad, the post–1975 public was less willing to see social dangers in terms of historical forces, instead preferring a strict moralistic division: problems were a matter of evil, not dysfunction" (p. 11). Much like how the Feast of Feasts focuses upon the past and future, but never the present, the New Right culture wars suggested that by returning to the values of the imagined past where authority was unquestioned, the future would be secured. In contrast, attempts to question the past were seen as disrupting a "natural" way of life. The Feast of Feasts is the clearest exploration of how doctrine and tradition serve certain interests at the expense of others, but it is not the only one. In season two, Father Blackwood makes his plans perhaps too explicit with his "five facets of Judas," which preaches men's dominance over women ("Chapter 16: Blackwood"). Blackwood's reforms represent the 1980s returns to tradition while Edward Spellman could be seen to represent a more 1960s liberal figure. Spellman's Manifesto emphasized love and pleasure (he advocated that magic "can and should be used for pleasure, for gain, and to satiate the senses"), while Blackwood's Facets of Judas focuses on patriarchal authority ("Chapter 16: Blackwood").

Sabrina is the first to realize Father Blackwood's danger. As an outsider who was not introduced to traditions from birth, but brings with her a set of external knowledges that make traditions seem strange, Sabrina is a kind of detective in the show. She encounters and reluctantly ends up participating in most of the rituals, but with a highly critical eye and frequently interrogating why something happens. By focusing on the power of individuals to shape religious doctrine, *CAOS* sidesteps being anti-religion, per se, but only against particular institutional interpretations. The critique can be applied to any hierarchical institution.

Sabrina is able to expose corruption because she never takes the New Right's approach of seeing problems as the actions of pure evil, but rather as a matter of dysfunction which allows an evil person to succeed. By taking what is often seen as "the embodiment of evil" and showing the Church of Night as simultaneously (1) a community of people trying to make sense of how to live, (2) a community that can be led into doing unjust things because of bad leadership, and (3) a community with a structure enabling abuse and corruption, it complicates the viewers' notions of "evil" and emphasizes the need to investigate "the will that sustains … and the strategic intent that supports" (Foucault, 1990). The 1980s media refusal to investigate causes and simply embrace the idea of evil over examining the will created injustice, while Sabrina's holding the will behind evil people accountable results in justice, such as saving Prudence from being killed at the Feast of Feasts and eventually ousting Blackwood from his position of power.

Conclusions

Perhaps the Satanic Ritual Abuse moral panic would have been quelled much more easily if there had been a Sabrina figure or figures who had the institutional power Sabrina holds within the admittedly much smaller community of the Church of Night who questioned the will behind the discourse of Satanic Panic, rather than excitedly relaying its details in the 1980s, to understand why it was occurring. Instead, the tabloid news media performed the role of Prudence, a true believer in what they were told. What is striking in the 1980s media coverage of Satanic Ritual Abuse is no one ever asks why people would be into child sacrifice. There was no attempt to understand why Satanists participate in such activities, only how the non–Satanist should protect themselves from evil, an evil that was framed by the worst activities imaginable, child sexual abuse, torture, and cannibalism. The lack of questioning has resulted in child sacrifice to continue being a common theme in moral panics and conspiracy theories, such as the QAnon linked #SaveTheChildren. *CAOS* never presents Satanism as the "embodiment of evil," an evil with the only purpose to invert the good, because to be on the lookout for such evil distracts from actual injustice.

The potentially critical reading of *CAOS* is limited, as season two ends with new leadership in both the Church and Hell, as Lilith replaces Satan and Zelda replaces Blackwood. For *CAOS's* critique to really stick, as Katie Stobbart outlined in her essay in this collection, there would have to be a challenge to the systems that allowed for corruption, and not simply hope that better leadership will right all wrongs, which has been a primary downfall of religious and political responses to the New Right's "culture war." *CAOS* sees injustice and abuses of power as the matter of bad individuals and not bad systems. It only actually hints at how the systems work when it demonstrates how they can be twisted by individuals rather than allowing viewers to understand why the villains exist in the first place. *CAOS* hints at the critical tools necessary, but ultimately redirects the criticism toward the safety of individuals. Such limitation is important because the social and media conditions conducive for a moral panic have not changed. The Satanic moral panic concluded more because moral panics often have a limited lifespan, especially one where physical evidence was nearly non-existent, not because its enabling conditions changed. The focus of the culture wars shifts, but the war does not end. The internet has only intensified the spread of sensational news, while also becoming the subject of many moral panics itself (Molloy, 2013). The deeper examination of complex social structures Hall et al. (1978) advocated for remains no closer to being our reality but it could be if, like Sabrina, we investigate past received wisdom.

Note

1. This lottery is also an example of how *CAOS's* world raises more questions than it answers, as 14 families would be too small a group to continue this tradition for very long without running out of candidates.

References

Andrade, G. (2018). "Anton LaVey's Satanic Philosophy: An Analysis." *Intermountain West Journal of Religious Studies* 9(1), 28–42.
Cronin, B. (2018, February 9). "Comic Legends: Did Stan Lee Try to Have a Comic Book Starring Satan?" *Comic Book Resources*. https://www.cbr.com/son-of-satan-marvel-comics-stan-lee/.
Desilver, D. (2018, August 7). "For Most U.S. Workers, Real Wages Have Barely Budged in Decades." Pew Research Center. https://www.pewresearch.org/fact-tank/2018/08/07/for-most-us-workers-real-wages-have-barely-budged-for-decades/.
Diamond, E. (1988, December 7). "Winners and Sinners: Media." *New York Magazine* 21(50), 44.
Dyrendal, A., Lewis, J.R., & Petersen, J.A. (2016). *The Invention of Satanism*. Oxford University Press.
Foucault, M. (1990). *The History of Sexuality, Vol. 1: An Introduction*. Trans. R. Hurley. Vintage. (Original work published 1976.)
Frank, T. (2004). *What's the Matter with Kansas: How Conservatives Won the Heart of America*. Metropolitan Books.
Greene, H. (2018). *Bell, Book, and Camera: A Critical History of Witches in American Film and Television*. McFarland.
Hall, S, Critcher, C., Jefferson, T., Clarke, J., & Roberts, B. (1978). *Policing the Crisis: Mugging, the State and Law and Order*. Macmillan.
Hobsbawm, E. (1983). "Introduction: Inventing Traditions." In E. Hobsbawm & T. Ranger (Eds.). *The Invention of Tradition*, 1–14. Cambridge University Press.
Hughes, S. (2017). "American Monsters: Tabloid Media and the Satanic Panic, 1970–2000." *Journal of American Studies* 51(3), 691–719.
Jenkins, P. (2008). *Decade of Nightmares: The End of the Sixties and the Making of Eighties America*. Oxford University Press.
Laycock, J.P. (2015). *Dangerous Games: What the Moral Panic Over Role-Playing Games Says about Play, Religion, and Imagined Worlds*. Berkeley: University of California Press.
Levin, I. (2012, November 5). "'Stuck with Satan': Ira Levin on the Origins of Rosemary's Baby." The Criterion Collection. https://www.criterion.com/current/posts/2541--stuck-with-satan-ira-levin-on-the-origins-of-rosemary-s-baby.
Lewis, J. (2002). *Hollywood v. Hard Core: How the Struggle Over Censorship Created the Modern Film Industry*. New York University Press.
Marx, K. (2005). *The 18th brumaire of Louis Bonaparte*. Trans. D.D.L. Mondial Books. (Original work published 1852.)
Molloy, P. (2013). "Sexual Predators, Internet Addiction, and Other Media Myths: Moral Panic and the Disappearance of Brandon Crisp." In C. Krinsky (Ed.), *The Ashgate Research Companion to Moral Panics* (pp. 189–206). Routledge.
Nathan, D., & M. Snedeker. (1995). *Satan's Silence: Ritual Abuse and the Making of a Modern American Witch Hunt*. iUniverse.
Pazder, L., & M. Smith. (1980). *Michelle Remembers*. Pocket Books.
Prendergast, M. (2017). *The Repressed Memory Epidemic*. Springer.
Quinlan, S.M. (2014). "Demonizing the Sixties: Possession Stories and the Crisis of Religious and Medical Authority in Post-Sixties American Popular Culture." *The Journal of American Culture* 37(3), 314–331.
Rich, N. (2013, April 4). "The Nightmare of the West Memphis Three." *The New York Review of Books*.
Rodriguez McRobbie, L. (2014, January 7). "The Real Victims of Satanic Ritual Abuse." *Slate*. https://slate.com/technology/2014/01/fran-and-dan-keller-freed-two-of-the-last-victims-of-satanic-ritual-abuse-panic.html.
Romano, A. (2016, October 30). "The History of Satanic Panic in the US—and Why It's Not Over Yet." *Vox*. https://www.vox.com/2016/10/30/13413864/satanic-panic-ritual-abuse-history-explained.
Rubin, M. (1999). *Thrillers*. University of Cambridge Press.

Sharbutt, J. (1988, October 27). "Cauldron Boils Over Geraldo's 'Devil Worship': 'Satan' Wins Ratings, Loses Advertisers." *Los Angeles Times.* https://www.latimes.com/archives/la-xpm-1988-10-27-ca-449-story.html.

Trott, J., & Hertenstein, M. (1992). "The Tragic History of Mike Warnke." *Cornerstone Magazine* 21(98). http://www.answers.org/satan/warnke1.html.

About the Contributors

Dessa **Bayrock** is a PhD candidate in the Department of English at Carleton University. She is the author of *Citizen of Riverdale*, an interactive choose-your-own-adventure-style fanfiction game built through Twine.

Kirsten **Bussière** is a doctoral candidate and part-time professor in the Department of English at the University of Ottawa. Her dissertation examines representations of space, time, and memory in contemporary post-apocalyptic fiction.

Hannah Meghan **Celinski** is an assistant professor and department head of Arts and Integrated Studies at the University of the Fraser Valley. Her PhD research is focused on the role of legacy in learning.

Heather **McAlpine** is an associate professor in the English department at the University of the Fraser Valley. She teaches nineteenth-century British literature and has published on the pre–Raphaelite movement.

Kaarina **Mikalson** studied mundanity and the politics of the everyday in contemporary Canadian comics. She was the project manager and co-director of Canada and the Spanish Civil War, which studies anti-fascism in Canada's literature and history.

Brett **Pardy** teaches in media and communication studies at the University of the Fraser Valley. His research focuses, through a critical theory lens, on the emotional impact of media on learning and unlearning conceptions around racism, masculinity, community, and mental health.

Whitney Tiffany **Renville** is a PhD student at North Dakota State University. Her research interests include disability in popular culture and rural subcultures. She teaches English and special education in South Dakota.

Sarah **Stang** is an assistant professor of game studies in Brock University's Centre for Digital Humanities. Her research primarily focuses on gender representation in both digital and analog games.

Katie **Stobbart** is a queer feminist poet from New Westminster. She earned her Honors BA in English from the University of the Fraser Valley.

W. Ron **Sweeney** teaches comics courses at the University of the Fraser Valley. He enjoys talking about the best and worst superheroes in existence.

Melissa **Wehler** has published essays in a variety of edited collections on topics including the gothic, feminism, and popular culture. She works at the University of Pittsburgh.

Mat **Wenzel** is a poet and teacher. He is an instructor of writing at TCU in Fort Worth. His creative and scholarly work engages with Queer theory as lived experience and as literary analysis.

Jess **Wind** is completing a PhD in language and literacy education at the University of British Columbia. Their research explores games, media, and fan spaces through queer, feminist, and anti-racist perspectives.

Index

ableism 43*n*13, 177
ace 52; *see also* Jones, Jughead
actors 31
adaptive intelligence 180
adults 111–12, 127, 129–32, 135
Adventure 36
The Adventures of You on Sugarcane Island 39
Afterlife with Archie 23, 176
"Against Worldbuilding" (Michel) 161–2
ageism 63–5
Aguirre-Sacasa, Roberto 8, 9*n*1, 12, 22, 43*n*14, 161, 176
Alaniz, Jose 174
alcohol 129–30
All the Rebel Women (Cochrane) 107
alternate universes 1–2, 18–20, 42*n*3, 49; *see also* fanfiction
Amash, Jim 20
Ambrose 159, 162
Americans with Disabilities Act (ADA) 178, 188*n*1
Amick, Mädchen 5
Andrews, Archie: agency in comics 13–14; and Cheryl's attempted rape 105, 116; choices and death 25; choices in comics 14, 15, 19; choosing Betty or Veronica 13, 18–19, 25*n*3; as cipher 13; death of 11–12, 20–5; extortion 120; gaybaiting kiss 156; and Griffons and Gargoyles 24; as iconic 12–14, 20; jamming with Pussycats 143; kidnapped by Nick 120; as queer 43*n*14; updating 3–4, 12–13; and Vixens dancing 126; *see also* Archie comics; *Riverdale*
Andrews, Fred 21, 24
anger 66
anti-racism 6
"Apocalypse Now!" 23
apologies 111, 113–14
archetypes 87

Archie comics: Archie's agency in 13–14; audience of 45; classic titles 9*n*2; as collaboration 54; and comics code 139; and consumption 140; and diversity 148; as dormant 12; as experimental 17; girls as readers of 140; history of 45; as history of comics 3; individuality in characters 181–2; *Life with Archie* as history of 20; as low brow 2; as old-fashioned 3; and *Riverdale* 23; updating Archie 3–4; video games 42*n*4
Archie comics (2015) 12–13
Archie Comics Publications Incorporated 45, 49
Archie Crossover Collection 22
Archie: 1941 23
Archie's Madhouse 175
Archie's Weird Fantasy 43*n*14
Archive of Our Own 51
#Aro-AceJugheadOrBust 156
Around the World in Eighty Days (Verne) 144
"As Much as I Want" (Elsinor) 52
asexuality 51–2, 156
Authors and Owners (Rose) 46
avatars 39, 43*nn*12–13

bad girls 142–3
The Badlands of Hark (Stine) 36
Baldwin, James 197
Banet-Weiser, Sarah 150, 151
banshees 89
Bates, Laura 106–7
Bayrock, Dessa 28–9, 42, 55, 56, 58
Beaty, Bart 2, 3, 13, 14, 25*n*3, 141, 148, 174, 177
#BelieveSurvivors 110
#BelieveWomen 110
Bell, A. 57
Bennet, Jessica 70–1
Berlinger, Joe 197

207

208 Index

Betty and Veronica 140
Betty's Serpent Dance: and adults 127, 129–32; agency 137; body as currency 136; choreography 133–4; dance as sacrifice 134; FP guiding 127, 130–1, 135, 136; gaze and physical engagement 126; lingerie 132; overview 124–5; performativity 132–3, 134; as prescribed transaction 129; privilege of 135; Serpents demonstrating 127–8; as televised 125; voice as phantom 132
Beverly Hills 90210 5
Bewitched 190
"Beyond the Closet as Raceless Paradigm" (Johnson) 166
Bible 89–90
Black Hood 22, 24, 112
Blackness 148, 151
Blackwood, Faustus: and Madam Satan 72; overview 199, 201; and Sabrina 81; on Satanism 198; and Zelda 64, 68–70, 72, 96
Blossom, Cheryl 53–4, 105, 109–10, 114–15, 116–18
Blossom, Penelope 117–18
Bodies That Matter (Butler) 128–9
body projects 187
book history 4–5
book overview 1–2, 6–7
"boys will be boys" 110–11, 116, 117
Braidotti, Rosi 102
brand names *see* product placements
Breaking the Frames (Singer) 15–16
British Colombia 4
Brokaw, Tom 198
Bromfield, Asha 148
Bruns, Axel 150
Bryant, Tim 43n11
Buffy the Vampire Slayer 62
Bughead 51, 59
Burke, Tarana 105, 106, 110
Burton, Nylah 95
Butler, Judith 128–9
Button, Ben 161

Canadian Copyright Act 47–8
cancelled programs 8
capitalism 46, 140, 144, 151–2; *see also* consumption
Carvalho, Diana 91
Cattel, Alec 179
Chamberlain, Prudence 107
characters (general) 3–4, 17, 49
Cheu, J. 184
Cheyne, Ria 184
Chick, Jack 196

child-eating 89
child sacrifice 196
children 196–8
Children's Institute International 196
Chilling Adventures of Sabrina (*CAOS*): agency in 80–1, 185, 186; "Chapter 1: October Country" 94; "Chapter 2: The Dark Baptism" 94; "Chapter 3: The Trial of Sabrina Spellman" 64–5; "Chapter 5: Dreams in a Witch House" 164; "Chapter 7: Feast of Feasts" 73–5, 199–201, 202n1; "Chapter 9: The Returned Man" 164; "Chapter 10: The Witching Hour" 93, 164; "Chapter 16: Blackwood" 160–1; "Chapter 20: Tales from the Dark Side" 59; "Chapter 20: The Mephisto Waltz" 169; and "Chapter 100: The Jughead Paradox" 1–2; coming out 165–7; criticized on Indigeneity 176; criticized on race 176; exploitation in 73; failures of Sabrina 159–65, 167–70; Feast of Feasts 73–5, 200–1, 202n1; feminism as ineffectual 73, 75–6, 79; feminist nightmare in 68–70; free will 198–9; homophobia 157; men in power 71–3; nuclear families 64, 65–8; and older women 63–5; overview 62; praised for queerness 155–6, 176; and *Riverdale* 1–2, 3, 161; and Satanism 190–2, 198–201, 202, 202n1; sidelined characters 76–8, 157, 162–3, 183, 185–6; utopias 178; violence as childish 79; vs. *Sabrina the Teenage Witch* 190; witchyness as queerness 157, 160; world building 160–2; *see also* disabilities; Lilith/Madam Satan
Chilling Adventures of Sabrina (graphic novel) 176, 177–8
"*The Chilling Adventures of Sabrina*'s Non-Binary Character Deserves Better" (Stern) 157
Chilton, Natalie 14
Chion, Michel 89
Choose Your Own Adventure (CYOA): and Citizens of Riverdale game 38–9; and death 43n11; illustrations 43nn12–13; as narrative expansion 32; overview 32; popularity of 42n6, 43n11; pronoun use 39, 43nn12–13; reader as co-creator 39; and video games 35–7, 40–1
"Choreographies of Gender" (Foster) 129
choreography 126, 129, 133–4; *see also* dance
Christianity 191–2, 193–4, 195, 199
Church of Satan 193–4, 195
Cinderella 94

Citizen of Riverdale game 28–9, 32, 37–40, 41, 55, 56, 58
Clair, Nick St. 105
class 141, 142, 150; *see also* privilege
Clayton, Chuck 108, 109, 111–12, 116
clothing styles 141–2
Cochrane, K. 107
co-creation *see* collaborations/co-creation
coercion 114
Cohen, J.J. 85
collaborations/co-creation 32, 37–8, 39, 41, 54, 56, 57
comic history 3
Comics Code Authority 139
communal canons 58–9
concealment 41
Concerned Children's Advertisers 145, 146
consent 113
consumer awareness 145–6
consumption: actors in ads 151; of *Archie* comics 140; clothing 140; and consumer awareness 145–6; and counterculture 147–8; and diversity 148; make-up 142–3; product placements 143, 144–5, 149–51, 152; self-branding 150–1, 152–3
consumptive viewers 126, 136
continuity 16
contradictions 16
control 43n11
Coody, Elizabeth Rae 87
Cooper, Alice 129–30, 135, 142–3
Cooper, Betty: Archie choosing 13, 18–19, 25n3; and Black Hood 120; clothing styles 141–2; Dark Betty 142–3; gaybaiting kiss 156; and Jughead 51; make-up 142–3; ponytail of 141; and slut-shaming 109–10, 111–12; *see also* Betty's Serpent Dance; *Riverdale*
Cooper, Polly 142–3
co-option 147–8
copyright 46–9
counterculture 147–8, 192, 195
Covid pandemic 8
Covino, Deborah 102
Creed, Barbara 86, 100
crisis utopias 178
critical viewing 145
Crowther, Will 36
Cuban Missile Crisis 43n11
cults 191, 193, 195, 197–8; *see also* Satanism
cunning 179, 182

Dahl, Stephan 144, 145
dance 125–6, 128–9, 131; *see also* Betty's Serpent Dance

Dark Betty 142
Dark Phoenix Sabrina 168
Day, K. 116
daycares 196–7
death 11–12, 15–16, 20–5, 43n11, 182–3
Death, Disability, and the Superhero (Alaniz) 174
The Death of Archie: A Life Celebrated (Kupperberg) 20
DeepDownBelow 53, 54
demons 88, 90–2, 163–4; *see also* Lilith/Madam Satan
Devil Worship: Exposing Satan's Underground 193, 198
The Devil's Rain 195
"The Dialectical Gaze" (Murphy) 128
Diamond, A. 186-7
disabilities: ableism 43n13, 177; acceptance of 173–4, 181; bodies' incompatibility with surroundings 185; as character traits 177; in *Chilling Adventures of Sabrina* (graphic novel) 178; and confinement 179; cultural locations of 178; death preferable to 182–3; defining 179–80; and fear 183; as focus 183; impairment vs. disabling society 173; as isolating 179, 183, 184; medical model 177, 179–80, 183–4, 185–6; mythologizing 182; as plot devices 186; and popular culture 184; Sabrina with 173, 176, 180–1, 182, 184–5; and social codes 182; social model 177, 184; "wholeness" and denial 176
"Disability in Theory" (Siebers) 182
diversity 148
Doiley, Dilton 23
Dolmage, Jay 175, 180, 181, 182
Douglas, Jane Yellowlees 56
Du Jour 144
Dungeons & Dragons 32, 36; *see also* Griffons and Gargoyles
Dyrendal, A. 193–4, 196

Eagle, Lynne 144, 145
Easter eggs 29, 161
Echols, Damien 197
Eco, Umberto 14–17, 24
economics 48–9, 58
education 140
Ehrenberg, Shantel 131
Elman, J. 186, 187
Elsinor 52
Ensslin, A. 57
"Enter the Aleph" (Ndalianis) 17
Epistemology of the Closet (Sedgewick) 166

Index

Epstein, Jeffrey 135–6
Eve 90, 91, 93, 100
Everdeen, Katniss 75–6, 78–9
The Everyday Sexism Project 107
evil 200, 201–2
The Exorcist 194
extortion 120

failure 159–65, 167–70
fair use 48–9
fanfiction: author's opposed to 49; as collaboration 32, 37–8, 41, 54; defined 49; as exclusively online content 47; inspirations for 28; legalities of 46, 47–9; and logic 28; and narrative control 33–4; original medium of 47; as participatory 32, 58; and sexuality 51–4; as transmedial storytelling 34, 42–3n6; *Twilight* 42n5; *see also* hypertext; narrative expansion
fans: and digital access 34–5, 41; as disappointed 2–3; and gossip 34; online communities 47, 49; reaction to Betty's pole dancing 130; and Superman's death 16; as visible 59
fantasy 24
fanzines 47
fashion spreads 140
Faust (Goethe) 91
Feast of Feasts 73–5, 200–1, 202n1
female voices 89
femininity 174
feminism: collective 96–7; fourth wave 106–7, 108; and internet 107; of Lilith/Madam Satan 94, 95, 98–100; nightmare in *CAOS* 68–70; rage in Sabrina 62; *Riverdale* and #MeToo movement 111; Sabrina as ineffectual 73, 75–6, 79; white saviors 77–8; and witchcraft 70–1; *see also* #MeToo movement; *Riverdale* and #MeToo movement
Feministing 106–7
femme fatales 87, 99
Fifty Shades of Grey (James) 42n5
Fighting Fantasy series 38
films 194
Fiske, J. 49
Ford, Christine Blasey 110
foreshadowing 11
forgiveness 24
Foster, Susan 129
Foucault, Michel 177, 178, 192
Fountain, E. 187
Francavilla, Francesco 19, 22–3, 176
Frank, Thomas 200
Fraser Valley 4

free will 198–9
Friedrich, Gary 195

gamified fictions 31, 37, 39, 57; *see also* narrative expansion
Garber, Megan 110, 135
gaslighting 117–18
gaze *see* Betty's Serpent Dance
gender 39, 56–7, 140
The Gender Knot (Johnson) 101
gender roles 65–8, 72, 85, 127, 128, 159–60
girl power 147
Girl Power (Meltzer) 146–8
Glen Ridge rape case 109
Goddesses and Monsters (Caputi) 88
Goldstein, Jessica 160–1, 165–6, 168
Goldwater, Jon 12
Gorelick, Victor 20, 21
gossip 34
Gossip Girl 142
Greendale, overview 177–8
Greene, Heather 194–5
Grey, Heather Laura 126
Griffiths, K. 111
Griffons and Gargoyles 24, 191

Halberstam, Jack 137n1, 157, 158, 163, 169
Hall, Kimberly Ann 152
Hall, Stuart 192–3, 202
Hariri-Kia, Iman 157
The Haunting of Hill House (Jackson) 68–9
Hawhee, D. 180, 184, 187
Hawkes, L. 179, 183
Hawthorne, Sian Melville 174
hegemony 192
Hellstrom, Damion 194–5
Henderson, Erica 51, 52
Hendrix, Grady 35, 36
Henesy, Megan 62
Hephestus 181
Herrera, Sylvia 23
heteronormativity 53–4, 126–8, 137n1, 157–9
heterotopias 178
high schools 109, 111–12
Hobsbawm, Eric 199–200
Holloway, Patrice 153n1
homogeneity 13
homophobia 20, 21, 157
House Hippo 145
housewives 68–70
Hughes, John 5
Hughes, S. 196
The Hunger Games 74–6, 78–80
Hurwitz, S. 88

Index 211

hush money 118
hypertext 30–1, 35, 42n5, 55–7; *see also* fanfiction; interactive fictions

iconicity 13, 16, 20, 25
In a Queer Time and Place (Halberstam) 137n1
incest 93
innocence 11, 12–13, 21
interactive fictions: co-creating meaning 32, 37–8, 41; and concealment 41; decisions and actions 56; and digital access 35, 41, 47, 58; *see also* fanfiction; hypertext; narrative expansion; video games
internet 35, 41, 47, 58, 108; *see also* #MeToo movement; social media
intersectionality 76, 79
invented traditions 200
inviting gaze 128

Jackson, Shirley 68, 74
Jackson, Steve 38
Jailhouse Rock sequence 126–7
James, E.L. 42n5
Jenkins, Henry 34, 49
Jenkins, Philip 192, 200
Jessica Jones 78, 79–80
Jewish mythology 85
Joaquin 156
Johnson, Allan 101
Johnson, E. Patrick 158
Joho, Jess 77
Jola, Corinne 131
Jones, Forsythe Pendleton, III (FP) 127, 129, 130–1, 135, 136
Jones, Jessica 78
Jones, Jughead: as asexual 51–2, 156; and Betty's Serpent Dance 133, 136; on innocence of Riverdale 21; locked in bunker 23; paradox of universes 1–2; as werewolf 23; see also *Riverdale*
Jones, Sara Gwenllian 46
Jones, S.G. 54
Josie and the Pussycats (band) 105, 116, 143–4
Josie and the Pussycats (film): clothing styles 141, 148–9; MegaRecords transformation of band 148–9; overview 139–40; as product 146; product placements 143, 144–5; racism 151; and riot grrrl 147; stores in 141
Josie and the Pussycats (TV show) 153n1
Jughead comics 156
Jughead No. 4 51
Jughead: The Hunger 23

Kanake, S. 179, 183
Katz, Rebecca 47, 48
Kavanaugh, Brett 110
Keller, Dan 191
Keller, Frances 191
Keller, Kevin 12, 19, 20, 21, 59
Kennedy, Pat 20
Kennedy, Tim 20
Kilgrave 78
Kinkle, Harvey 159, 163, 164, 169, 176, 181–2
Kinkle, Tommy 173, 180, 185
Koenitz, Hartmut 33, 35–6
Kraus, Daniel 36, 39
Kristeva, Julia 86
Kupperberg, Paul 18–19, 20

Lady Lilith (Rossetti) 91
lamia 89
Langsdale, Samantha 87
Latinx 148
LaVey, Anton 193–4, 195
Law, Hayley 148
"'Leaving my girlhood behind'" (Henesy) 62
Lebling, David 35, 38–9
Lee, Stan 195
"The Less I Know the Better" (DeepDownBelow) 53, 54
Levin, Ira 194
Lewis, J.R. 193–4, 196
LGBTQIA+: Archie as queer 43n14; asexuality 51–2, 156; bisexuality 53–4; *CAOS* praised for 155–6; coming out 164–7; expectations 167; failure as 157–8, 167; gaybaiting 156; non-binary people 167; readers' choosing partners 58; in *Riverdale*'s first minute 155; slash fiction 40, 49, 53–4; straight saviors 77, 166; witchyness as 157, 160; *see also* homophobia; Keller, Kevin; Putnam, Theo
Life with Archie: The Married Life 16, 18–20, 25
Lilith (Jewish mythology) 85, 88–92, 93, 96, 100–1
Lilith (magazine) 101
Lilith/Madam Satan 63–4, 72, 83–4, 92–102
Lilitu 85, 88
Lindgren, Maria 55
Lindgren Leavenworth, Maria 33
The Lion, The Witch, and the Wardrobe (Lewis) 92
lipstick 142–3
Lipton, Jacqueline 49

Lipton, J.D. 49
The Little Mermaid 94
Lodge, Hiram 24
Lodge, Veronica: Archie choosing 13, 18–19, 25n3; clothing styles 142; gaybaiting kiss 156; and Nick 112, 113–14, 118; and slut-shaming 108–10, 111–12; and survivorship 116, 117–18; see also *Riverdale*
logic 28
"The Lottery" (Jackson) 74, 75–6
low brow art 2
Lucifer (Gaiman) 92

MacDonald, Shana 78
Madam Satan/Lilith 63–4, 72, 83–4, 92–102
Madej, Krystina 36
make-up 142–3, 144, 149–50, 152
Manduley, Aida 119
Manson family 195
Marvel Comics 195
Marx, Karl 191
"Mary Sue" narratives 32, 40
Mason, Moose 19
McAlpine, Heather 4
McCloud, Scott 13
McCoy, Josie 116, 141, 143–4, 148, 149, 150–1; see also various *Josie and the Pussycats*
McLaughlin 187
McMartin Preschool 196
McRuer, Robert 182
Medusa 91
MegaRecords 148–9
Melody 141, 143, 148
Meltzer, Marisa 146–7
membership 128, 129
Mendes, Camila 121, 149
Mephistopheles 91
Metacritic 2
metis 180–1, 184–5, 187
#MeToo movement: charges 115–16; in *Jessica Jones* 79–80; non-apology apologies 114; overview 71, 105, 106, 107–8; *Riverdale* actors 121; and survivorship 119, 121; victim-blaming 110
Michel, Lincoln 161–2
Michelle Remembers (Smith and Pazder) 196, 199
Milano, Alyssa 105, 106
Mildred 75
Milk, Harvey 166
Miller, Nicholas E. 30–1
Milton, John 173
Missal, D.J. 41
"The Missionaries" 81

Misskelley, Jessie, Jr. 197
Mitchell, C.L. 177, 178, 186
Mogilevich, Mariana 145–6
Monfort, Nick 40
Monroe, Marilyn 126
monsters 86–7, 88, 94
monstrous-feminine: denial of sex and reproduction 96; and departure from norms 89, 100, 182; as full of disgrace 98; as liberating 102; overview 86–7, 94–5; remixed and remediated 100; reproducing parthenogenetically 91; women's screams 89
The Monstrous-Feminine (Creed) 86
Monstrous Women in Comics (Langsdale and Coody) 87
moral panic 24, 191, 192, 193, 195–8, 201–2
Morningstar, Lucifer 92–3, 95, 96–7, 99
Moss, Molly 137n1
mothers 94
Motion Picture Association of America rating system 194
Motion Picture Production Code 194
Moulin Rouge 125–6
Muggs, Ethel 108–9, 111, 112
Munford, Rebecca 68, 69
Muñoz, J.E. 158
Murphy, Alexandra G. 125, 128
Murry, Ashleigh 148, 149
"The Myth of Superman" (Eco) 14–16
"The Myth of the Underage Woman" (Garber) 135
mythic time 15, 17, 19
mythology 85, 87–92, 161; see also Lilith/Madam Satan
myths 17–18

Nana Ruth 179, 183
narrative expansion 29, 31–2, 33–4, 40
narrative vs. interactivity 35–6
Navar-Gill, Annemarie 156
Ndalianis, Angela 17
Nelson, Ted 30, 55
neoliberalism 67
New Age spirituality 195
New Right 190, 193, 200–1
Nomadic Subjects (Braidotti) 102
non-binary people 167; see also Putnam, Theo
normativity 148, 175, 178
nostalgia 5
novel time 15, 19
nuclear families 65–8

Obama, Barack 107
The Omen 194

Index 213

oneiric climate 16, 17, 19, 24
Otto, Miranda 67
ownership 45, 46–7

pageants 128
Pandora 100–1
Paradise Lost 197
"The Paratext of Fanfiction" (Lindgren) 55
Parfitt, Clare 125
parodies 5, 24
passive viewers 126, 127, 133, 136
pastiche 2, 17, 30, 50
patriarchy/misogyny: and ancient stories 101; and the Bible 89–90; *CAOS* tropes 95; disobedience as demonic 91; Faustus and Zelda 68–70; fear of the feminine 85, 86, 96; Lilith (Jewish mythology) rejecting 97; and movement 129; rewritings of myths 88–9; violence in dismantling 78–9; witches challenging 62, 70–1; and women working together 96–7; *see also Chilling Adventures of Sabrina*; dance; #MeToo movement; *Riverdale* and #MeToo movement
Pazder, Lawrence 196, 197, 198
performativity 128–9, 132–3, 134
performer gaze 128, 129, 133, 136
Perry, Luke 5
Petersen, J.A. 193–4, 196
Petsch, Madelaine 120–1, 149
pinups 140
plot 22
Poharec, L. 186–7
Poitevin, Kimberly 151
pole dancing *see* Betty's Serpent Dance
Policing the Crisis (Hall) 192–3
ponytails 141
Pop's Diner 20
popular culture 2, 17, 29–30, 50, 147, 184
post-feminism 67, 80, 153
power: and gender boundaries 85; girl power 147; in lipstick 143; of older women 65; patriarchal power and women 68–9, 71; of Prudence 76–7; rape as 115; of Sabrina 80–1; of wealth 114
Prance, Sam 156
precarity 151–2
pregnancy 143
prestige 49
privilege 115–16, 117–18, 135
product placements 143, 144–5, 149, 152
pronouns/gender 39, 43n12, 56–7
prop placement 145
Prudence 71, 75, 76–7, 199–200
Putnam, Jesse 173, 177, 178, 179–80, 183, 185
Putnam, Theo 77, 79, 157, 160, 162–3, 164–6
Pythagoras 101

Queer Art of Failure (Halberstam) 157
queer gaze 137n1
queer studies 158–9
queerness 158; *see also* LGBTQIA+
Quinlan, Sean M. 195
Quinn, Harley 186–7

racism 111, 116; *see also* whiteness
Rand, Ayn 194
rape 80, 91, 109, 114–18; *see also* #MeToo movement
reactionary conservatism 192, 193, 198, 200–1
reader reception theory 33
Reagan, Ronald 193
reality 20–1, 22, 24, 161–2
the Reaping 74–5
Reinhart, Lili 121, 134, 136, 151
representation 51–4, 58
repressed memories 197
reproduction 86–7, 91, 96
resetting/reboot 0, 3, 13, 14, 15, 16
retaliation 111, 115, 119–20
Reynolds, Dee 131
Riesman, Abraham 156
Ringwald, Molly 5
riot grrrl 140, 146–8
ritual abuse 191, 195–6, 198, 202; *see also* moral panic; Satanism
rituals 73–5
Rivera, Geraldo 198
Riverdale: as act of co-creation 41; Archie's death 24–5; blackwashing 148; and *CAOS* 1–2, 3, 161; "Chapter 3: Body Double" 142–3; "Chapter 13: The Sweet Hereafter" 21–2; "Chapter 18: When a Stranger Calls" 105; "Chapter 18: When a Stranger Calls" (*Riverdale*) 105; "Chapter 20: Tales from the Dark Side" 59; "Chapter 21: House of the Devil" 124–36; "Chapter 37: Fortune and Men's Eyes" 126–7; "Chapter 100: The Jughead Paradox" 1–2, 3; Cheryl's attempted rape 105; clothing styles 141–2, 143–4; in comics 23; dance 126; dance and heteronormativity 126–8; deaths in 21–2; disappointment of fans 2–3; diversity 148; fanfiction as unique 49; first minute of 155; gaybaiting 156; and iconicity 16; and Jughead's sexuality 51–2, 156; make-up 142–3; moral panic commentary 191; as narrative expansion 29; as not imaginary 1, 5; number of

viewers 2; overview 3, 46; product placements 143, 144, 149–51, 152; resets in 22; self-branding 150–1, 152–3; and *Stranger Things* 42n3; undergrads' reaction to 139; vs *Archie* comics (2015) 13; *see also* Betty's Serpent Dance; various characters
Riverdale (town), overview 177
Riverdale: A Land of Contrasts conference 28–9, 30
Riverdale: All New Stories (comic series) 23
Riverdale and #MeToo movement: apologies 111, 113–14; "Chapter 3: Body Double" 108–12; "Chapter 18: When a Stranger Calls" 112–20; justice 119–20; Nick as predator 112–13; Nick as rapist 114–15; Nick's privilege 115–16, 117–19; overview 105–6; Petsch's PSA 121; sexual harassment in 108–12; survivorship 116–21
Rivers, Nicola 107
Road to Riverdale 23
Robbins, Trina 140
Rocko's Diner 4
roll playing games (RPG) 43n11; *see also* Dungeons & Dragons; Griffons and Gargoyles
Romero, Ariana 115
Rose, Mark 46
Rosemary's Baby 190, 194–5
Ross, Marlon B. 166
Rossetti, Dante Gabriel 91
Rotton Tomatoes 2
Russell, John G. 148
Ryan, Marie-Laure 33–4

Sabrina the Teenage Witch 175–6, 190
St. Clair, Nick 105, 111, 112–20
Saint-Gelais, Richard 42n6
Samael 92–3
Santos, Cristina 87, 95
Satan 72, 80–1, 194–5, 198–9; *see also* Morningstar, Lucifer
Satan Seller (Warnke) 195
The Satanic Bible 194
Satanic cults 191, 193, 195, 197–8; *see also* Satanism
Satanic milieu 193
The Satanic Rites of Dracula 195
Satanism: and *CAOS* 190–2, 198–201, 202, 202n1; Church of Satan 193, 194–5; moral panic 24, 191, 192, 193, 195–8, 201–2; *see also Chilling Adventures of Sabrina*
Satan's School for Girls 195

satire *see Josie and the Pussycats*
scholarship 6
Schwabach, Aaron 48–9
Scratch, Nick 97–8
Scream 5
second-person perspective 39, 56
Sedgwick, Eve 166, 174
Seibers, Tobin 181, 182
self-awareness 5, 30–1, 49
self-branding 150–1, 152–3
self-referencing 29–30; *see also* hypertext
Serpent Dance *see* Betty's Serpent Dance
serpents 87, 88, 89, 91, 93
Serpents (gang) 127–8, 134–5, 136
sex-trafficking rings 135–6
sexual assault: "boys will be boys" 110–11, 116, 117; in *CAOS* 80; and Jessica Jones 80; and nuanced language 135; public call outs and feminism 71; reporting 118, 120; tactics of predators 112; *see also* #MeToo movement; *Riverdale* and #MeToo movement
sexual harassment 108–10
sexuality: and disability 175, 186; freedom of witches 95–6; as monstrous 91, 94–5; over-confidence of 124; reality of teenagers 124, 135; as weapon 96, 113; *see also* Betty's Serpent Dance
Shadowhunters 92
Shears, Peter 145
shooting locations 4
Singer, Marc 15–16, 17
Sinofsky, Bruce 197
slash fiction 40, 49, 53–4
slut-shaming 108–10, 111–12, 113
Smallville 17–18
Smith, Michelle 196, 199
Snow White 94
Snyder, Sharon L. 177, 178, 186
social media 106, 107, 140, 150
Somerville, Siobahn 158
Sons of Satan 72
soullessness 185
"The Spectator's Dancing Gaze in *Moulin Rouge!*" (Parfitt) 125–6
Spelling, Aaron 195
Spellman, Edward 200, 201
Spellman, Hilda 64–7, 199
Spellman, Sabrina: in *Afterlife with Archie* 176; agency of 80–1, 186; in *Archie's Madhouse* 175; as childish 79; in *Chilling Adventures of Sabrina* (graphic novel) 176; curing disabilities 183–4; as Dark Lord's sword 81; as disabled 173, 176, 180–1, 182, 184–5; failures of 159–65, 167–70; and Feast of Feasts 74, 75; as

isolated 187; and Lilith/Madam Satan 93–4, 97–8; overview 62, 175; and queer possibilities 157; questioning Satanism/rituals 200–1; in *Sabrina the Teenage Witch* 175–6, 190; vs. Prudence 76; see also *Chilling Adventures of Sabrina*
Spellman, Zelda 64–70, 162, 164, 199
spin-offs 3, 18; see also hypertext
spinsters 63–4
Sprouse, Cole 52, 156
staining 148
Stanfill, Mel 156
Staples, Fiona 12–13
Star Wars 24, 25
Stepford wife-ism 68
stereotypes 77, 128, 133
Stern, Kaila Hale 157
Steubenville rape case 109
Stine, R.L. 36
storylines 3, 4, 8
Stranger Things 42n3
Street Cents 146
strip clubs 128
subliminal messages 145
succubus 88
supercrips 174, 182
superheroes 14–17, 187
Superman 14–17
supermarket check outs 3
Supernatural 92
survivorship 110–11, 115, 116–21; see also #MeToo movement; *Riverdale* and #MeToo movement
Sweeny, W. Ron 4
Sweet Pea 136
Swinehart, Christian 36

tabloid news 196, 201–2
Tangled 94
teen sick lit 186, 187
teenagers 3, 187
televangelists 199
Thomas, Roy 195
time 15, 16, 17, 19, 22
Todd, John 196
Topaz, Toni 53–4, 136
torture 111
tourism 4
toxic masculinity 66
transgender gaze 137n1
transgender people *see* Putnam, Theo
transphobia 157, 162–3
True Blood 92
Trump, Donald 71, 107
Tucker, Nicholas 36, 43n11
Twelve-Cent Archie (Beaty) 2, 13, 177

Twin Peaks 5
Twine program 32
Twitter 4, 5

Ulrich, Skeet 5
Unbecoming Female Monsters (Santos) 87
"underage women" 135
Understanding Comics: The Invisible Art (McCloud) 13
Uslan, Michael 18
Ussher, Jane 87
utopias of deviation 178

Valenti, Jessica 106–7
Valerie 141, 143, 148, 151–2, 153n1
Verne, Jules 144
Vesey, Alyxandra 153
victim-blaming 110–11
video games 31–2, 35–7, 39, 40–1; see also Citizen of Riverdale game
viewers, numbers of 2
Vixens 126–8
The Voice in Cinema (Chion) 89
Vuic, Kara Dixon 126

Waid, Mark 12–13, 23
Waking the Witch (Grossman) 71
Waldorf, Blair 142
Walker, Rosalind 178
Walker, Roz: character in *CAOS* 176; in *Chilling Adventures of Sabrina* (graphic novel) 178; confronting Sabrina 164–5; as marginalized 77, 183, 185–6; overview 173–4, 179
Wardwell, Mary 63–4, 81, 160
Warnke, Mike 195, 198
Waters, Melanie 68, 69
Watson, Lachlan 157, 166–7
werewolves 23
The West Memphis Three 197
whiteness 148, 150–1
Whyte Wyrm 129–30; *see also* Betty's Serpent Dance
Wiccan 3, 65
Wind, Jess 5, 30
witchcraft 62, 70–1, 77, 195; see also *Chilling Adventures of Sabrina*
world building 161–2
World War II 23

Youtube 150

Zdarsky, Chip 51, 52
zombies 23
Zork 35–6, 39
Zuckoff, Aviva Cantor 101

www.ingramcontent.com/pod-product-compliance
Lightning Source LLC
Chambersburg PA
CBHW032043300426
44117CB00009B/1165